CN01472231

Setting up a CCM
BUSINESS in
EUROPE

WITHDRAWN

Publicité par caissons lumineux en parkings souterrains

EDF
Electricité
de France

Regus

KOGAN
PAGE

First published in English in 1999

Kogan Page Limited
120 Pentonville Road
London
N1 9JN
UK

Kogan Page Limited
163 Central Avenue, Suite 4
Dover
NH 03820
USA

© Corine Moriou, 1999

The right of Corine Moriou to be identified as the author of this work has been asserted by Corine Moriou in accordance with the Copyright, Designs and Patents Act 1988.

Although the information contained in this guide has been verified to the best of our ability, it is subject to periodic revision. Therefore, we cannot guarantee that this information will remain valid over time. We recommend that readers contact the organizations listed at the end of each chapter.

   Readers who have information or experiences to share are encouraged to send their contributions in writing (French or English) to the author, care of Kogan Page.

Translated from the French by Peggy Ganong.

First published in France as *Créer Son Entreprise en Europe* by Lamy/Les Echos in 1997.

To order a copy of the French original, contact:
Editions Lamy
187/189 quai Valmy
75490 Paris CEDEX
Telephone: (33) (01) 44 72 12 12

British Library Cataloguing in Publication Data
A CIP record for this book is available from the British Library.

ISBN 0 7494 3027 3

Typeset by Saxon Graphics Ltd, Derby
Printed and bound by Thanet Press Ltd, Margate

Contents

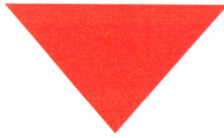

Foreword

It is generally accepted that the creation of new businesses is vital to the continued prosperity and growth of Europe. They provide new products and services, speed up structural change, increase competition and stimulate the commercial transactions on which improved living standards and job creation depend.

Promoting entrepreneurship and creating a business environment that encourages the creation and growth of new businesses has therefore moved centre-stage in European enterprise policy.

In this respect the birth of the Euro is a real opportunity for European enterprises. The opportunities for cross border trade will increase dramatically for European enterprises. It will lead to reduced costs and provide a stable framework which will make it easier to do business abroad.

It will give a major impetus to the Single Market. The free movement of goods, services and people has opened up a market of 370 million consumers for business, and the mutual recognition of qualifications has made it easier to create a business in another Member State.

However, despite the convergence process towards Europe as a single economic entity, differences persist between Member States concerning enterprise registration procedures, fiscal rules and labour legislation. It is the lack of knowledge and the difficulty in obtaining information on these national provisions that entrepreneurs consider the biggest hurdles to benefiting from the Single Market. According to a recent survey only a quarter of companies say they have all the information they need to do business or start up a company in the Single Market.

This well-researched guide is a timely contribution to tackling the information gap by providing at a glance information on legal, fiscal and social rules as well as support programmes for setting-up a business in the European Union. It is also a kind of 'First-Stop-Shop' as it provides contact details of various institutions and agencies an entrepreneur will come across in his or her venture. *Setting up a Business in Europe* is therefore a most welcome contribution to our efforts to make it easier to become an entrepreneur in Europe. I hope it will find a great many users.

Guy Crauser, Director General of DG XXIII
Enterprise Policy, Distributive Trades, Tourism and Social economy
European Commission

Foreword

Day after day, one step at a time, Europe is being built. Starting in the middle of the 1980s, this movement picked up considerably and, for nearly five years now, the Single Market has been a reality. The advent of the euro will further boost economic integration. Nobody will be left untouched by this sea change.

The single currency is absolutely vital if Europe is to compete on an equal footing with its principal rivals, on our continent and throughout the world. Not only will the euro offer our enterprises a domestic market of 370 million inhabitants, it will also remove the climate of insecurity linked to currency fluctuations.

This change also provides a fantastic business development opportunity for European companies operating within this vast market. In particular, small- and medium-sized businesses will find it easier to seek out new niches to conquer.

At the same time, investing in European Union member states remains a complex affair. First of all this is because the legal framework of the Single Market, despite the great strides that have been made, has still not been completed. Europe had set itself the objective of adopting the final measures, as outlined in an action plan, by 1 January 1999. Secondly, even in areas where community law is complete, each country has its own administrative, tax and legal practices – not to mention its own linguistic and cultural ones.

A guidebook of this kind is thus particularly valuable for the would-be investor. It provides all the information needed to organize an investment in any one of the 15 European Union member states. Corine Moriou has made a significant contribution to the construction of Europe, and deserves our sincere gratitude.

Pierre Moscovici

Pierre Moscovici
French Minister delegate for European affairs

Acknowledgements

Many thanks to the following individuals for their invaluable support in getting this book published:

Viviane de Beaufort
Professor at ESSEC and author of *Acquérir une entreprise en Europe*.

Geneviève Brame, consultant at HSD Ernst & Young and author of *Living and Working in France*.

Pascal Grandchamp, solicitor
SOFFAL law firm.

Arnaud de Roucy, solicitor
JDP law firm.

Olivier Riffaud, solicitor
JDP law firm.

François-Xavier Robichet, solicitor
IDEFT law firm.

Jacques Thiriet
RDE, consultancy specialized in business start-ups and takeovers.

Guy-Martial Weijer, solicitor
Nauta Dutilh law firm.

I would also like to thank all the solicitors and experts in the 15 countries of the European Union, whose details appear at the end of this book.

Finally, my personal gratitude goes to the following:

François Roussely, Chairman of EDF, and Jean-François Paulet of the Centre EDF Entreprises Tertiaires;

Laurent Ledermann, Chairman and CEO of LGA.

Fabienne Meyer, Regional Marketing Manager, Regus.

I am grateful to them for their sponsorship, which is proof enough that the information in this guide is of value for small, medium-sized and large enterprises.

Jean Marchand, Managing Director of the monthly publication *Réussir A l'Etranger,* for giving me the opportunity to solicit the testimonials from entrepreneurs that are featured in this book.

Peggy Ganong for her professional and personal qualities as a translator.

Patrick Lejoncour, Head of Marketing at Kogan Page, who supported me throughout this project, and the entire team at Kogan Page, which contributed to its successful completion.

Last of all, I am grateful to the individuals from the member states that I have met over the last few years, whose generosity and insight have enriched this work.

Introduction

*E*leven countries joined the euro bandwagon as of 1 January 1999. Three others have opted out for the time being (the UK, Denmark and Sweden) and, despite making great strides toward fulfilling the conversion criteria, Greece must wait for the next round.

Today, 'Euroland' is the economic and commercial powerhouse of the planet, with 290 million inhabitants (versus 268 million in the United States and 126 million in Japan), 19.4 per cent of world GDP (19.6 per cent for the United States and 8.2 per cent for Japan) and 18.6 per cent of world trade (16.6 per cent for the US and 8.2 per cent for Japan).

Just as Southeast Asia is beginning to see the light at the end of the tunnel, the devaluation of the Brazilian real has plunged Latin America into recession. The Japanese economy continues to contract, but in more limited fashion. The Russian crisis appears to be more serious than initially anticipated, and is having repercussions in eastern and central Europe. As for the United States, there may be signs of a slowdown to come.

With the single currency, the Single Market is beginning to take shape. The Euro Area has become a top priority for any company looking for favourable business development conditions. The European Union currently enjoys low inflation (1.5 per cent in 1999), historically low interest rates and high levels of consumer confidence. Even the unemployment rate has fallen, from a peak of 11.2 per cent in 1994 to 10 per cent in 1998.

Within the 15 EU member states, the vast majority of businesses are small to medium-sized: 99 per cent employ fewer than 50 people and together account for half of all jobs and nearly half of all revenues. Out of 15.8 million businesses, only 31,000 are considered large corporations.

The pace of foreign investment has picked up since 1995, and even more sustained growth is expected in the coming years. For large corporations, establishing a presence abroad is becoming more important than exporting goods and services, which is rising only moderately from one year to the next. Mergers and acquisitions remain the preferred routes to penetrating target markets, followed by the establishment of local plants and joint venture agreements.

Small and medium-sized businesses have been less involved in the trend towards globalization, and hence have developed an approach that differs from that adopted by multinational groups. Nonetheless, they must gain access to external markets in order to effectively compete with foreign rivals on their home soil. While the introduction of the euro has made competitive devaluation a thing of the past, it has also ushered in the era of transparent pricing and accelerated international trade.

Small and medium-sized businesses (SMEs) have several options to choose from in this new environment: they can develop distribution networks, buy an existing company in cooperation with a local firm, or create a new legal entity.

This guide does not discuss the procedures for establishing liaison or branch offices, subsidiaries or joint ventures, or for taking over an existing firm. Numerous publications on these subjects already exist.

All European SMEs that decide to set up operations in another country must comply with local legal, labour, tax and financial regulations in force. And while the European Commission is taking steps to harmonize legislation throughout the European Union, there is still a long way to go before a common set of regulations will apply in the member states. In many cases, European directives are not immediately transposed nationally. This does not make things easy for the Euro-entrepreneur.

Replacing local rules with a set of supranational regulations is not currently on the agenda. Tax harmonization, however, is expected to become one of the Commission's most pressing projects as the euro advances. But for the moment, for want of a unanimous view on the part of the member states, even this project is at a standstill.

While many works are already available on Community law, this guide focuses on the basic points of entry that are of vital importance in each of the member states. To facilitate comparisons, each chapter is laid out in the same way, and there are a number of tables at the back of the book.

Potential investors are warned, however, against drawing hasty conclusions about countries where they may be interested in setting up a business. In addition to the tax, labour or financial advantages, there are other key criteria that need to be weighed, such as market conditions, partnership opportunities, standard of living and personal factors, that entrepreneurs must define for themselves. Readers are strongly urged to contact local solicitors, chartered accountants, bankers and other experts in the country of their choice.

This guide is intended to prepare future entrepreneurs to deal with the local experts they will meet when the time comes to bring their project into existence.

Setting up a business abroad is not an impossible dream. The model that served our parents is no longer viable. It is time to imagine other ways of working and other avenues of personal growth. Going to work for a large corporation in order to work abroad as an expatriate is increasingly reserved for the happy few. What other opportunities are there for those who want to work abroad? It is a question of choice as well as of circumstances.

For each of the 15 countries discussed in this guide, we have included the testimonial of individuals working in a variety of business areas (information technology, telecommunications, advertising, temporary employment, plastics, agri-food, medicine, fashion, music, art, etc.). These testimonials were published in 1998 and 1999 in the French monthly publications *Réussir à l'étranger* and *Défis* (Bubble Gun). They are intended to enlighten, but not to provide the basis for generalizations on any of the countries discussed.

I have deliberately decided to showcase companies of all sizes and degrees of fame: *ex nihilo* start-ups (LGA, Oy J-F Galtat Wines, Bubble Gun, Odyssey Com), the professions (SOS Doctors), greenfield projects (Décathlon, Plastic Omnium), franchises and corners (Naf-Naf, Museal), and subsidiaries (Louis Vuitton, Adecco, Gemplus, MPO, LA CIE, la Fonte Ardennaise, Groupe Bazin).

The entrepreneurs whose career paths we present have certain things in common: they are under the age of 40 and have advanced degrees. Most of them began working abroad and have never worked in their native country. Some of them got their first taste of expatriate life while serving in the military (the French CSNE or national service performed in a foreign subsidiary or office of a French company). They either run their own company or are running a foreign subsidiary of a French-based group in which they share the profit. They seized the opportunities that presented themselves or made things happen to suit their aspirations. They are curious about the world around them, appreciate independence and like living in a foreign land. They are opportunistic, full of energy and highly creative. They all express a high degree of professional satisfaction. And some of them are already thinking about putting down roots in another country. . . maybe even beyond Europe.

We wish every success to the next group of candidates.

1

Setting Up a Business in Austria

CZECH

Gmund

Krems

SLOVAKIA

Linz

Wels

Vienna ✪

Steyr

Baden

Eisenstadt

GERMANY

Salzburg

Wiener Neustadt

Kufstein

Kitzbühel

Eisenerz

Bruck

Bregenz

Innsbruck

Feldkirch

Bludenz

Landeck

Graz

HUNGARY

Lienz

SWITZERLAND

ITALY

Villach

Klagenfurt

SLOVENIA

CROATIA

Key statistics

Total surface area:	83,858 square kilometres
Population:	8 million
GDP growth:	3.3% (1998)
Per capita GDP:	23,406 euros (1998)
Public deficit/GDP ratio:	−2.1% (1998)
Public debt/GDP ratio:	63.1% (1998)
Inflation:	0.9% (1998)
Unemployment:	4.4% (1998)

Austria offers investment subsidies to encourage foreign inflows that involve technology transfer, business start-ups and job creation. Germany is the principal foreign investor in Austria, accounting for more than one-third of the total investment inflow.

Austria's membership of the European Union created additional interest in the country as an attractive place to invest, not only because of its high per capita income, but also as it is a gateway to Central and Eastern Europe. In 1998, both Hewlett Packard (US) and Winterthur (Switzerland) established their headquarters for Eastern Europe in Vienna.

France, which is Austria's number four supplier and its number six client, has become the seventh-largest investor, behind Germany (42 per cent), Switzerland (11 per cent), the United States (10 per cent), the Netherlands, Italy and the United Kingdom.

Most foreign investment is concentrated in the automotive, metallurgical, oils and chemicals, wood and paper, and textiles industries. In addition to manufacturing, foreign investment extends to the banking, finance, retail and tourist trades.

Companies controlled by foreign shareholders employ 280,000 employees, 9 per cent of Austria's total workforce.

Recent foreign investments include EDF (France), which has acquired an equity interest in ESTAG, thereby becoming the first foreign operator in the Austrian electrical power industry; Gemplus (France) has acquired Ski Data; Mannesman (Germany) has established a position in telecommunications; Gruner and Jahr (Germany) has acquired News and TV Media; and Magma International (Canada) has acquired Steyr-Daimler-Puch.

Regulations governing foreign investment

Foreign companies may establish operations in Austria under the same terms as Austrian firms. Direct investments require no prior government approval, although for statistical monitoring purposes, the National Bank (the Austrian Central Bank) must be notified.

Banks and insurance companies wishing to set up operations must obtain the prior approval of the Ministry of Finance (*Bundesministerium für Finanzen*).

No restrictions apply to the repatriation of dividends, interest and capital to the investor's country of origin.

Real estate acquisitions require the prior approval of the local land use authority (*Grundverkehrsbehoerde*).

A permit is required to build production facilities. Delivery is subject to compliance with both technical and environmental protection regulations.

Principal legal forms

It is possible to conduct business in Austria by establishing a representative office, a branch office or a subsidiary. Subsidiaries must adopt one of the country's existing legal forms.

The limited-liability company (GesmbH) and the corporation (AG) are the most widely used legal forms in Austria. Around 80 per cent of all subsidiaries set up by foreign companies in Austria are GesmbH.

■ Limited-liability company (GesmbH – Gesellschaft mit beschränkter Haftung)

Requirements of a GesmbH:

— minimum of two founding shareholders (sole proprietorship is permitted);
— minimum capital of 500,000 schillings (36,336.42 euros) fully subscribed, half of which must be paid in at the time of incorporation;
— incorporating instruments must be notarized.

Flexible management:

— one or more managers, who may but need not be shareholders;
— a supervisory board (*Aufsichtsrat*) is necessary only if declared capital exceeds 1 million schillings (€72,672.83), and if there are more than 50 shareholders or an annual average of more than 300 employees. Minimum of three members, who must be individuals and who are appointed by the shareholders. For such companies, the works council may appoint one-third of the supervisory board;
— the presence of an independent auditor (*Wirtschaftsprüfer*) is now required;
— shareholders' liability is limited to the capital invested.

■ Corporation (AG – Aktiengesellschaft)

Requirements of an AG:

— minimum of two shareholders;
— minimum capital of 1 million schillings (72,672.83 euros), fully subscribed and 25 per cent paid in at the time of incorporation;
— incorporating instruments must be notarized.

Corporate governance is divided into two bodies:

— an executive board (*Vorstand*), whose members may not also be members of the supervisory board (*Aufsichtsrat*);
— a supervisory board, which appoints and supervises the executive board; its make-up and role are similar to those of a GesmbH;
— the presence of an independent auditor (*Wirtschaftsprüfer*), appointed by the annual general meeting of the shareholders, is mandatory;
— shareholders' liability is limited to the capital invested.

Other legal forms

■ General partnership (OHG – Offene Handelsgesellschaft)

Requirements of an OHG:

— minimum of two partners, who may be corporate entities;
— partners' liability is joint and several and unlimited with respect to the debts of the entity.

■ Limited partnership (KG – Kommanditgesellschaft)

Requirements of a KG:

— active partners are personally liable for the debts of the entity;
— limited sleeping partners' liability is limited to the capital invested.

■ GesmbH & Co KG – Gesellschaft mit beschränkter Haftung & Co Kommanditgesellschaft

Requirements of a GesmbH & Co KG:

— this is a type of KG in which the active partner is a GesmbH whose liability is limited to its assets;
— sleeping partners' liability is limited to the capital invested;
— this form combines two distinct advantages: the tax status of a partner-ship with limited liability for both active and sleeping partners.

Administrative procedures

Establishing a GesmbH is relatively straightforward. Setting up an AG is somewhat more complex and entails the following procedures.

■ Drafting the articles of incorporation, the bylaws and miscella-neous instruments

The articles of incorporation and bylaws are drawn up by a notary, and must contain the following information: legal form and corpo-rate name, business purpose, registered office, start-up date, number of shareholders, authorized share capital and its division among the share-holders.

Other required documents:

— proof that capital has been paid in by the shareholders;
— where applicable, details of in-kind contributions;
— a list of members appointed to the supervisory and executive boards, certified by notarized instrument;
— certified samples of the managing directors' signatures;

— for regulated businesses, a government licence;
— itemized statement of start-up costs;
— statement from the tax authorities certifying that no unpaid taxes are due.

■ Applying for registration

The application for registration is filed with the commercial register (*Firmenbuch*) of the district court under whose jurisdiction the company's registered office falls. As soon as the articles of incorporation and bylaws are signed, the company acquires existence as a company being formed (*in Gründung*), but it is entry into the commercial register that confers corporate personality or legal existence.

■ Announcements

All entries in the commercial register are automatically published in the Official Gazette (*Zentralblatt für Eintragungen in das Firmenbuch*).

■ Principal organization/incorporation costs

Registration fees are fixed at 1 per cent of the initial invested capital, and publication fees amount to 10,000 schillings (726.73 euros). The cost of incorporating an AG, including notary and legal expenses, totals from 10 to 15 per cent of the initial capital invested.

To these amounts may be added legal expense fees, which vary depending on the nature and complexity of services rendered and which are negotiated between the client and solicitor.

Human resources/labour law

■ Employment contract

Permanent

A written contract signed between the employer and the employee, containing a required minimum of information on job requirements and working conditions.

Fixed-term

Concluded for a single three- or six-month term that is not renewable.

■ Length of the working week

Legal maximum of eight hours a day and 40 hours a week. Collective bargaining agreements entitle eligible employees to a 38.5-hour week.

■ Overtime regulations

Overtime is limited to:

— two hours per day;
— 10 hours per week;
— 60 hours per year.

Under certain circumstances, these limits may be exceeded.

■ Annual vacation period

Thirty days per year, increasing to 36 days for employees with more than 25 years of continuous service.

■ Wages

There is no statutory guaranteed minimum wage. Industry-wide collective bargaining agreements generally set a minimum wage.

In general, the annual wage is divided into 14 months: 12 months of salary plus a summer bonus (*Urlaubsgeld*) and a year-end bonus (*Weihnachtsgeld*).

■ Social security

All employees must be covered by social security, which provides the following benefits: sickness and maternity (*Krankenversicherung*), family allowance (*Familienbeihilfe*), disability and old age (*Pensionsversicherung*), unemployment (*Arbeitslosenvericherung*) and worker's compensation (*Unfallversicherung*).

■ Mandatory social security contributions

Employer contributions: around 21.5 per cent of gross salary, with a fixed ceiling. Revised annually.

Employee contributions: around 17.6 per cent of gross salary, with a fixed ceiling. Revised annually.

■ Employing foreigners

Nationals of the European Union do not need permits to work in Austria. Non-EU nationals may obtain work permits from the local labour office upon presentation of an employment contract. The permit is valid for one job, one year and one province.

When the initial one-year permit expires, the holder may apply for a two-year permit (*Arbeitserlaubnis*). Although holders of this permit may change jobs, the permit is valid for one province only. After this second permit expires, its holder can apply for a five-year permit (*Befreiungsschein*) that secures access to work anywhere in Austria.

Employers are generally required to demonstrate that the foreign workers they wish to hire have skills that are not available on the Austrian employment market.

Paying taxes

■ Tax on registered capital (Gesellschaftsteuer)

One per cent plus the registration fees.

■ Corporate income tax (Körperschaftsteuer)

The corporate tax rate is 34 per cent, and the minimum amount payable is 50,000 schillings (€3,633.64) for an AG and 25,000 schillings (€1,816.82) for a GesmbH.

■ Personal taxes (Einkommensteuer)

The tax rate rises progressively from 10 to 50 per cent (five brackets).

■ Withholding at source on wages (Pay-As-You-Earn)

Employers withhold personal income taxes at source, calculated on the basis of the wages paid to employees. This is the Pay-As-You-Earn (PAYE) system.

■ Value-added tax (Umsatzsteuer)

The VAT levied on goods and services features several rates:

— Zero rate;
— Reduced rate: 10 per cent;
— Standard rate: 20 per cent.

■ Real estate tax (Grundsteuer)

Generally rates of 1/1,000 or 2/1,000 multiplied by a municipal coefficient of up to 500 per cent.

Investment incentives

The Austrian Business Agency (ABA), which has offices in Vienna and New York, is a good place for the potential investor to obtain general information. In 1997, the ABA advised 62 foreign companies, including 22 German, nine US and seven Italian investors. In an attempt to satisfy demand, the Agency now devotes greater resources to SMEs.

Companies with investment projects can also contact their local banks, the relevant ministries or the regional development office in the area in which they plan to locate.

Large-scale projects are submitted to Investkredit (*Österre-ichische Investitionskredit*), a bank that offers advice on location and potential partners, as well as information on available incentives and long-term business financing.

Regional incentives

Of the nine *Länder*, the most heavily subsidized are Burgenland (preferential support area in the southeast), Styria, Lower Austria and Carinthia. The European Recovery Programme (ERP) offers special incentives for regions such as these, which are considered under-industrialized, targeting innovative enterprise projects. Österreichische Kommunalkredit offers 30-year loans with a five-year grace period for repayment.

In areas that are not designated support areas, local and regional authorities sometimes offer low-interest rate loans and guarantees for the acquisition of real estate and equipment, as well as for the construction of plants and innovative projects.

The European Recovery Programme

The European Recovery Programme (ERP) provides subsidized loans for four different types of projects: national, export-oriented, infrastructures and special growth and technology. Loan amounts range from 5 million to 200 million schillings (€363,364.17 to €1,453,566.83), covering up to 75 per cent of the cost of the investment (both tangible and intangible).

In general, loans are granted for a term of eight years with a three-year grace period. The interest rate is 2.5 per cent or 4 per cent. Loans must be secured by a mortgage, a bank guarantee or the Austrian Guarantee Fund.

Successful applicants must (i) present projects that will improve production or human resources, or that will create jobs; (ii) demonstrate that they are financially sound (sales trends, cash flow, exports); or (iii) that their project will have a positive impact on the environment or Austrian subcontractors.

The ERP Technology Programme is designed to foster industrial research and co-operation between Austrian and foreign businesses, as well as with research institutes, particularly in connection with the Eureka Programme.

The BUERGES programme for small businesses

This programme is designed to help small businesses (fewer than 500 employees) by providing loans of up to 5 million schillings

(€363,364.17), or 10 million schillings (€726,728.34) under certain circumstances. Investments covered under the programme include new processes, energy savings, improvements in tourism, recreation and transportation infrastructures and co-operative projects with other businesses.

These guaranteed loans cover up to 70 per cent of investment costs and offer low interest rates for periods of up to 10 years.

A second BUERGES programme designed to encourage exports offers guaranteed low-interest rate loans.

■ The Seed Financing Programme

This programme targets businesses that have been in operation for less than two years. It is designed to help these businesses implement a global concept, conduct market research and draw up a financing plan for the production and marketing of the product.

A combination of low-interest rate loans and grants available under the programme covers up to 75 per cent of investment costs, to a ceiling of 6 million schillings (€436,037). Loans are granted for a term of seven years with a three-year grace period.

■ Innovation incentives

The Research Promotion Fund for Industry and Commerce encourages innovation and technology transfer by helping businesses turn discoveries and innovations into marketable products. The Fund provides grants or loans that cover up to 50 per cent of investment costs, attractive terms and a guarantee.

■ Environmental protection

Environmental protection is an important issue in Austria. Investors are advised to obtain information on environmental legislation in force when selecting production sites.

Various programmes fund measures taken by businesses to protect or improve the environment. They are financed by the government and administered by Österreichische Kommunalkredit.

Funding is available for projects involving waste water treatment, pollution reduction and environmental clean-up, and takes the form of low-interest rate loans with grace periods.

Louis Vuitton Österreich GesmbH

One of the first luxury brands to set up operations in Austria.

We respect to the letter the values that matter to Austrians: creativity – the Austrians are the Italians of the German-speaking world – and quality.

Olivier Dupont, Managing Director

In 1996, the famous brown canvas with the 'LV' monogram celebrated its 100th birthday. With annual sales of more than 8.8 billion francs in 1997, and retail successes in Paris and London, LVMH group subsidiary Louis Vuitton Malletier SA announced its intention to open 15 megastores around the world.

For now, the primary objectives in Austria are quality driven. And the strategy seems to be paying off in this small nation of 8 million inhabitants with ample purchasing power.

'The main reason we have been successful to date is that we were one of the first luxury brands to set up operations in Austria,' explains Olivier Dupont, Managing Director of Louis Vuitton Österreich GesmbH. 'We believed in this market's potential before anyone else did.' The first retail outlet opened for business in Vienna in 1985. Carry-on luggage, handbags, accessories, small leather goods and scarves found immediate success with demanding customers who appreciate beautiful and tasteful objects.

In a country where music and art are second nature, Louis Vuitton naturally extended its presence to Salzburg in 1988 and Kitzbühel in 1993. Overall, the Austrian subsidiary employs 15 people whose average age is around 30.

'Clients tend to be younger and there are now nearly as many males as females who come into our shops. Since 1995, the local clientele accounts for the bulk of our revenues. When the Asian crisis hit, business from foreign sources dried up. Japanese travellers passing through Vienna have become more cautious. They now buy one bag instead of two.'

Born in the 19th century, the inventor of the famous travelling trunk built his success on a policy of integrated manufacturing and distribution. Louis Vuitton currently has 240 exclusive boutiques around the globe, including around 60 in Europe. Selling through independent distributors is out of the question.

Because it has chosen to forgo subcontracting, Louis Vuitton maintains better control over costs and can offer its customers high quality goods at a reasonable price. Some customers are willing to pay more for custom-ordered goods, which carry a 20 per cent to 30 per cent higher price tag.

At 35 years of age, Olivier Dupont has already been places. After graduating from HEC, one of France's most prestigious business schools, and picking up an advanced degree from the same school in International Management, Olivier learned about marketing in his second year of study at McGill University in Montreal before fine-tuning his finance skills at the University of Cologne. In 1986, Peat Marwick offered him a job at its Düsseldorf office developing the portfolio of business with foreign corporations operating in Germany. Seven years later, he went to work for one of the firm's clients, Louis Vuitton, also based in Düsseldorf. In 1996, he took over at the helm of the Austrian subsidiary.

'Along the way, I married a German woman,' he says. 'Because I also manage our Swiss subsidiary, which operates six retail outlets, we live in Geneva. In fact, we divide our time between the two countries, and take advantage of our free time to sail and hike.'

Useful addresses in Austria

Austrian Business Agency (ABA)
Opernring 3
A 1010 Wien
Tel.: (43 1) 58 85 80

Central Bank
Österreichische Nationalbank
Otto Wagner Platz 3
A-1090 Wien
Tel.: (43 1) 40 42 00

Chamber of Commerce
Hessenplatz 3
4010 Linz
Tel.: (43 732) 780 00

Chamber of Commerce
Wiedner Hauptstrasse 63
A-1000 Wien
Tel.: (43 1) 50 10 50

Commercial Register
Handelsgericht Wien Firmenbuch
Riemergasse 7
A-1010 Wien
Tel.: (43 1) 51 52 80

Government of the Province of Salzburg
Chiemseehof
5010 Salzburg
Tel.: (43 662) 80 420

Government of the Province of Styria
Salzamtgasse 3
8010 Graz
Tel.: (43 316) 87 70

Ministry for Social Management
Information Service for Labour Market Inquiries
Stubenring 1
A-1010 Wien
Tel.: (43 1) 712 63 49

Ministry of Economic Affairs
Investors' Information Centre
Stubenring 1
A-1010 Wien
Tel.: (43 1) 711 00 55 55

Ministry of Finance
Bundesministerium für Finanzen
Himmelpfortgasse 9
A-1010 Wien
Tel.: (43 1) 51 43 30

National Social Security Office
Hauptverband der Österreich
Sozialversicherungstrager Kundmanngasse 21
A-1030 Wien
Tel.: (43 1) 71 13 20

Österreichische Investitionskredit
Renngasse 10
A-1013 Wien
Tel.: (43 1) 53 135

Vienna Business Agency (WWFF)
Ebendorferstrasse 2
A-1000 Wien
Tel.: (43 1) 4000 86 794

Vienna Economic Research Fund
Ebendorfersstrasse 2
A-1082 Wien
Tel.: (43 1) 40 00 86 70

Notes

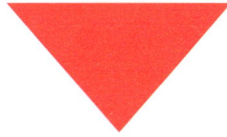

2

Setting Up a Business in Belgium

Key statistics

Total surface area:	30,528 square kilometres
Population:	10 million
GDP growth:	2.9% (1998)
Per capita GDP:	€21,801 (1998)
Public deficit/GDP ratio:	−1.3% (1998)
Public debt/GDP ratio:	117.3% (1998)
Inflation:	1% (1998)
Unemployment:	8.8% (1998)

Belgium is divided into three self-governing regions: Flanders, Wallonia and the Brussels capital. The country has a well-developed commercial tradition and an excellent communications network. Brussels, capital city of the European Union, lies at the heart of a highly cosmopolitan political and business environment.

Belgium favours foreign investment that will develop cutting-edge skills or result in innovative products intended for export, particularly in the areas of information technology and multimedia. Favourable tax treatment also provides an incentive to multinational groups to establish their European headquarters or distribution hubs.

Of Belgium's 100 top industrial or commercial enterprises, 65 per cent are controlled by foreign shareholders. Two-thirds of all foreign investments are made by European Union member nations, with the Netherlands, France and Germany the clear-cut leaders. The United States and Japan top the list of foreign investors from outside the European Union.

More than half of all capital investments are in service-related fields, while industrial investments mostly concern the chemicals, petro-chemicals and automotive industries.

Recent foreign investments of note: Airtours (UK) bought tour operator Sun International; RSL Communications (US) bought ET Belux; Masco (US) acquired the radiator manufacturer Vasco; ING (Netherlands) took control of Banque Bruxelle Lambert and the Belgium-Dutch insurance group, Fatés, took control of the Generale de Bank.

Regulations governing foreign investment

No preliminary approvals are required for foreign direct investment in Belgium. However, setting up a business in certain sectors might require government authorization or license. These include: banking, insurance, road transport, the manufacture and sale of food products, the opening of department stores and small retail shops, the cutting and polishing of diamonds.

For statistical monitoring purposes, investors are required to furnish information on these transactions via their bank, which transmits the supporting documents to the Institut Belgo-Luxembourgeois. Repatriation of capital and profits is freely permitted.

Foreign investors practising a business that requires registration with the registrar of companies or the handicrafts council must provide proof of their entrepreneurial fitness in the form of a diploma, a training certificate, practical experience, etc. The local trade council issues the certificate of compliance.

Building permits are required prior to the commencement of industrial construction and are delivered once an environmental permit has been issued. The latter is granted on the basis of compliance with environmental standards.

Principal legal forms

It is possible to conduct business in Belgium by establishing a representative office, a branch office or a subsidiary. Subsidiaries must adopt one of the country's existing legal forms. For small- and medium-sized businesses, the most widely used forms are the limited-liability company and the corporation.

■ Limited-liability company (SPRL/BVBA – Besloten vennootschap met beperkte aansprakelijkheid)

Requirements of an SPRL/BVBA:
— minimum of two founding shareholders (sole proprietorship is permitted in the case of an SPRLU);
— minimum share capital of 750,000 Belgian francs (€18,592.01), fully subscribed and one-third paid;
— strict formalities at the time of incorporation (notarized instrument).

Flexible management:
— minimum of one manager, who may be but need not be a shareholder, but who must be an individual;

— annual general meeting;
— presence of one or more independent auditors is mandatory, depending on the size of the company;
— shareholders' liability is limited to the capital invested.

■ Corporation (SA/NV – Naamloze vennootschap)

Requirements of an SA/NV:
— minimum of seven shareholders;
— minimum capital of 2,500,000 Belgian francs (€61,973.38), fully subscribed, and at least 25 per cent paid in.

Fairly cumbersome management:
— board of directors with a minimum of three members (two for companies with only two shareholders); one or more managers, who may be but need not be members of the board;
— annual general meeting of the shareholders;
— presence of one or more independent auditors is mandatory, depending on the size of the company;
— shareholders' liability is limited to the capital invested.

Other legal forms

■ General commercial partnership

Requirements:
— minimum of two partners;
— partners' liability is joint and several and unlimited.

■ Limited partnership

Requirements:
— Active partners' liability is joint and several and unlimited.
— Sleeping partners' or contributors' liability for debts of the entity is limited to capital invested.

■ Co-operative corporation (SC)

Two legal forms:
— the unlimited-liability co-operative corporation (SCRIS) (used by groups of companies);
— the limited-liability co-operative corporation (SCRL).

This legal form resembles that of the SPRL with capital of 750,000 Belgian francs (€18,592.01), but there are at least three partners and there are fewer legal restrictions.

Administrative procedures

The following formalities must be accomplished to establish an SPRL or an SA.

■ Preparing the articles of incorporation and bylaws

The articles of incorporation and bylaws must contain the following information: legal form and corporate name, business purpose, registered office, life of the company, amount of capital, names and details of signing members (individuals or corporate entities), corporate governance structure.

■ Drafting the financial plan

A financial plan covering two years of operation must be drawn up (preferably by an accountant) and held in the custody of a notary. In the event of subsequent financial difficulties or insolvency, this document may serve as proof of the founding shareholders' liability if the latter have failed to invest sufficient capital to sustain the company as a going concern.

■ Opening a bank account

The paid-in capital is deposited with a bank into a blocked account, and the bank issues a certificate to this effect.

◼ Drafting the articles of incorporation and bylaws

For both the SPRL and SA, this is done in the presence of a notary (authentic instrument). For an SCRI, the articles of incorporation and bylaws may be drafted under private signature.

◼ Filing the incorporating instrument

Within two weeks of the signature of the incorporating instrument, it must be filed with the clerk of the commercial court of the district of the company's domicile.

◼ Publishing the incorporating instrument

The court clerk submits an abstract of the articles of incorporation and bylaws for publication in the official gazette (the *Moniteur Belge*). The language of publication depends on where the company's registered office is or where it plans to do business.

◼ Registering the company

The company then obtains its Register of Commerce number.

◼ Principal organization/incorporation costs

For an SA with initial capital of 2,500,000 Belgian francs (€61,973.38), costs include:

— tax on registered capital of 0.5%;
— registration with the Register of Commerce (3,000 Belgian francs) (€74.37);
— announcement in the *Moniteur Belge* (6,000 Belgian francs for 10 pages) (€148.74);
— notary fees, which vary depending on share capital from 0.85% (for the first 1,500,000 Belgian francs) to 0.02% (above 62,500,000 Belgian francs).

To these amounts may be added legal expense fees, which vary depending on the nature and complexity of services rendered and which are negotiated between client and solicitor.

Human resources/labour law

■ Employment contract

Permanent

A written contract signed between the employer and the employee, containing a required minimum of information on job requirements and working conditions.

Fixed-term

A written contract of a maximum term of two years, renewable only under special circumstances.

■ Length of the working week

Thirty-six to 38 hours in many industries.

■ Overtime regulations

Restrictions on working time:
— Nine hours maximum per day;
— 45 hours maximum per week.
— Premium of 25 per cent over the regular hourly wage for overtime, rising to 100 per cent on Sundays and legal holidays.

■ Annual vacation period

Twenty days.

■ Paid leave and public holidays

Ten days.

■ Wages

A minimum wage has been set under the terms of national collective bargaining agreements. A minimum monthly wage has been set for full-time workers 21 years of age and over.

■ Social security

Sickness and maternity, disability, old age and survivor benefits, on-the-job accidents and occupational diseases, unemployment and family allowance are provided for.

■ Mandatory social security contributions

Employer contributions: around 33 per cent of gross salary.

Employee contributions: around 13 per cent of gross salary.

Contributions for family allowances, paid vacations, on-the-job accidents and occupational diseases are fully paid by the employer.

■ Employing foreigners

Nationals of the European Union do not need permits to work in Belgium, but they must submit a statement from their employer certifying that they are employed full-time. After completing a probationary period, they are entitled to a five-year, renewable residence permit.

For non-EU nationals, the employer must request a work permit from the regional office of the Ministry of Labour. The work permit is granted for one year and is renewable.

Foreign executives and researchers may qualify for favourable tax treatment in certain cases.

Paying taxes

■ Tax on registered capital (Voornaamste Registratierechten)

Both initial capital and capital increases are taxed at a rate of 0.5 per cent.

■ Corporate income tax (Vennootschapsbelasting)

Standard rate: 39 per cent (40.17 per cent)*;

— reduced rate if profits are below 13 million Belgian francs (€322,261.58).
— from 0 to 1 million Belgian francs: 28% (28.84%)*
— from 1 to 3.6 million Belgian francs: 36% (37.08%)*
— from 3.6 to 13 million Belgian francs: 41% (42.23%)*

Note: Not all companies qualify for the reduced rate.

*A 3% 'crisis tax' (CCC) has been added on to the corporation tax.

Personal taxes

Progressive rate from 25 per cent to 55 per cent (seven brackets).

A three per cent 'crisis tax' has been added on to the personal income tax.

Value-added tax (BTW – Belasting over de toegevoegde waarde)

Depending on the nature of goods and services:
— Zero rate;
— Reduced rate: 1%, 6%, 12%;
— Standard rate: 21%.

Local taxes

A variety of taxes at diverse rates are in force, levied on building construction, manufacturing sites, roads, personnel employed, polluting companies, etc. Given that the sums involved are very low, their impact is not significant.

Investment incentives

Incentive packages are granted on the basis of the type of company, its sector of activity and the region of domicile (Brussels, Flanders, Wallonia). While they essentially target small and medium-sized firms, larger undertakings may qualify if their investment project creates jobs or leads to environmental improvements.

Certain areas in Belgium (such as the provinces of Hainaut, classified as Objective 1, and Limbourg, Objective 2) have been given priority status by the European Union and thus receive special structural fund grant money.

◼ Regional incentives

The three regions manage their own programmes of financial investment incentives. They are extremely numerous and can be very interesting.

Capital grants may include interest subsidies that vary with the region and the nature of investment project.

Grants are not subject to self-financing requirements in Brussels or Wallonia.

The regional incentive grant may not exceed 21 per cent of the amount invested.

In addition to this type of incentive, regions may offer exemptions from real estate taxes on a case-by-case basis.

◼ Tax incentives

Co-ordination centres

Favourable tax treatment is offered to foreign groups of companies that set up headquarters in Belgium, provided that the activity of the so-called co-ordination centre is restricted to co-ordination and management services rendered for the sole benefit of some or all of the companies comprising the group.

Set up as Belgian subsidiaries or branch offices, they are subject to a reduced taxable base equal to eight per cent of their operating expenses, excluding personnel and financial costs. In addition, dividends distributed and interest and royalties paid are exempt from withholding at the source.

Foreign executives working in co-ordination centres are entitled to very favourable tax treatment. Throughout their assignment in Belgium, they are not taxed on worldwide income at Belgian rates. Instead, they are subject to non-resident income tax solely on income earned in connection with their position in Belgium.

To obtain this status, centres must be approved by an inter-ministerial committee, which bases its decision on the following criteria:

— capital of at least 1 billion Belgian francs (€24,789,352.48);
— consolidated annual revenues total at least 10 billion Belgian francs (€247,893,524.77), of which 500 million or 20 per cent must be earned outside the parent's home country;
— the group has at least four foreign subsidiaries in four different countries;
— the co-ordination centre employs at least 10 people in Belgium within two years of the start of operations.

Co-ordination centres are authorized to engage in the following kinds of activity, solely for the benefit of the group to which they belong: advertising, scientific research, accounting, etc. They may not engage in commercial or production-related activities.

More than 300 companies, in particular US, UK and French, have opted for this tax status. To qualify, companies must file an application with the *Administration centrale des contributions directes*.

Distribution centres

Distribution centres, which co-ordinate the international export from Belgium of raw materials and finished goods, may also qualify for favourable tax treatment.

Subsidiaries and branch offices of foreign companies set up for the purpose of purchasing raw materials or for packaging or storing merchandise are entitled to privileged tax treatment in the form of an income tax assessment of five per cent of operating costs.

Since a reform was introduced in 1994 aimed at enabling Belgium to compete more effectively with the Netherlands and Luxembourg in attracting foreign investors to set up distribution centres, these centres may exercise certain management and administrative activities (such as invoicing and financial, banking tax and customs services). They may also sell finished goods and merchandise to other companies in their group, provided that any purchases made from other Belgian companies permit the latter to earn a normal profit margin on the sale.

Inspired by the Dutch model, the Belgian authorities no longer consider as operating expenses the cost of services provided by third parties (such as transportation), provided that they are invoiced at prevailing market prices.

This favourable tax status is granted provided that the distribution centre assumes no business risks, or that such risks are deemed negligible.

Service centres

Service centres must limit themselves to planning or auxiliary activities on behalf of other companies in the group to which they belong. Call centres whose role is to provide information to customers or contribute passively or actively to the sales process fall into this category. The tax advantages are similar to those that apply to co-ordination and distribution centres, and are offered for a period of five years.

The Belgian holding: non-taxable dividends and capital gains

Favourable tax status is granted to Belgian companies that have an equity stake of at least five per cent in a company that distributes dividends to it, or that paid at least 50 million Belgian francs (€1,239,467.62) to acquire the equity interest in question. In particular:

— 95 per cent of all dividends received are tax exempt;
— capital gains on the sale of equity interests are not taxed;
— a registration tax of 0.5 per cent of the capital invested in the Belgian company is levied.

Such companies are not required to be pure holding companies (the holding of equity securities).

Foreign credits attached to dividends may not be used by the Belgian holding company.

To qualify for this favourable tax status, the subsidiary of the Belgian holding company must be subject to tax on corporate income similar to that levied in Belgium.

An 'anti-abuse' proviso introduced in the Act of 23 October 1991 disqualifies dividend payments made by:

— companies established in countries with a more advantageous income tax system;
— holding or financing companies that qualify for privative tax status in their country of domicile;
— investment firms;
— companies established abroad which distribute dividends that do not meet the requirements of this provision.

Accelerated depreciation

Large companies that set up operations in development areas are entitled to accelerated depreciation (twice the rate in force in Belgium) if they opt for the double straight-line depreciation method.

Small firms (those employing fewer than 50 people or with annual revenues of less than 200 million Belgian francs (€4,957,870.50)) may effect an immediate write-down of their investment costs.

Investments in energy saving and scientific research equipment may be straight-line depreciated in three years (33.3 per cent per year). This entitlement also applies to industrial assets that are considered strategic for the Belgian economy.

Business start-up costs may be 100 per cent depreciated in the company's first year of operation.

Research incentives

Interest-free advances are available to cover up to 50 per cent of all expenses incurred in the development of prototypes or new manufacturing processes. These loans are refunded only when the product or process begins to generate a profit.

A tax deduction of 440,000 Belgian francs (€10,907.32) is granted for each additional employee hired to work in a scientific research centre, doubling to 880,000 (€21,814.63) for highly qualified researchers.

Hiring subsidies

Grants and reduction in social charges are offered to companies that hire the long-term unemployed, unskilled workers, and workers over the age of 50 who have been replaced by part-time younger workers.

Companies that hire young employees without previous experience are entitled in the first year to a 10 per cent reduction in the reference wage specified in the relevant collective bargaining agreement. The second year, their social charges are reduced by 10 per cent. They also qualify for reduced social security charges (from 10 per cent to 50 per cent) under the wage moderation scheme, which does not require that they hire the unemployed.

Employers are offered financial incentives to introduce flexi-time arrangements such as part-time work, reduced working hours and sabbatical leave.

The National Employment Office offsets some of the costs of training workers at technical training institutes or production sites by contributing up to 45 per cent of wages and social charges and up to 50 per cent of related travel and accommodation expenses.

Useful addresses in Belgium

Belgian National Bank
boulevard de Berlaimont, 14
B-1000 Brussels
Tel.: (32 2) 221 21 11

Brussels Chamber of Commerce and Industry
500, avenue Louise
B-1050 Brussels
Tel.: (32 2) 648 50 02

Deux Flandres
Congrescentru-Citadelpark
B-9000 Gand
Tel.: (32 91) 22 29 47

Fédération des Entreprises de Belgique
4, rue Ravenstein
B-1000 Brussels
Tel.: (32 2) 515 08 11

General VAT Administration
Cité Administrative de l'Etat
Tour Finances, bte 39
Boulevard du Jardin Botanique 50
B-1010 Brussels
Tel.: (32 2) 210 26 11

Institut Belgo-Luxembourgeois du Change
boulevard de Berlaimont, 5
B-1000 Brussels
Tel.: (32 2) 219 46 00

National Employment Office (ONEM)
boulevard de l'Empereur, 7
B-1000 Brussels
Tel.: (32 2) 515 41 11

National Social Security Office
boulevard Waterloo, 76
B-1000 Brussels
Tel.: (32 2) 509 31 11

Provinces of Antwerp and Limbourg
Huidevettersstraat, 45
B-2000 Antwerp
Tel.: (32 3) 232 39 57

Provinces of Hainaut and Namur
boulevard Tirou, 9
B-6000 Charleroi
Tel.: (32 71) 31 00 02

Provinces of Liège and Luxembourg
rue Saint-Rémy, 1
B-4000 Liège
Tel.: (32 41) 23 02 78

■ Ministries

Ministry of Economic Affairs
Office for Foreign Investments
square de Meeus 23
B-1040 Brussels
Tel.: (32 2) 506 51 11

Ministry of Finance
Wetstraat, 12
B-1000 Brussels
Tel.: (32 2) 233 81 11

Ministry of the Brussels Region
Office for Foreign Investments
rue du Champ de Mars, 25
B-1050 Brussels
Tel.: (32 2) 513 97 00

Ministry of the Flanders Region
Leuvenseplein, 4
B-1000 Brussels
Tel.: (32 2) 507 38 51

Ministry of the Middle Classes
Administration de la Réglementation
2ème Direction
Tour Sablon
Rue J Stevens 7
B-1000 Brussels
Tel.: (32 2) 504 62 11

Ministry of the Wallonia Region
Rue Royale, 67
B-1000 Brussels
Tel.: (32 2) 218 27 00

■ Regional organizations

Flanders Foreign Investment Office (FFIO)
Leuvenseplein 4
B-1000 Brussels
Tel.: (32 2) 2 227 53 11

Office for Foreign Investors in Wallonia
Avenue du Prince de Liège, 7
B-5100 Namur
Tel.: (32 8) 132 14 53

Plastic Omnium Automotive NV

I was attracted by the chance to take responsibility for a greenfield project and by the opportunity to gain access to the automotive industry in an international group that is rapidly expanding.

Peter Naeye, Managing Director

To better meet the needs of its client Opel, the French group Plastic Omnium built a plant near Antwerp, in Herentals. The foundation was laid in June 1997, and the company now employs 180 people, including 40 managers and support staff.

Peter Naeye, 38, was born in Louvain and trained as an electrical-mechanical engineer. Today he is in charge of this new plant. 'After graduation, I began working in the Development Department at Philips Consumer Electronics, where I was project manager in the audiovisual segment based in Austria. Later on, I was head of quality, organization and productivity in Hasselt and plant manager in Louvain. When Plastic Omnium approached me about designing and launching the Herentals plant, I was attracted by the chance to take responsibility for a greenfield project and by the opportunity to gain access to the automotive industry in an international group that is rapidly expanding.'

With 80 subsidiaries in 18 countries and a workforce of nearly 9,000, the Plastic Omnium group has several core businesses: automotive parts (interior, exterior and fuel systems); equipment and services for local governments and private companies that handle waste, recreation and recycling; supplying technical parts and anti-rust cladding made of high-performance plastics used in a number of industries; and medical and pharmaceutical parts and sets.

This family business founded by Pierre Burelle 50 years ago posted revenues of 9 billion French francs in 1998. Half of its revenues are now earned outside France via its international subsidiaries mainly based in Europe.

'We chose Flanders in order to be close to our customers and prospects. In addition, this location gives us excellent positioning with respect to both German and French automakers. The Flanders Foreign Investment Office (FFIO) supported us throughout the project development phase, helping us put the deal together and negotiate grants with the Flemish government. We were awarded 150 million Belgian francs, which is considerable,' says Peter Naeye.

'To manufacture the bumper for the new Opel Astra – we're the exclusive supplier – as well as the fuel system, our guiding principle is the tight flow model, based on the notions of "just in time" and "zero defect". Half of our shop floor workers are women; we appreciate their precision. The average age of our managers is 30, and I made them speak French to facilitate communications within the group. Since I got here, I have the feeling that I have worked as much in two years as I would have worked in four years elsewhere. Years count double – but so does experience!'

To keep in shape, this married father of four allows himself an annual skiing vacation of one week. His favourite resorts are Tignes and Val Thorens.

Notes

3

Setting Up a Business in Denmark

North Sea

Skagen

Frederikshavn

Torshavn

Faroe Islands

Thisted

Alborg

SWEDEN

Skive

Viborg

Randers Grena

Holstebro

Herning Silkeborg

Ringkobing

Arhus

Horsens

Helsingor

Hillerod

Copenhagen

Vejle

Holbaek
Kalundborg

Frederica
Esbjerg Kolding

Middlefart

Koge

Ribe

Odense

Slagelse

Haderslev

Nyborg

Korsor

Naestved

Svendborg

Baltic Sea

Vordingborg

GERMANY

Nakslov

Nykobing

Key statistics

Total surface area:	43,094 square kilometres
Population:	5.3 million
GDP growth:	2.7% (1998)
Per capita GDP:	€29,448 (1998)
Public deficit/GDP ratio:	0.8% (1998)
Public debt/GDP ratio:	58.1% (1998)
Inflation:	1.9% (1998)
Unemployment:	5.1% (1998)

Denmark, the European Union's only Scandinavian member country until 1995, has opted out of the Euro Area for the time being, but is expected to join in 2001. This small country provides an excellent spring-board for foreign businesses interested in securing access to the markets of Northern Europe. The motor and rail link announced for 2000 between Copenhagen and Malmö (Sweden) has sparked interest in the Danish capital on the part of investors, who are keen to improve their distribution channels into the Nordic and Baltic nations. Although the country is sparsely populated, Danish consumers enjoy high purchasing power.

Some 2,200 Danish companies are in the hands of foreign share-holders. These foreign-held firms employ 140,000 people (10 per cent of private sector employment overall) and contribute 17 per cent to total revenues earned by companies established in Denmark.

The major foreign equity holdings are in the electronics industry, where nearly one-third of all companies are controlled by foreign shareholders. The foreign investment community is led by the Netherlands, the United Kingdom, Germany, Norway, Sweden and the United States.

The Invest in Denmark Office has identified six key sectors for foreign investors: telecommunications and information technologies, call centres, retail distribution centres, the environment, agri-business, and pharmaceuticals. Out of 169 projects in 1996 (the last year for which statistics are available), 45 per cent were European, 37 per cent were US and 19 per cent were Asian.

The list of recent foreign investors includes DHL Worldwide Express (US), Dell Computer (US), Structural Bioinformatics (US), American Power Conversion (US), Itochu (Japan), Laboratorium Visby (Germany), Robert Bosch (Germany), Nokia (Finland), United Biscuits (UK), France Telecom (France) and Gemplus (France).

Regulations governing foreign investment

Foreign direct investment (from inside and outside the European Union) is freely permitted. What restrictions there are pertain to foreign investment in the national defence industry and in mining, oil, and the public service sectors.

Foreign investors are expected to comply with stringent local regulations governing sanitation and safety, the environment and consumer protection. In some cases they must obtain a permit to build, which is processed within three months at the most.

The acquisition of real property by foreign investors requires the prior approval of the Ministry of Justice, unless this property is purchased for direct use in industrial or commercial operations. This requirement was enacted to prevent foreign tourists from buying up too many Danish summer cottages.

Principal legal forms

It is possible to conduct business in Denmark by establishing a representative office, a branch office or a subsidiary. Subsidiaries must adopt one of the country's existing legal forms.

The ApS (*Anpartsselskab*) is the legal form most widely used by investors in Denmark, although the A/S (*Aktieselskab*) form is used as well, by both large corporations and SMEs.

■ Limited-liability company (ApS – Anpartsselskab)

Requirements of an ApS:

— at least one founder (an individual or a corporate entity), who must be a Danish resident or an EU national;
— minimum capital of 125,000 kroner (€16,820.52), fully subscribed and paid in when the company is formed.

Relatively flexible management:

— an executive board composed of one or more members, who must be Danish residents or EU nationals;
— a board of directors with a minimum of three members (at least half and a minimum of two must be Danish residents or EU nationals residing in an EU country) is mandatory if share capital exceeds 300,000 kroner (€40,369.24) or if the workforce exceeds 35;

— annual general meeting of shareholders;
— mandatory audit of financial statements by one or more independent auditors;
— shareholders' liability is limited to the capital invested.

■ Corporation (A/S – Aktieselskab)

Requirements of an AS:

— at least one founder (an individual or a corporate entity), who must be a Danish resident or an EU national;
— minimum capital of 500,000 kroner (€67,282.07), fully subscribed and paid in.

Relatively cumbersome management:

— a board of directors with a minimum of three members, who may be but need not be shareholders, but who must either be Danish residents or nationals of an EU member country;
— an executive board composed of one or more members, who must be Danish residents or EU nationals;
— annual general meeting of shareholders;
— mandatory audit of financial statements by one or more independent auditors, at least two if the company is listed;
— shareholders' liability is limited to the capital invested.

Note: If one of the managing directors is an EU national, or if the majority of the members of the board of directors are EU nationals, permission can be obtained from the Ministry of Justice to appoint a non-EU national to an executive management position.

Other legal forms

■ General commercial partnership (IS – Interessentskab)

Requirements of an IS:

— minimum of two partners;
— no statutory requirements regarding minimum capital;
— partners' liability is joint and several and unlimited with respect to third parties.

■ Limited partnership (KS – Kommanditselskab)

Requirements of a KS are:

— two types of partners;
— active partners, whose liability is unlimited;
— limited sleeping partners, whose liability is limited to the capital invested;
— this legal form is often used for maritime and real estate activities.

■ Co-operative corporation (Amba – Andelsselskab med begraensetanswar)

This legal form is mainly used in the agricultural sector.

Administrative procedures

Setting up an ApS or an A/S entails the following procedures.

■ Drawing up the articles of incorporation and bylaws

The incorporating instrument is composed of two documents:

— a charter of incorporation (bylaws), drawn up and signed by the founding members, which includes the names and addresses of the founding members, the names of the members of the board and independent auditors, draft articles of incorporation and details on the shares offered for subscription;
— the articles of incorporation themselves, containing the following information: corporate name, business purpose, registered office, share capital, par value of shares, shareholder voting rights, the transferability of shares, powers vested in the annual meeting of the shareholders and rules for calling shareholders' meetings and the powers vested in the directors, officers and independent auditors of the company.

■ Approving and signing the articles of incorporation and bylaws

The organizational meeting resolves to form the company and elects its managing directors and independent auditors.

■ Registering with the Danish Commerce and Companies Agency

The application for registration must be filed by the members of the board of directors or the executive board. The company acquires full legal status only after registering with the Danish Commerce and Companies Agency. The founding members are personally and jointly liable for all transactions effected in the name of the company between the date on which corporate instruments are signed and the date of registration.

It takes three to four months to complete the procedures required to set up an A/S or an ApS. It is for this reason that many investors prefer to acquire a registered but inactive company (see inset below on acquiring a ready-made company).

■ Publishing the notice of incorporation

The Danish Commerce and Companies Agency takes care of the required publication in *Statstidende*, the official gazette.

■ Principal organization/incorporation costs

Registration fees for establishing a company are as follows:

— a fixed fee of 3,000 kroner (403.69 euros) for an A/S;
— a fixed fee of 2,300 kroner (309.50 euros) for an ApS;
— a tax on registered capital of 0.4 per cent.

To these amounts may be added legal expense fees, which vary depending on the nature and complexity of services rendered and which are negotiated between client and solicitor.

They generally come to around 20,000 kroner (2,691.28 euros).

Acquiring a 'ready-made' company

It is possible to acquire a ready-made company in Denmark, ie a registered company that has exercised no activity since it was established.

This practice is widespread in Denmark, since it enables investors to dispense with incorporation processing delays. In addition, founding members avoid being held personally liable for company transactions in the interim between company formation and registration, a process that can take several weeks.

A meeting of the shareholders is called to approve the amendments required in view of the company's future business activity.

It costs around 7,000 kroner (€941.95) to acquire a ready-made ApS and around 13,000 kroner (€1,749.33) to acquire an A/S.

Human resources/labour law

■ Employment contract

Permanent

A written contract signed between the employer and the employee, containing a required minimum of information on job requirements and working conditions.

Fixed-term

There are no restrictions on the maximum term of fixed-term employment contracts.

■ Length of the working week

The legal maximum is 40 hours.

■ Overtime regulations

Overtime regulations and compensation vary from one sector to another.

■ Annual vacation period

Five weeks a year.

■ Paid leave and public holidays

Ten paid public holidays a year.

■ Wages

There is no statutory minimum wage.

Wages are fixed in employment contracts or by collective bargaining agreements for various employment categories and industries.

■ Social security

Workers receive benefits covering sickness and maternity, old age and disability, on-the-job accidents, unemployment and family allowances.

■ Mandatory social security contributions

The Danish social security system is largely financed through direct taxes. Social security contributions are factored into income taxes. Certain mandatory contributions are not based on wage levels, such as the supplemental retirement contribution (ATP) of 2,700 kroner (€363.32) a year. The employer covers two-thirds of the total.

The contribution to the vocational training fund for unemployed young people totals around 1,200 kroner (€161.48) per annum.

■ Employing foreigners

Nationals of the European Union and non-member Nordic nations (Norway and Iceland) do not need a permit to work in Denmark. Nationals of other countries must obtain both a work permit and a residence permit from the chief of police in their district of domicile. Foreigners with recognized, needed skills generally have no problem obtaining these permits.

Paying taxes

■ Tax on registered capital (Kapitaltilforselsafgift)

One per cent tax rate on capital increases.

■ Corporate income tax (Selskabskat)

Standard rate: 32 per cent.

■ Solidarity tax (Arbejdsmarkedsbidrag)

A special 2.5 per cent tax that is deductible from taxable corporate income.

Employers are taxed on the basis of their revenues, less exports and assets acquired in Denmark.

■ Personal taxes

Three brackets ranging between 41 per cent and 58 per cent.
Voluntary church tax of 0.7 per cent on net taxable income.

■ Withholding at source on wages

Employers withhold personal income taxes at source, calculated on the basis of the wages paid to employees.

■ Value-added tax (Mervaerdiagift)

Zero rate.
Standard rate: 25 per cent

■ Municipal and provincial real estate taxes (*Kommunal/ Amtskommunal Grundskyld*)

Levied on land only. Tax rates of 0.6 per cent to 2.4 per cent (municipal) and 1 per cent (provincial).

Investment incentives

Potential investors should contact the Invest in Denmark Office set up by the Ministry of Business and Industry to attract and support foreign investment by helping businesses analyse opportunities in Denmark. It provides services ranging from preliminary studies to business start-up assistance, and can also identify potential partners and put foreign investors in contact with the relevant government organizations. Since investment incentives are limited in Denmark, investors are advised to have other reasons for establishing a business there.

Most incentive packages are designed to stimulate research and development, energy savings, venture capital and exports. The government seeks to promote certain sectors such as pharmaceuticals, biotechnology, biogenetics, information systems and technology and environmental protection and energy savings. Special incentives exist for under-developed regions.

Regional incentives

Some regions have set up special incentive programmes to foster job creation through the development and upgrading of existing businesses. Among them, the counties of Nordjylland, Lolland, Bornholm, the Faeroe Islands and part of the Aarhus Islands, Viborg, Ringkoebing, Sonderjylland, Funen and Storstroms.

These development incentives are awarded by the Danish Agency for Development of Trade and Industry (*Erhvervsfremme Styrelsen*), and finance around 30 per cent of productive investment costs. In addition, low-interest rate loans with a three-year grace period are granted for a period of 10 years. Those seeking such loans can apply directly to the European Investment Bank or via a local bank or financial institution.

Loans are also available from the Nordic Investment Bank for investments in Scandinavian countries.

Government incentives

Research and development

The Danish Agency for Development of Trade and Industry also offers tax-free grants, loans or venture capital investments that cover up to 50 per cent of the costs related to new product design, feasibility and

48

market studies, and patent expenses. In return, companies receiving this aid must show that the new product will create new jobs and boost exports.

The Eureka programme covers up to 50 per cent of the total investment outlay and hiring subsidies are also available to firms that offer three-year contracts to young researchers. Special amortization schedules are provided to foster research and development.

Incentives targeting the service and industrial sectors

The government has implemented a programme aimed at creating jobs in small service firms, offering training and advisory services to self-employed consultants, accountants, legal professionals and architects. Self-employed individuals who work at home are also eligible under the programme.

Investment projects that lead to energy savings may qualify for reduced interest rate loans from Finance for Danish Industry that range from 100,000 to 3 million kroner (€13,456.41 to €403,692.44) and cover up to 70 per cent of costs. 'Green jobs' created in the areas of energy, food and water may qualify for special employment subsidies.

Export incentives

The Danish Export Promotion Council (EPC) provides grants to businesses seeking to develop new export markets. EPC grants cover 40 per cent of costs for two years, rising to 60 per cent over three years if the company is exporting for the first time to difficult markets.

Loans and equity interests are offered by the Industrialization Fund for Developing Countries and the Industrialization Fund for Central European Countries to firms that invest in emerging markets and eastern and central European countries, respectively.

Community incentives

Denmark receives regional structural funding grants from the European Commission under Objectives 2 and 5b. Objective 2 (economic conversion of declining industrial regions) covers the northern region of Jutland. Funding supports technological development, measures designed to improve competitive posture and those aimed at reducing structural weaknesses in the regional economy. Objective 5b-eligible regions (economic diversification of vulnerable rural areas) include North and South Jutland, Viborg, Ringkoebing and the islands.

Denmark also receives non-regional funding available under Objective 3 (to combat long-term unemployment and help young adults find jobs), Objective 4 (to help workers adjust to changes in the industrial fabric) and Objective 5a (agriculture and fishing).

Useful addresses in Denmark

Agency for Employment
Arbejdsmarkedsstyrelsen
Hesselogade 16
DK-2100 Koberhaum 0
Tel.: (45 39) 27 19 22

Competition Council
Noregarde 49
DK-1165 Copenhagen K
Tel.: (45 33) 93 90 00

Copenhagen Capacity
Kongens Nytorv 6
DK-1050 Copenhagen K
Tel.: (45 33) 33 03 33

Danish Agency for Development of Trade and Industry
Erhvervsfremme Styrelsen
Tagensvej 137
DK-2200 Copenhagen N
Tel.: (45 35) 86 86 86 86

Danish Chamber of Commerce
Det Dansk Handelskammeret
Boersen
DK-1217 Copenhagen K
Tel.: (45 33) 32 52 16

Danish Commerce and Companies Agency
Erhvervs-OG Selskabsstyrelsen
Kampmannsgade 1
DK-1780 Copenhagen V
Tel.: (45 33) 12 42 80

Danish Industries' Federation
Industriraadet
H.C Andersens boulevard 18
DK-1787 Copenhagen V
Tel.: (45 33) 77 33 77

Distribution Council Denmark (DCD)
Amaliegade 45
DK-1256 Copenhagen K
Tel.: (45 33) 36 01 80

Environmental Protection Agency
Miljostyrelsen-Strandgade 29
DK-1401 Copenhagen K
Tel.: (45 32) 66 01 00

Finance for Danish Industry and Handicrafts
Finansieringsinstituttet for Industri OG Haandvaerk
La Cours Vej 7
DK-2000 Frederiksberg
Tel.: (45 38) 33 18 88

Industrialization Fund for Developing Countries
IFU- Bremerholm 4
DK-1069 Copenhagen K
Tel.: (45 33) 14 25 75

Invest in Denmark
Slotsholmsgade 10–12
DK-1215 Copenhagen K
Tel.: (45 33) 92 45 52

Ministry of Environment and Energy
Hojbro Plads 4
DK-1200 Copenhagen K
Tel.: (45 33) 92 76 00

Patent Office
Helgeshoj Alle 81
DK-2630 Taastrup
Tel.: (45 43) 50 80 00

Regional Development Fund
Industri-OG Handelsstyrelen
Sondergade 25
DK-8600 Silkeborg
Tel.: (87 45) 20 40 60

Ellinas Phone Rentals ApS

The ability to make contact swiftly is increasingly what gives businesses a competitive edge.

Hervé Soursou, Managing Director of OdysseyCom ApS

'I'd wanted to set up my own business since I was 18 years old. Undoubtedly looking for freedom and a challenge,' says Hervé Soursou. Today, the 27-year-old entrepreneur runs OdysseyCom, the company he established in Copenhagen.

While a student at France's Ecole Nationale d'Ingénieurs de Metz (an engineering school), Hervé Soursou did a few internships at Alcatel subsidiaries, where he discovered his passion for telecommunications. But before settling on this business, he took a few detours that in fact came in handy when he set about establishing his own company.

'As part of my military service, I worked for a subsidiary of GTM Entrepose in Rotterdam, where I was an engineer on an offshore pipeline-laying project for platforms all over the world. Two years later, still working in the same field, I went to Norway to work for Coflexip Stena Offshore Norge. My work has taken me all over the place – Europe (England, Spain), North and South America (US, Argentina, Mexico). I've always loved to travel and get to know other people and cultures. One of the things I noticed on my travels was that not being reachable by phone at all times was a real handicap for business people. The ability to make contact swiftly is increasingly what gives businesses a competitive edge.

'Businesses that set up operations in Scandinavia often choose Denmark as their launching pad because of its central location. This is why I decided to do market research in partnership with the Copenhagen Business School to identify telephone installation needs for this small country with a population of 5 million, which attracts scores of business people – especially Japanese and American. The cell phones in these countries are not compatible with Scandinavian standards, which, like the rest of Europe, are GSM-compatible.'

And thus OdysseyCom came to life at the beginning of 1999. Initially capitalized at 125,000 kroner, this ApS rents multi-standard satellite and cellular phones by the day, the week or the month. The rental fee does not include the cost of the calling, of course. It is also possible to send or receive faxes and e-mail messages. To promote his services, Hervé Soursou made use of existing conduits to VIPs: the airlines, vehicle rental outfits and the major hotels, not to mention travel agencies and trade show and seminar organizers. After all, what better publicity could one get? Denmark attracts thousands of conference participants every year.

For Danish residents who go to Asia, the United States and Latin America, OdysseyCom rents mobile phones via a reservation centre that is open around the clock.

In Angola, Tierra del Fuego, Nepal – basically wherever the terrestrial network does not extend, satellite telephones have become essential. Reporters and emergency medical personnel cannot get along without them in the mountain and desert regions where their work often takes them.

'I'm really happy living in Denmark, where there is much less stress than in France. Business is made easier by the professional, friendly attitude that reigns here. The only downside is that I've got to get my Danish up to speed. As soon as the subject is money, you've got to speak the local language to be truly effective,' concludes Hervé Soursou.

Notes

4

Setting Up a Business in Finland

Barents Sea

NORWAY

Ivalo

Muonio

Kolari

SWEDEN

Kelloselka

Kemijarvi

Rovaniemi

RUSSIA

Tornio

Kemi

Taivalkoski

Gulf of Bothnia

Oulu

Raahe

Ylivieska

Kajaani

Pietersaari

Kokkola

Iisalmi

Nurmes

Lieska

Vaasa

Seinajoki

Aanekoski

Hattuvaara

Joensuu

Kasko

Virrat

Varkaus

Parkano

Jamsa

Mikkeli

Pori

Gulf of Bothnia

Rauma

Lahti

Kuovola

Imatra

Forssa

Vaalimaa

Turku

Hyvinkaa

Salo

Porvoo

Kotka

Mariehamn

✪ **Helsinki**

Hango

Gulf of Finland

Baltic Sea

Key statistics

Total surface area:	338,144 square kilometres
Population:	5.1 million
GDP growth:	5.3% (1998)
Per capita GDP:	€21,877 (1998)
Public deficit/GDP ratio:	1% (1998)
Public debt/GDP ratio:	46.2% (1998)
Inflation:	1.4% (1998)
Unemployment:	11.4% (1998)

The Finnish economy is currently enjoying a rate of growth that places it among Europe's top performers. Unlike its Scandinavian neighbours Denmark and Sweden, Finland opted to join the Euro Area in 1999.

Larger than Italy but sparsely populated, Finland remains the world's leading producer of wood and paper products. In just a decade, the country has managed to diversify into highly sophisticated industries such as shipbuilding, medical equipment, telecommunications and electronics. Sectors such as consumer goods (food, wine, multimedia, etc) and services (restaurants, travel, leisure, etc) are expanding rapidly, and demand for imported goods has skyrocketed in the last two years.

The Invest in Finland Bureau offers information and advice to enterprises interested in setting up operations in Finland.

Finland's geographic location makes it attractive for companies interested in penetrating the Baltic, Scandinavian and Russian markets. By 2010, trade between the Baltic Sea nations is expected to increase 10-fold.

Foreign investment in Finland has been boosted by two noteworthy developments in the past few years. The first was the privatization programme launched in 1992, and the second was the passage in 1993 of a liberal new investment code.

Foreign corporations have primarily strengthened their equity interests in the high-tech industry and have shown a great deal of interest in the transport, advertising and building/civil engineering industries. Today, business opportunities can be found in the fields of multimedia and subcontracting for the electricity, electronics and shipbuilding sectors.

Finland's biggest foreign investors are from the United States, Sweden, Switzerland, the Netherlands and the United Kingdom.

Recent foreign investments include Catella (Sweden), Carnegie (Sweden), Skandinaviska Enskilda Banken (Sweden), Hennes and Mauritz (Sweden), Aker Maritime (Norway), Union Bank of Switzerland, Gardner

Denver (US), Emery Worldwide (US), US Filter (US) and McWhorter Technologies (US).

Regulations governing foreign investment

Foreign companies may freely make direct investments in Finland. They may freely acquire existing Finnish companies, except in a limited number of cases. The Ministry of Trade and Industry (MTI) must grant prior approval to any investor seeking to acquire at least one-third of the voting rights in a major company if the investor is not a national of a European Union or OECD country. This concerns companies with a work-force of more than 1,000, or whose revenues exceed 1 billion markka (€168,187,926.46), regardless of the sector of activity. In addition, the Ministry of Defence must approve all investments in the national defence sector, regardless of the investor's nationality. Special licensing or approvals must be obtained for investment in the banking, insurance and television broadcasting industries. Foreign firms may freely acquire real estate.

Principal legal forms

It is possible to conduct business in Finland by establishing a representative office, a branch office or a subsidiary. Subsidiaries must adopt one of the country's existing legal forms.

The limited liability company (*Osakeyhtiö* – OY) is the most widely used legal form in Finland, for both subsidiaries of foreign groups and indigenous firms. A company law reform that went into effect in September 1997 draws a distinction between companies that invite the public to subscribe to shares (OY) with minimum share capital of 500,000 markka (€84,093.96) and companies capitalized at a minimum of 50,000 markka (€8,409.37).

■ Osakeyhtiö (OY)

Requirements of an OY:

— at least one founder (may be an individual or a corporate entity), who must be a resident of a European Economic Area (EEA) country or have obtained the prior approval of the Ministry of Trade and Industry (MTI);

— minimum share capital of 50,000 markka (€8,409.37), fully subscribed and 50 per cent paid in;
— relatively simple administrative procedures.

Relatively flexible management:

— *a board of directors composed of at least one member and one deputy member if share capital is under 500,000 markka (and a minimum of three members if share capital is more than 500,000 million markka);
— if share capital is 500,000 markka (€84,093.96) or more, a managing director must be appointed, who may be but need not be a member of the board of directors (optional in other cases);
— at least half of the members of the board of directors as well as the managing director must be residents of an EEA country (unless an exception has been granted by the MTI);
— one or more independent auditors must be appointed by the shareholders, depending on the size of the company;
— shareholders' liability is limited to the capital invested.
— Supervisory board composed of at least five members, depending on the articles of association.

Other legal forms

■ General commercial partnership (Avoin Yhtiö)

Requirements:

— minimum of two partners, may be an individual or a corporate entity;
— partners' liability is joint and several and unlimited with respect to third parties.

■ Limited partnership (Kommandiitetiyhtiö)

Requirements:

— active partners' liability is unlimited;
— limited partners' liability is limited to the capital invested.

Administrative procedures

Setting up an OY entails the following procedures.

■ Drafting the deed of incorporation and articles of association

A patent search is recommended to ensure that the corporate name chosen is available in order to avoid any delay in the registration.

Company founders draw up the incorporating instrument, which must be dated and signed.

Subscribed capital is deposited into a bank account.

■ Holding the organizational meeting of the shareholders

The founders call an organizational meeting to decide on the formation of the company, and to elect its first directors and other managers, if any.

■ Registration

Within six months of having signed the deed of incorporation, a registration application form (in Finnish or Swedish) must be completed in duplicate and sent to the National Board of Patents and Registration. This form must be accompanied by a statement from the bank certifying that the capital mentioned in the deed of incorporation and articles of association has been deposited into a bank account.

The company acquires a corporate entity after registration, and becomes liable for all obligations stemming from the incorporating instrument or contracted after the organization meeting has been held. It takes from two to four months to process the registration application.

■ Publishing requirements

A notice of incorporation is published in the official gazette once the company is registered.

■ Principal organization/incorporation costs

A fixed fee of 1,400 markka (€235.46) is charged to register an OY with the National Board of Patents and Registration. It costs around 500 markka (€84.09) to process requests made to the Ministry of Trade and Industry (MTI) for exemption from the aforementioned residency requirements for members of the board.

Incorporation may involve legal expenses, which vary depending on the nature and complexity of services rendered.

Human resources/labour law

■ Employment contract

Permanent

A written contract signed between the employer and the employee, containing a required minimum of information on job requirements and working conditions.

Fixed-term

A written contract of a maximum term of five years under exceptional circumstances.

■ Length of the working week

The legal maximum is 40 hours; the working week is generally 35 to 38 hours under the terms of various collective bargaining agreements.

■ Overtime regulations

Restrictions:

— 200 hours maximum per annum for weekday overtime;
— 120 hours maximum per annum for weekend overtime.

Compensation:

— on weekdays and Saturdays, the bonus is 50% for the first two hours and 100% for additional hours worked;
— on Sundays and holidays, the bonus is 150% for the first two hours and 200% for additional hours worked.

■ Annual vacation period

Four to five weeks a year, depending on seniority. Collective bargaining agreements may provide for additional vacation days.

◼ Public holidays

Eleven paid holidays a year.

◼ Wages

There is no statutory minimum wage.

Wages are fixed in employment contracts or by collective bargaining agreements for various employment categories and industries.

Employees receive a vacation bonus of 50 per cent of their monthly wage.

◼ Social security

Social security benefits are available to all residents and cover sickness and maternity, disability, on-the-job accidents, retirement, unemployment and family allowances.

◼ Mandatory social security contributions

More than 40 per cent of wage costs, of which around 10 per cent are paid by the employee.

◼ Employing foreigners

Nationals of the European Economic Area do not need a permit to work in Finland. They are granted a five-year residence permit. Nationals of other countries must obtain both a work permit and a residence permit from the Finnish embassy or consulate in their country of residence before coming to Finland. These permits are generally granted for a one-year period and can be renewed without difficulty. Foreign executives and high-level technicians working for foreign companies based in Finland generally have no problem obtaining the required permits.

For others, obtaining the permit to live and work in Finland is more difficult in practice given the current level of unemployment, although there is no legislation restricting the employment of foreigners.

Paying taxes

■ Corporate income tax (Yhteisön tulovero)

The corporate income tax rate is 28 per cent.

■ Personal taxes

Personal taxes include:
— a progressive national income tax, with seven brackets from 0% to 38%;
— a local tax of 15% to 20%;
— a church tax of 1% to 2.25%.

> Note: The combined burden of social security contributions and income taxes in Finland is among the highest in the European Union, just behind Denmark and Sweden. Mandatory withholdings come to 45.5% of GDP.

■ Value-added tax (Arvonlisävero)

There are three rates that apply to goods and services:
— Zero rate;
— Reduced rates: 12% and 17%;
— Standard rate: 22%.

■ Real estate taxes (Kiinteistövero)

0.2 per cent to 0.8 per cent depending on the municipality.
Deductible from taxable corporate income.

■ Capital tax (Varallisuusvero)

OY are not subject to this tax.
A tax of 1 per cent is levied on the net worth of the branches of non-resident companies.

Investment incentives

Finland has adapted its incentive system to the European Union's regional policy objectives. Foreign companies compete on an equal footing with indigenous businesses for the investment incentives offered by the Finnish government. These incentives primarily promote the establishment of SMEs in regions that require development support. They may take a variety of forms including outright grants, loans, guarantees, tax breaks and training subsidies.

For information on available aid, the relevant regional organization or the Invest in Finland Bureau should be contacted.

■ Regional incentives

Finland is divided into four development areas for the purpose of regional incentives.

Area I (the northern and eastern regions and a small portion of the southwest) is the most economically disadvantaged region and therefore receives the highest subsidies. Area II comprises central Finland to the south of Area I and the Aland Islands. Area III, which receives less government development support, covers parts of the western coast and central Finland.

In addition to Areas I-III, regions that have undergone deep industrial change are grouped into Structural Adjustment Areas. These areas are primarily located in the provinces of Vaasa, Pirkanmaa, Häme, Satakunta and Varsinais-Suomi.

Regional incentive programmes target small and medium-sized companies involved in production, tourism or services.

MTI investment grants cover a percentage of total investment costs for the acquisition of land, premises and equipment, and vary depending on location:

— Area I: 25 to 45%;
— Area II: 15 to 30%;
— Area III: 0 to 20%;
— Structural adjustment areas: 0 to 20%.

Eligible firms should contact one of the 15 Regional Centres for the Development of the Economy and Employment.

Grants are also available to cover transportation costs, calculated on the basis of the area and the distance. Large companies are entitled to no more than 40 per cent of the grants awarded to SMEs.

For information:
— Area I: 9 to 31%
— Area II: 7 to 29%
— Area III: 5 to 27%.

■ Other incentives

Kera financing

The Finnish Regional Development Fund (Kera) finances business start-ups and SMEs and provides development capital to high-tech ventures. Kera has 15 regional offices and venture capital subsidiaries in Finland.

Kera grants micro-loans of up to 100,000 markka (16,818.79 euros) to firms employing no more than five people and low-interest rate loans to women entrepreneurs as well as to those who invest in or form partnerships with fledgling companies. However, two-thirds of the loans granted by Kera concern the industrial sector, and cover from 20 per cent to 70 per cent of total investment costs. Applications generally take from two to four weeks to process.

■ MTI grants

The Ministry of Trade and Industry (MTI), with regional offices throughout the country, offers development grants that enable SMEs to make fixed asset investments (machinery and equipment, buildings and real estate, etc), improve the quality of their products or streamline production, management and marketing processes. The grant may cover up to 15 per cent of the total investment outlay.

To qualify, companies must employ no more than 250 people and earn annual revenues of 120 million markka (€20,182,551.18) maximum (or have total assets of no more than 60 million markka (€10,091,275.59)).

MTI grants are also available for business start-ups and very small undertakings, defined as those with a workforce of less than 50 and annual revenues of no more than 30 million markka (or total assets of no more than 12 million markka). This type of grant covers up to 15 per cent of approved investment costs and 45 per cent of wages paid in the first year of operation. The maximum grant amount is 100,000 markka (€16,818.74) for each new job created, up to a ceiling of three.

Finally, MTI provides research and consulting aid for both business start-ups and existing firms seeking to expand into new business areas.

■ Research and development incentives

The Technology Development Centre (TEKES) offers grants and loans to foster the development and subsequent commercialization of high-tech products.

Grants may cover up to 50 per cent of approved investment costs, including wages, sub-contracting, raw materials, travel and patent and trademark licensing, while loans cover up to 60 per cent of the total. It takes two months to process applications.

The Finnish National Fund for Research and Development (SITRA) makes equity investments in high-tech firms in Finland, but also in other European countries and the United States if commercial ties or technology transfer potential exist. When considering an investment, the Fund examines the applicant firm's competitive position, international marketing potential and the quality of its management.

SITRA usually makes investments of €91,508.05 to €2,745,241.58 over a period of five to 10 years.

MTI also awards grants for technology projects in the fields of energy and the environment, covering up to 50 per cent of approved costs.

■ Skilled labour and training

The Labour Ministry and its 15 regional offices offer advice on where to establish a business and provide information on workforce skills (education and skills level).

It can organize vocational training programmes and provide funding for all or a portion of the related costs.

■ Export incentives

The Ministry of Trade and Industry offers grants to SMEs that cover up to 50 per cent of approved costs of training, market research, international patent protection, sales and marketing brochures and travel abroad for the purpose of prospecting and attending trade shows.

The Finnish Fund for Industrial Co-operation (Finnfund) makes equity investments in companies of around 25 per cent and offers medium- and long-term loans. The JOP and ECIP programmes provide additional funding.

Finnevera provides export-credit guarantees to facilitate transactions.

Useful addresses in Finland

Bank of Finland
Snellmaninaukio
PO Box 160
FIN-00100 Helsinki
Tel.: (358 9) 18 31

Finnish Export Credit
Eteläesplanadi 8
PO Box 123
FIN-00131 Helsinki
Tel.: (358 9) 13 11 71

Finnevera
Vuorimiehenkatu 1
PO Box 1010
FIN-00101 Helsinki
Tel.: (358 10) 52 170

Finnish National Fund for Research and Development (SITRA)
Vudermaankatu 16 B
PO Box 329
FIN-00121 Helsinki
Tel.: (358 9) 61 89 91

Finnish Regional Development Fund (Kera)
Vilhonkatu 5
PO Box 249
FIN-00101 Helsinki
Tel.: (358 20) 460 34 00

Helsinki Chamber of Commerce
Kalevankatu 12
FIN-00100 Helsinki
Tel.: (358 9) 22 86 01

Invest in Finland Bureau
Aleksanterinkatu, 17
FIN-00106 Helsinki
Tel.: (358 9) 69 69 125

National Board of Customs
Ratakatu 1 B, Pl 512
FIN-00101 Helsinki
Tel.: (358 9) 61 41

National Board of Patent and Registration
Arkadiankatu, 6A
FIN-00100 Helsinki
Tel.: (358 9) 693 95 00

The Research Institute of the Finnish Economy
Lönnrotinkatu, 4B
FIN-00120 Helsinki
Tel.: (358 9) 609 900

Statistics Finland
FIN-00022 Tilastokeskus
Tel.: (358 9) 173 41

Technology Development Centre
TEKESPO Box 69
FIN-00101 Helsinki
Tel.: (358 10) 52 151

Ministries

Ministry of Finance
Unit for International Tax Affairs
Snellmaninkatu 1 A
FIN-00171 Helsinki
Tel.: (358 9) 16 01

Ministry of Labour
Fabianinkatu 32, Pl 524
FIN-00101 Helsinki
Tel.: (358 9) 185 62 19

Ministry of Trade and Industry (MTI)
Commission for Foreign Investment
Aleksanterinkatu, 4
FIN-00170 Helsinki
Tel.: (358 9) 160 35 37

OY J-F Galtat Wines Ltd

Wine importer: a new occupation in Finland.

I have just set up a joint venture, OY Vin Direkt Finland Ab, with a Swedish importer.

Jean-François Galtat, Managing Director

In 1996, Jean-François Galtat founded a company representing French wine producers in Helsinki. The timing was perfect. Until 1995, the public company ALKO had a monopoly on wine imports in Finland. A new business was born, and 120 licences were delivered to importers who were hopeful of making large profits. Unfortunately, not all of them had their feet on the ground or any solid knowledge of the wine industry.

This young agricultural engineer is the only French national present in this professional community. Other than the fact that he hails from a country that is known for its grands crus, Jean-François Galtat has other serious credentials: a specialist in winemaking and tasting, he began his professional career as a flying wine maker, spending four months in the northern hemisphere and four in the southern (Australia, New Zealand and Tasmania).

'I wasn't interested in getting tied up with a job straight away. I wanted to gain experience abroad and take advantage of my four months of vacation a year to travel with my Finnish girlfriend, whom I met while studying in Montpellier. Three years down the road, I didn't hesitate to start my own business in Finland rather than in France. The corporate tax rate is 28 per cent and the bureaucracy is much less cumbersome – even though I don't speak Finnish.

'My corporation (OY) was set up in less than two months with initial capital of 15,000 markka, before the 50,000 markka requirement was enacted. Legally, I'm a commercial agent since my clients pay me a commission. This varies from 5 per cent to 10 per cent of the transaction. I pay a great deal of attention to the image of the products that I offer, with upbeat packaging (labels in English) and good value for money.

'Amongst my bestsellers: Wild Pig Red, which sells for 34.90 francs a bottle, which is a real feat when you consider that excise taxes come to around 15 francs and the VAT is 22%. My wines are sold to a network of 250 ALKO outlets and to restaurants, as well as to the maritime company Silja Line, which carries 6 million passengers a year. It is the second largest operator behind London Heathrow Airport. Since 1994, the economy has improved and young people in Finland have got into the habit of dining out and ordering good wine with their meals. In fact, one or two restaurants open every month in Helsinki. My business is developing and I have just set up a joint venture, OY Vin Direkt Finland Ab, with a Swedish importer to strengthen the sale of prestigious French wines to upscale restaurant operators.

To get rid of the stress that comes with negotiating, I put on my skis and go off into the forest that surrounds my apartment.'

Notes

5

Setting Up a Business in France

Key statistics

Total surface area:	549,000 square kilometres
Population:	58.9 million
GDP growth:	3.2% (1998)
Per capita GDP:	€21,976 (1998)
Public deficit/GDP ratio:	–2.9% (1998)
Public debt/GDP ratio:	58.5% (1998)
Inflation:	0.4% (1998)
Unemployment:	11.9% (1998)

Eager to create or save existing jobs and attract new technologies, the French government encourages foreign investors who seek to establish or take over businesses in France.

Centrally located in Europe, France is an attractive place to do business, offering many advantages: industrial and scientific know-how, an extensive rail (the TGV or high-speed train) and inland transport infrastructure, a vast telecommunications network, a highly-skilled labour force, and 'quality of life' and cultural attractions that appeal to expatriate workers. In Europe, only the United Kingdom attracts more foreign investment capital than France does.

The government now offers tax incentives to encourage businesses to set up their corporate or logistical headquarters in France.

The chronic under-capitalization of some of France's small- and mid-sized companies (PME) makes them enticing targets for foreign investors, and a relatively transparent regulatory environment helps ease the entry.

According to information published by the Délégation à l'Aménagement du Territoire et à l'Action Régionale (DATAR), the French government body responsible for fostering foreign investment, the 445 foreign investment projects launched in 1998 will create or save 29,411 jobs. This represents an increase of 21.5 per cent in the number of projects compared to 1997.

North America (the United States and Canada) accounted for 111 investment projects and 8,782 jobs. Europe was the source of 310 projects and 18,534 jobs (63 per cent of all new or created jobs), with Germany the number one foreign investor with 78 projects, followed by the Benelux countries (67 projects) and the United Kingdom (47 projects). Despite the financial crisis that has shaken the Far East, Asia and in particular Japan (14 projects) maintained respectable levels of investment inflow, especially considering the absence of a large-scale project such as Toyota's investment in Valenciennes in 1997.

The Nord-Pas-de-Calais region attracts the most foreign investment, ahead of Ile de France, Rhône-Alpes and Alsace and Lorraine. The automotive industry is the primary target of investment decisions.

France's strength in the high-tech arena is showcased by the electronics, information systems and technology and telecommunications industries. Consultancy and high value-added services are also posting rapid growth.

Recent foreign investments worth citing include the Japanese automaker Toyota, which is pouring 4 billion francs into the construction of a factory in the Nord-Pas-de-Calais region; the Japanese cosmetics giant Shiseido, which is building a manufacturing unit near Orleans; and Photo Print, a German electronic-card designer that plans to set up operations in Pulversheim (located in the Haut-Rhin region).

Sykes Enterprises, an American firm, has announced plans to set up a call centre in the Essonne; Siemens SAS is installing an international semi-conductor research and development centre in Sophia-Antipolis; ITT Automotive (US) is building an assembly unit in the Moselle for its automobile fluid-injection system; Colgate Palmolive has chosen France as the site for its European headquarters; and the Dutch firm Intervet International plans to locate its veterinary products R&D centre in the Maine-et-Loire region.

Foreign investment in France for 1998 includes Alcore Brigatine (US) in the Pyrénées Atlantiques, Oxford Automotive (US) in the Nord, the Calvados and the Cher regions, NTN Transmissions Europe (Japan) in the Sarthe, Eagle Witzenmann (Japan) in the Moselle and Koyo Seiko (Japan) in the Loir-et-Cher and outside Lyons.

Regulations governing foreign investment

■ The voluntary scheme

Regardless of nationality, foreign investors are free to do any of the following in France:

— establish branch offices or new companies;
— extend the activity of branch offices or existing companies;
— effect capital increases without increasing existing equity shareholdings, and increases in the equity shareholding by investors that already hold more than two-thirds of the capital or voting rights in a French corporation under foreign control;

— carry out mergers, partial business transfers, disposals or takeovers on a leasing-management basis of business between French companies under foreign control and belonging to the same group;
— engage in transactions involving loans, advances, guarantees, consolidations or abandonment of debts granted to a French company by the foreign investor controlling it;
— invest in real estate, with the exception of commercial property development;
— invest up to 10 million francs (€1,524,459.90) in the handicrafts, hotel or retail trade, as well as in freight services, gravel pits and mines;
— acquire agricultural land that is not used to produce grapes and/or wine.

■ Preliminary filings

Investments that fall outside those listed above must be submitted for the prior approval of the French Treasury Department (*Direction du Trésor*) at the time they occur.

An investment is considered to 'occur' when any transaction that substantiates the agreement between the contracting parties is effected, in particular the conclusion of the agreement, the official announcement of the purchase or exchange offer or the acquisition of an asset that qualifies as a direct foreign investment in France.

When any one of these events occurs, the application should be sent to the Ministry of the Economy, Treasury Department, Bureau D 3 (*Ministère de l'Economie, Direction du Trésor, Bureau D 3*).

■ Advance approval scheme

Foreign investments are subject to prior approval when they are made in the following sensitive industries:

— activities that contribute to the exercise of government authority in France, even on an occasional basis only;
— investments that involve public policy, health or security;
— investments made in the field of arms research, production or trade, including munitions, powders and explosive substances designed for military purposes, or military hardware.

Investors may consider that approval has been granted after one month from the date on which the application is filed, unless the Minister of the Economy requests that the projected transaction be postponed.

■ Administrative report

An administrative report drawn up on a special standard form must be sent to the Treasury Department for the following transactions:

— the establishment of companies, branch offices or new business undertakings when the amount involved exceeds 10 million francs;
— those approved by the Minister of the Economy that involve a sensitive industry;
— the winding-up of foreign direct investments in France.

Certain types of business are regulated, such as restaurants, tobacco shops/bars, licensed drinking establishments, pharmacies and hair salons.

Principal legal forms

It is possible to conduct business in France by establishing a representative office, a branch office or a subsidiary. Subsidiaries must adopt one of the country's existing legal forms.

For small- and medium-sized businesses, the limited-liability company (SARL) is the most widely used legal form, while the corporation or public limited form (SA) is better suited to larger undertakings.

■ Limited-liability company (SARL – Société à Responsabilité Limitée)

Requirements of an SARL:

— minimum of two founding shareholders (if the EURL (*Entreprise Unipersonnelle à Responsabilité Limitée*) form is opted for, sole proprietorship is permitted) and a maximum of 50;
— minimum share capital of 50,000 francs (€7,622,45), fully subscribed and paid in;
— incorporation by private signature or notarized instrument.

Flexible management:

— minimum of one manager who may be but need not be a shareholder;
— annual general meeting of shareholders;
— shareholders' liability is limited to the capital invested;

— presence of an independent auditor mandatory when certain threshold levels are surpassed (revenues, balance sheet amounts, workforce);
— for tax and social security purposes, non-majority or 50/50 owner-managers may be considered employees.

An SARL may take the form of a mutual fund or investment trust (*société à capital variable*). Ten per cent of capital must be paid in.

■ Corporation (SA – Société anonyme)

Requirements of an SA:

— minimum of seven shareholders;
— minimum capital of 250,000 francs (€38,112.25), half of which must be paid in when the company is established, and the rest within five years of the company's registration (minimum capital of 1,500,000 francs (€228,673.53) for companies that effect public offerings);
— incorporation by private signature or notarized instrument.

Two possible forms of governance:

— a board of directors (three to 24 members, who must be shareholders); or
— an executive board (seven members maximum, may be but need not be shareholders) and a supervisory board (three to 24 members, who must be shareholders);
— presence of an independent auditor mandatory;
— shareholders' liability is limited to the capital invested;
— for tax and social security purposes, the chairman-CEO (or the chairman of the executive board) may be considered an employee.

Other legal forms

■ General commercial partnership (SNC — Société en nom collectif)

Requirements of an SNC:

— minimum of two partners;
— no minimum capital requirement;
— partners' liability is joint and several and unlimited.

■ Partnership limited by shares (SCA – Société en commandite par actions)

Requirements of an SCA:

— active partners' liability is joint and several and unlimited;
— limited sleeping partners' liability is limited to the capital invested;
— this legal form, rarely used, makes it possible to raise capital from outside sources while restricting governance and management to a closed circle of individuals.

Note: The limited partnership form (*société en commandite simple*) is also permitted.

■ Partnership (Société civile)

Requirements:

— minimum of two partners;
— no minimum capital requirement;
— partners' liability is unlimited in respect of capital invested;
— this legal form is recommended for the joint practice of a profession and for real estate and agricultural activities.

■ Société d'exercice libéral (SEL)

Requirements of an SEL:

— a corporation (ie created with capital) in the form of an SARL (*SELARL*), SA (*SELAFA*) or partnership (*SELCA*);
— minimum capital between 50,000 and 250,000 francs (€7,622.45 to €38,112.25) depending on the legal form;
— partners practising a profession or other activity, with more than half of the capital and voting rights held by the professionals in the practice;
— partners' liability is limited to the capital invested;
— subject to corporate income tax.

■ Société par actions simplifiée (SAS)

Requirements of an SAS:

— minimum of two shareholders, French or foreign corporate entities with a minimum capital of 1.5 million francs;
— minimum capital of at least 250,000 francs or the equivalent value in another currency;

— very flexible management and organization;
— particularly suited to large co-operative ventures between large enterprises.

Administrative procedures

The following procedures must be followed to establish a business in France.

■ Drafting the articles of incorporation and bylaws

A preliminary patent search is recommended in order to verify that the corporate name is available.

The articles of incorporation and bylaws must include the following mandatory items: corporate name, business purpose, registered office, life of the company, legal form, amount of share capital and each member's contribution, the names of the founding managers.

■ Paying in of capital

Capital is deposited into a blocked capital account with a retail bank, the Deposit and Consignment Office (*la Caisse des Dépôts et Consignations*) or a notary.

■ Signing the articles of incorporation and bylaws

The founders or their proxy-holders sign the articles of incorporation.

■ Signing the 'état des actes accomplis'

A statement of the instruments drawn up in the name and on behalf of the company to be incorporated must be signed.

■ Publishing the incorporating instrument

A notice of incorporation (*avis de constitution*) is published in an official gazette (*journal d'annonces légales*).

■ Filing the business registration form

The business registration is filed with the *Centre de Formalités des Entreprises* (CFE).

The CFE is a 'one-stop shop' at which all required filings can be made using a single document.

The CFE carries out most of the legal, social security and tax procedures with the appropriate organizations. The CFE office of jurisdiction is located:

— in the local Chamber of Commerce and Industry office under whose jurisdiction the company's registered office is located (if the company is involved in a retail or industrial activity or is a professional practice);
— in the local Trade Council office (*Chambre de Métiers*) under whose jurisdiction the company's registered office is located (if the company's business involves handicrafts or is mixed (handicrafts and retail)).

■ Publishing the notice of incorporation

The notice of incorporation is published in the *Bulletin officiel des annonces civiles et commerciales* (BODACC).

■ Principal organization/incorporation costs

For an SARL with initial capital of 50,000 francs, incorporation costs total around 5,000 francs (€762.25), broken down as follows:

— registration with the French Corporate and Trade Register (*registre du commerce et des sociétés*): about 1,300 francs (€198.18);
— announcement in a legal bulletin: from 1,500 to 3,000 francs (€228.67 to €457.35);
— licensing: a fixed excise tax of 1,500 francs (€228.67).

For an SA with initial capital of 250,000 francs, incorporation costs total around 7,000 francs (€1,067.14), broken down as follows:

— registration with the French Corporate and Trade Register (*registre du commerce et des sociétés*): about 1,300 francs (€198.18);
— announcement in an official gazette: from 3,500 to 4,000 francs (€533.57 to €609.80);
— licensing: a fixed excise tax of 1,500 francs (228.67 €).

Legal expense fees may be added to these amounts, generally around 12,000 francs (€1,829.39) for an SARL and around 25,000 francs (€3,811.23) for an SA. Expenses are negotiated between client and solicitor, and vary depending on the nature and complexity of services rendered.

Human resources/labour law

■ Employment contract

Permanent

A written contract signed between the employer and the employee, containing a required minimum of information on job requirements and working conditions.

Fixed-term

A written contract of a maximum term of 18 months, which may be extended to 24 months under exceptional circumstances. It may be renewed only once, and may not exceed a total of two years.

■ Length of the working week

Legal maximum of 39 hours.

A reform is under way to reduce the legal working week to 35 hours as of 1 January 2000 for companies with more than 20 employees, with an extension granted to others until 1 January 2002.

■ Overtime regulations

130 hours per annum maximum. Premium of 25 to 50 per cent over the regular hourly wage for overtime.

■ Annual vacation period

For each month worked, the employee accumulates 2.5 workable days of paid vacation, or five weeks per year. Certain industry-wide collective bargaining agreements grant additional annual vacation days.

■ Paid leave and public holidays

Eleven days per year.

■ Wages

A legal minimum wage exists.

Actual wages may be higher, depending on the terms of industry-wide collective bargaining agreements or specific wage agreements.

■ Social security

Health and maternity, death and disability, old age, supplemental retirement, unemployment and family allowance benefits are provided.

■ Mandatory social security contributions

Employer contributions: 30 to 45 per cent of gross salary.

Employee contributions: up to 25 per cent of gross salary.

■ Employing foreigners

Nationals of the European Union do not need permits to work in France. Within three months of their arrival in France, they must apply for a residence permit (*carte de séjour*).

The residence permit is initially valid for a five year period, and then 10 years upon renewal. Non-EU nationals must apply for a work permit from the Regional Labour, Employment and Professional Training Organization (*Direction Départementale du Travail et de l'Emploi et de la Formation Professionnelle*). They receive a one-year, renewable residence permit with the word 'salaried' on it.

Note: Foreigners who have been living in France without interruption for at least three years may apply for a 10-year residence permit. This permit is automatically renewed when the 10-year period expires.

Certain company executives and partners (non-EU nationals, those holding residence permits, etc) will require a business permit (*carte de commerçant étranger*), valid for one year and renewable, unless they are EU nationals or hold a 'carte de resident'.

Paying taxes

■ Tax on registered capital

Fixed excise tax on invested capital of 1,500 francs (€228.67) when the company is incorporated and in the event of a capital increase.

■ Corporate income tax (IS)

Basic rate: 33.13 per cent + a 'temporary contribution' of 10 per cent, which brings the global tax rate to 36.13 per cent.

For businesses whose annual revenues exceed 50,000,000 francs (€7,622,450.86), the tax rate is 33.13 per cent + 10 per cent + 10 per cent, ie an effective rate of 40 per cent.

For SMEs *(PME)*: 19 per cent + 10 per cent, ie an effective rate of 20.9 per cent for profits of up to 200,000 francs (€30,489.80), provided that such profits are recapitalized or appropriated to retained earnings for three years in a row.

■ Personal taxes (IR)

Progressive tax rate from 0 per cent, then from 10.5 to 54 per cent (seven brackets) excluding the CSG and CRDS global rate of 8 per cent.

■ General social contribution (Contribution sociale généralisée (CSG))

7.5 per cent is withheld at source on:

— income that qualifies as a wage;
— non-wage professional income;
— property income;
— investment income.

Replacement income (retirement pensions, unemployment benefits) is subject to a CSG tax rate of 6.2 per cent.

Of the 7.5 per cent that is withheld, 5.1 per cent (3.8 per cent for replacement income) is deductible from taxable income or profits on which it is levied.

■ Contribution to the reduction of the social security debt (Contribution au remboursement de la dette sociale (CRDS))

0.5 per cent withheld on the same taxable base as the CSG.

■ Business tax

— based on the annual rental value of fixed assets used by the taxpayer in connection with its business activity, plus an assessment of 18 per cent on the gross remuneration paid to personnel;
— standard 16% abatement on the defined taxable base;
— applicable rates vary from one municipality to the next;
— deductible from taxable corporate income.

Note: The assessment on payroll expenditures is being progressively abated from 1999 to 2002, and will be eliminated entirely in 2003.

■ Real estate tax

Levied on land and buildings.

Rates vary from one municipality to the next.

■ Value added tax (Taxe sur la valeur ajoutée (TVA))

— Reduced rate (mainly on food, books and certain services): 2.1%, 5.5%;
— Standard rate: 20.6%.
— Certain transactions are exempt from VAT (mainly exports).

Investment incentives

■ Tax incentives

Exemption from corporate income tax for start-ups

New businesses may qualify for an income tax exemption, depending on where they set up operations.

— Businesses located in listed regions (*zones prioritaires d'aménagement du territoire*):

— regions that are eligible for the land use planning subsidy (PAT – *prime à l'aménagement du territoire*);
— rural regions that have been granted priority-development status (TRDP – *territoires ruraux de développement prioritaire*);
— urban regeneration zones (ZRU – *zones de redynamisation urbaine*).

The exemption is 100 per cent for the first two years, 75 per cent the third year, 50 per cent the fourth year and 25 per cent the fifth year.

Eligibility requirements:

— the grant is available to companies planning to operate in the industrial or service sector, regardless of legal form (sole proprietorship or corporation).
— firms involved in real estate, agriculture, finance, banking, insurance and non-commercial professions are not eligible. As an exception to the foregoing, non-commercial professions are eligible for the exemption if they have been set up as a corporate-tax paying entity, provided that they employ at least three people at the end of the first financial year and throughout the period covered by the exemption.
— the registered office and all operations and facilities must be located in an eligible area.
— the business created must be genuinely new: companies set up as part of a restructuring, expansion, take-over or concentration do not qualify for this grant.
— not more than half of the company's share capital may be held by other companies.
— the company must be subject to actual bookkeeping and not a standard tax assessment.
— companies that are exempt from corporate income tax may also be exempted from the business tax and/or the real estate tax on buildings and/or taxes levied to cover Chamber of Commerce and Industry or Trade Council expenses for two years.

A competitive tax system to attract headquarters and logistical hubs

Multinationals that establish their European headquarters or logistics hub in France can receive a ruling from the French government on the tax status of their business that is not subject to subsequent revision. In this case, the government fixes their taxable base for corporate income tax purposes as a percentage of total annual operating expenses. The average rate is determined case-by-case.

In addition, some types of compensation paid by the headquarters (or logistics hub) to expatriate employees may, at the employer's request, be provided for by the headquarters (or logistics hub). In this way, the amounts paid out are not considered as taxable personal income and are taxed at the common corporate tax rate.

Exemption from corporate income tax in urban free-trade areas (zones franches urbaines)

Firms that set up in one of the 44 ZFUs in France (districts with more than 10,000 inhabitants in Bordeaux, Montpellier, Vaulx-en-Velin, Mantes-la-Jolie, etc) are exempt from income tax for five years, up to an annual ceiling of 400,000 francs (€60,979). They are also entitled to an automatic temporary exemption from the business and real estate tax and to reductions in the employer contribution to social security.

Exemption from the business tax

There are various measures that grant entitlement to exemption from the business tax:

— exemption from the business tax for new firms during the year in which they are incorporated, and a 50 per cent tax reduction the following year;

— a two-year exemption for new firms that qualify for the aforementioned exemption from corporate income tax. This measure applies only to new businesses or takeovers of companies in difficulty located in a listed region, and is granted at the discretion of the territorial authorities and/or government bodies concerned;

— an optional temporary exemption linked to land use planning in the *Zones d'Aménagement du Territoire* (ZAT) that are eligible for the *Prime d'Aménagement du Territoire* (PAT) and *Territoires Ruraux de Développement Prioritaire* (TRDP). It applies to start-ups, expansions, decentralization, conversions and takeovers of manufacturing sites in difficulty, scientific and technological research and design, engineering, administrative support and IT departments;

— the territorial authorities set the eligibility requirements, percentage and term of exemption;

— an automatic five-year exemption is granted in *zones de revitalisation rurale* and *zones de redynamisation urbaine* (rural and urban regeneration areas) for business start-ups and extensions.

Tax exemption in Corsica (under free-trade zone regulations)

Businesses already established in Corsica on 1 January 1997, or founded before 31 December 2001 may, under certain circumstances, qualify for a five-year exemption from both corporate and personal income taxes, up to a ceiling of 400,000 francs (€60,979.61) a year. They may also be eligible for exemption from the business tax and reduced employer social security contributions, subject to certain defined ceilings.

This applies to companies in the manufacturing, retail and handicrafts sectors, and to the professions, provided that the latter are subject to corporate income tax and that at the end of each applicable fiscal year there are at least three people on the payroll.

Regardless of the legal form (one-person business or a company), the enterprise must have the resources in Corsica needed to operate autonomously.

Exemption from the corporate income tax for business established in the DOM (Overseas Departments)

Businesses established in the DOM prior to 31 December 2001, as well as existing companies that establish a new business activity by the same date may qualify for total or partial exemption from corporate income tax for a period of 10 years. Prior approval is required. Approval is granted on the basis of the corporate purpose, the business plan and the number of jobs created.

Tax deduction for investments in the DOM-TOM (Overseas Departments and Territories)

Businesses that are subject to corporate or personal taxes may deduct investments made in a variety of sectors, notably manufacturing, fishing, tourism, alternative energy, agriculture, handicrafts, civil engineering, transport, industrial maintenance, audio-visual production, broadcasting and film-making.

Investments made in sectors that are not considered sensitive are subject to prior approval if certain thresholds are surpassed.

Research tax credit

For new businesses, the tax credit in respect of the start-up year is equal to 50 per cent of the research expenditure incurred over the year in question. In addition, the tax credit is equal to 50 per cent of research expenditure made in the first year in the course of which the company incurs such expenditure.

The company may obtain immediate repayment of the surplus tax credit earned in respect of the start-up year and in the following two years.

Job training subsidies

New firms are entitled to a tax credit equal to 25 per cent of training expenditures over their first year of operation, or over the first year in which such expenditures are made.

Tax reduction for equity investments

Unlisted companies

Under certain conditions, individuals who make a cash capital investment in an unlisted company, either at the time of its incorporation or when a capital increase is effected, may deduct 25 per cent of the invested amount from their taxable income, up to an annual ceiling of:

— 37,500 francs if they are single, widowed or divorced;
— 75,000 francs for married taxpayers filing a joint return.
This brings the maximum tax reduction to 9,375 francs or 18,750 francs (€1,429.21 or €2,858.42).

Innovative companies

Under certain conditions, individuals who invest in venture-type mutual funds (FCPI – *fonds communs de placement dans l'innovation*) are entitled to a tax reduction equal to 25 per cent of the invested sum, up to a ceiling of:

— 75,000 francs if they are single, widowed or divorced;
— 150,000 francs for married taxpayers filing a joint return.
This brings the maximum tax reduction to 18,750 francs or 37,500 francs (€2,858.42 or €5,716.84).

Unlisted warrants for entrepreneurs

Certain employees in innovative small and medium-sized firms may be entitled to entrepreneur warrants issued by new businesses issued by unlisted joint stock companies. These companies must not have been in operation for more than 15 years, and 75 per cent of the share capital must be held by individuals or corporate entities whose own shareholders are individuals. To qualify for the tax treatment granted to capital gains at the time of sale (taxed at a rate of 26 per cent), the employee holding such warrants must have continuous service of at least three years in the company on the date of sale. The proceeds of the sale are not subject to social security contributions.

■ Available grants

Regional Development Grant (Prime d'Aménagement du Territoire (PAT))

The Regional Development Grant (PAT) is an equipment subsidy granted to French and foreign companies planning operations in the industrial or service sector in PAT-eligible areas. The investment must be in excess of 20 million francs (exclusive of tax), and the project must involve a start-up, an extension or the conversion or takeover of a company in difficulty.

Eligible operations:

— In the industrial sector: creation of at least 20 permanent jobs over three years;
— In the service or research sector: creation of at least 10 permanent jobs over three years;
— Expansion of a business: at least a 50 per cent increase in the workforce over three years.

■ Grant amounts

In the industrial sector:

— standard rate zones: 50,000 francs (€7,622.45) maximum per job, up to a ceiling of 17% pre-tax of the investment;
— higher rate zones: 70,000 francs (€10,671.43) maximum per job, up to a ceiling of 25% pre-tax of the investment;
— zones that have been granted an exception to the foregoing include Corsica, Douai, Valenciennes, Avesnes-sur-Helpe and the Longwy PED (European Development Pole): 70,000 francs (€10,671.43) maximum per job, up to a ceiling of 33% pre-tax of the investment for Corsica and the PED, and up to a ceiling of 28% pre-tax for Douai, Valenciennes and Avesnes-sur-Helpe.

In the service sector:

— The number of jobs created and the location determine the amount of the grant.
— The investment amount is not taken into consideration.
— Companies are eligible for 70,000 francs maximum per job.

Industrial conversion companies (sociétés de conversion)

Some of France's largest employers have set up industrial conversion companies. They include EDF (DII), Charbonnages de France (SOFIREM), Usinor-Sacilor (SODIE), GIAT Industries (SOFRED), Thomson (GERIS) and Rhône-Poulenc (SOPRAN) among others. Their role is to encourage job-creating business location and development in areas that have been hit by industrial restructuring and downsizing. They invest in the investor's equity capital or provide non-guaranteed medium- and long-term loans at discounted rates.

Prime Régionale à la Création d'Entreprises (PRCE)

This regional job creation grant is available to companies that have been in business for less than one year, and which create the number of jobs stipulated by the regional government council. The professions are not eligible for this grant. The amount of the grant is limited to 150,000 francs (€22,887,35) and 200,000 francs (€30,489.80) in priority zones as defined by the regional government council.

Prime Régionale à l'Emploi (PRE)

The regional government council sets eligibility requirements for this grant. It applies to any project involving the establishment of a business, as well as the extension, take-over or conversion of an existing one. The amount of the grant is determined on the basis of the number of jobs created or protected, up to 30 jobs. The amount per job created varies from 10,000 to 40,000 francs (€1,524.49 to €6,097.96).

> Note: Not all French regions offer PRCE and PRE. They are gradually being eliminated and replaced by other types of grants such as refundable advances and equity capital grants or guarantees.

■ Innovation grants

The *Agence Nationale de Valorisation de la Recherche* (the ANVAR) offers grants to innovative projects, technology transfers, young people and independent inventors. The ANVAR also reviews applications submitted in connection with the European EUREKA programme, which funds joint projects between at least two industrial firms from different EUREKA member nations.

■ Business start-up grants

These grants are available to all entrepreneurs who are planning to set up a company or whose company has been set up within the last year. This subsidy may be used to finance up to 70 per cent of business expenditures, up to a ceiling of 200,000 francs.

The grant serves to finance the use of specialized consulting firms (market research, feasibility and design studies, financial, tax and industrial property advice) and certain start-up costs incurred by the entrepreneur (time spent, travel, etc).

■ Innovative projects grants

High-tech companies in operation for less than two years are eligible for these grants, which are delivered in the form of a zero-interest advance that is repaid if the innovation succeeds, and which may cover up to 50 per cent of expenses allowable by the ANVAR:

— internal expenditures: personnel costs, costs related to the purchase of parts and materials, licensing fees, the cost of building prototypes and scale models, technical testing and adjustment costs, demonstrations;
— external expenditures: subcontracting to specialized service providers, in particular laboratories or research firms under contract.

Business start-up and takeover grants for the unemployed

Those eligible for this grant include: those targeted by the *emploi-jeune* programme, those who qualify for the RMI (minimum revenue), those who qualify for other special allowances and to employees or laid-off workers of companies that are in receivership or bankruptcy who take over all or a portion of such a company, provided that all the grant money is invested in the project and that they assemble the necessary additional capital.

Beneficiaries who found a company receive social security coverage for a year and up to 40,000 francs (€6,097.96) per person, while those who take over a company in difficulty receive 500,000 francs (€76,224.51). The grant must be repaid within five years.

Loans, advances and interest-rate buydowns

Firms may turn to banks for project financing. In general, the banks require that the potential investor contributes 30 per cent of the total investment amount to qualify for a loan.

The BDPME (*Banque du développement des petites et moyennes entreprises*), which resulted from the combination of the CEPME (*Crédit d'équipement des PME*) and SOFARIS (*Société de caution mutuelle*), offers small and medium-sized firms medium to long-term loans with attractive terms. Under certain circumstances, local authorities may offer companies:

— long-term loans and advances that are more attractive than the average interest rate;
— interest-rate buydowns on loans;
— guarantees or security.

Le Fonds Régional d'Aide au Conseil (FRAC)

Companies setting up operations or planning to acquire a business in difficulty may apply to the FRAC for a consultancy grant. Applications must be obtained from the local authorities in the region of the company's domicile before arranging the consultancy. Available in certain regions only, the grant covers up to 50 per cent of the cost of a preliminary study, up to a ceiling of 100,000 to 200,000 francs (€15,244.90 to €30,489.80).

A grant covering up to 80 per cent of short-term consulting (one to five days), up to a ceiling of 25,000 francs (€3,811.23) is also available in certain regions.

■ Hiring subsidies

First-hire grants

Companies hiring their first employee on a permanent basis are exempt from employer social security contributions for two years. Those hiring an employee for a fixed term are eligible provided that the term of the employment contract is at least 12 months.

This grant supports self-employed individuals who have set up a one-person business, companies whose managers are not considered salaried employees for social security purposes and SARLs with minority or egalitarian management. This measure does not apply to the manager, his or her spouse (or unmarried partner) or dependants who are hired.

The exemption includes the employer contribution to social security, sickness, old age, worker's compensation and family allowances.

Note: Companies that have not hired any employees in the previous 12 months or since their start-up date (if within less than 12 months) are eligible for this grant.

Young-hire grants

Companies that hire young people between the ages of 16 and 26 are eligible for a full or partial exemption from social charges and/or an outright grant. To qualify, companies must comply with certain requirements concerning length of the training period, compensation and the type of employment contract.

Other types of grants

Companies subject to corporate income tax are eligible for a tax credit of 10,000 francs (€1,524.49) per net job created in 1998, 1999 and 2000. This tax credit is imputable to the 10 per cent corporate income tax contribution, up to a ceiling of 500,000 francs (€76,224.51) per fiscal year.

Other hiring grants and subsidies entitle companies to an exemption from mandatory employer contributions to social security and/or an outright grant:

— the *contrat de qualification,* normally reserved for young people under the age of 25, can in certain cases be extended to older adult job seekers, thus entitling the hiring employer to a grant of 5,000 to 20,000 francs (€762.24 to €3,048.98);

— exemption from employer social security contributions for recruitments that bring the total workforce to 50 maximum in urban regeneration and rural revitalization zones;

— exemption from employer social security contribution for recruitments that bring the total workforce to 50 maximum in urban free-trade zones;

— reduced social charges on low-wage earners and exemption from the family allowance contribution;

— 30% abatement on mandatory employer contributions to employment insurance, workers' compensation and family allowance benefits for the hiring of part-time workers.

An ANVAR grant is offered to companies that hire researchers.

Some regions offer an ARC grant for employers that hire unemployed management level staff. Eligibility requirements vary from one region to another.

Useful addresses in France

Agence Nationale de Valorisation de la Recherche (ANVAR)
43, rue Caumartin
75436 Paris CEDEX 09
Tel.: (33) 01 40 17 83 00

Agence Pour la Création d'Entreprises (APCE)
14, rue Delambre
75682 Paris CEDEX 14
Tel.: (33) 01 42 18 58 58

BDPME
Tour Atlantique
92911 Paris La Défense Cedex
Tel.: (33) 01 46 96 08 00

Centre National de Sécurité Sociale
URSSAF
3, rue Franklin
93100 Montreuil Sous Bois
Tel.: (33) 01 49 20 10 10

Délégation à l'Aménagement du Territoire et à l'Action Régionale
(DATAR)
Invest in France Network (IFN)
1, avenue Charles Floquet
75007 Paris
Tel.: (33) 01 40 65 12 34

Direction Départementale du Travail et de l'Emploi
49, rue de Réaumur
75003 Paris
Tel.: (33) 01 44 84 42 86

Direction Générale des douanes et des droits indirects
23 bis, rue de l'Université
75007 Paris
Tel.: (33) 01 40 04 04 04

**Direction Générale du développement scientifique
technologique et de l'innovation**
1, rue Descartes
75005 Paris
Tel.: (33) 01 46 34 35 35

Institut National de la Propriété Industrielle
26 B, rue St Petersbourg
75008 Paris
Tel.: (33) 01 53 04 53 04

Ministère de l'Economie, des Finances et du Budget
Direction du Trésor
Bureau D 3 – Télédoc 267
139, rue de Bercy
75572 Paris CEDEX 12
Tel.: (33) 01 44 87 72 85

Ministère de l'Environnement
20, avenue Ségur
75007 Paris
Tel.: (33) 01 42 19 14 53

Ministère des Affaires Etrangères
37, quai d'Orsay
75007 Paris
Tel.: (33) 01 47 53 53 53

Ministère du Travail et des Affaires Sociales
127, rue de Grenelle
75007 Paris
Tel.: (33) 01 44 38 38 38

Registre du Commerce et des Sociétés
Greffe du Tribunal de Commerce
1, quai de Corse
75004 Paris
Tel.: (33) 01 44 41 54 54

SOFARIS
Société Française pour la Garantie des Financements des PME
4, rue Cambon
75001 Paris
Tel.: (33) 01 42 97 57 37

LGA: market leader in parking lot billboards

We created a need, and today we are present in most of the major cities in France.

Laurent Ledermann, Chairman and CEO

When he founded LGA (Ledermann Guironnet et Associés) in 1976, Laurent Ledermann, then 25 years old, became the pioneer of underground parking billboards, much in the same way that Jean-Claude Decaux had earlier become known as the pioneer of street furniture.

While it is true that this company is not in the same league as billboard advertising giants such as Avenir, Giraudy and Dauphin, it holds a strategic position in today's market. Present in downtown areas throughout France, LGA offers advertisers the opportunity to get their message across on 3,500 backlights located at 250 different sites.

At the age of 20, Laurent Ledermann discovered at International Média the intricacies of selling advertising space. . . on paper tablecloths and napkins in cafes and restaurants. It was there that he met Georges Guironnet, also employed by the company.

The two young men pounced on the opportunity to take over the advertising management contract concluded by a firm based in Toulouse and Les Grands Travaux de Marseille (GTM), a subsidiary of the Lyonnaise des Eaux. GTM is the franchisee and builder of underground parking lots.

With a notarized loan of 200,000 French francs (30,490 euros), they founded an SARL and got started in the billposting business. They negotiated other contracts with underground parking lot operators, which are either mixed ownership corporations or private companies such as SOGEPARC or SANPAG. The terms of the deals are straightforward: they are paid either royalties of fixed amount per visual display unit or a percentage of earned revenues.

'During the day, we prospect for new clients, mainly small local business owners within a 100 to 300 metre radius of the parking lot in question. Unlike outdoor advertising above ground, billboards in underground parking lots are basically local media. A kind of last-minute reminder prior to purchase,' explains Laurent Ledermann.

'When we started out, it was easy to get a 30 per cent deposit up front, which enabled us to buy light boxes. I would install them and do maintenance work at night. It wasn't easy to delegate after that, having got my start in the field. It was quicker to do it myself than to explain how to do it! We created a need, and today we are present in most of the bigger cities in France, although Paris remains our biggest local market. To handle our

95

growth and cultivate ties with local partners, we set up agencies in Lyon, Marseille, Toulouse and Toulon. These local partnerships are crucial in our business. For the time being, the extent of our international development has been limited to the Belgian market, where we are present in the cities of Antwerp and Ostende.'

LGA has an impressive list of clients: BMW, Darty, Gaumont, Monoprix, Apple, Lancel, Jean Louis David and hundreds of others have signed on and regularly renewed their contracts. Advertisers generally commit to one- to three-year contracts covering several display units, or choose to embark on one- to two-week campaigns on 300 boards.

In 1989, Georges Guironnet started up a solar heating firm in Corsica and since then Laurent Ledermann has been alone at the helm of LGA, which employs around 20 people. Although he misses the synergies with his erstwhile partner, he continues to forge ahead on his own.

LGA has carved out a nice niche for itself in the advertising market, which is essentially a mass medium that provides an alternative to television. Given its specialization, this SME has never been a takeover target, but it is a strategic partner for many of the bigger advertising agencies.

'We've established a partnership relationship with France Rail Publicité, a subsidiary of the SNCF, based on the natural fit between station advertising display units and underground parking lot light boxes. The experiment got off to a positive start in Lille, and is expected to extend to other provincial cities.'

LGA aligned with More O'Ferrall, now controlled by the US firm Clear Channel, after the Jean-Claude Decaux group lost the stock market battle it waged to take over the British company.

French regulations place strict limits on billboarding in downtown areas. For example, on the celebrated Champs Elysées in Paris, only Decaux and LGA are present. More O'Ferrall and LGA decided to install new 4 x 1.80 display units, which are particularly well suited to singing the praises of the latest models brought to market by Ford, Fiat and Renault.

And since Laurent Ledermann is a CEO who loves innovation more than anything else, it is not surprising that other projects are in the works.

'Although it may seem contradictory, I would like to use my work as a way of encouraging people to use bicycles as a means of transport, by setting up a bike rental system.

People who live in the suburbs often park their cars far away from city centres and take the metro into town. I'd like to offer the bicycle as an alternative means of getting around – by renting them out of parking lots. Of course, it would be necessary to develop a self-service and deposit system.'

Laurent Ledermann is also interested in parking lot decor, and has asked various artists to do wall paintings. Examples include the ad for the stockbroker Money in the Paris Bourse parking lot, for McDonald's in Lyon and Castel Plage in Nice. He is also thinking of adapting visual display and projection techniques used in concerts to underground parking lots.

Could this be the parking lot of the third millennium? One thing is certain: the billboard business is undergoing a sea change. One of the walls in Laurent Ledermann's office features a statement that Vivendi CEO Jean-Marie Messier made to the press: Nobody can rest on their laurels any more.

And if he had done something else? He replies that he might have become a civil engineer. This son of a Polytechnique graduate likes the feel of construction sites. . . where the world of tomorrow is being built.

Notes

6

Setting Up a Business in Germany

DENMARK

Baltic Sea

North Sea

Kiel •

• Rostock

• Schwerin

• Hamburg

• Emden   • Bremerhaven

Bremen •

POLAND

• Hanover

Potsdam • ⭐ Berlin

• Magdeburg

NETHERLANDS

• Halle

• Dusseldorf

• Leipzig

Dresden •

• Koln

Erfurt •

Chemnitz •

Bonn •

• Suhl

BELGIUM

Frankfurt

Wiesbaden •

CZECH

• Mainz

LUX.

• Nurnberg

Saarbrucken •

Regensburg •

• Stuttgart

FRANCE

• Augsburg

• Munich

AUSTRIA

• Freiburg

SWITZERLAND

Key statistics

Total surface area:	356,978 square kilometres
Population:	82 million
GDP growth:	2.8% (1998)
Per capita GDP:	€23,284 (1998)
Public deficit/GDP ratio:	−2.1% (1998)
Public debt/GDP ratio:	61% (1998)
Inflation:	1% (1998)
Unemployment:	9.4% (1998)

The economic powerhouse of Europe, Germany reunified is the European Union's most densely populated country, with a market of 82 million consumers and a GDP of €23,284 billion.

The significant GDP growth recorded in the last three years has been export driven. At the same time, unemployment has climbed as high as 12.6 per cent for the country as a whole and to 20 per cent in the former East Germany (with more than 4 million job seekers).

With more than 2,500 companies operating in Germany, France is the country's number one foreign investor, followed by Switzerland, Austria and the United States.

It was during the privatization of the east German economy that France moved to the head of the class of foreign investors, neck and neck with the United States.

Large French corporations such as Lafarge-Coppée, Air Liquide, Valeo and Accor very rapidly set up operations in the former East Germany.

After having posted average growth of 6 per cent since 1991, the new provinces recorded a lower rate of economic growth than their west German counterparts in 1997 (1.6 per cent versus 2.2 per cent). Only two east German provinces (*Länd*), Saxony and Thuringia, have continued to achieve sustained growth.

Both business takeovers and genuine start-ups in the five new *Länder* are beginning to slow down, even though substantive tax breaks are still being offered by the government to spur business development.

Recent foreign investment in Germany includes Intermarché (France), which has become a shareholder in Spar, the electrical consortium formed between the Southern Co (US) and German groups Veba and Viag; the acquisition of Wayss and Freytag by the Hollandsche Beton Groep; the AE Bishop (Australia)/Mercedes-Benz partnership in the automotive parts sector; the joint venture between Motorola (US) and Siemens to build a plant in Dresden; and Mercer International (a company with a Swiss-Canadian shareholder base), which is installing a paper mill in east Germany.

Regulations governing foreign investment

There are no legislative restrictions on foreign direct investment. No preliminary filings or approvals are required. For statistical monitoring purposes, those who establish businesses must report their investment to the local branch of the Bundesbank (*Ländeszentralbank*) in the *Länd* in which they plan to invest. Capital repatriation and profit remittance are freely permitted. A special licence must be obtained to do business in certain sectors such as banking, real estate, transport and insurance.

Until the end of 1994, the *Treuhandanstalt Gesellschaft* was charged with privatizing state-owned concerns in the former East Germany. When it was dismantled, its activity was divided among three companies:

— the *Beiteiligungs Management-gesellschaft* (BMG) monitors companies that have not yet been privatized;
— the *Treuhand Liegenschaftgesellschaft* (TLG) sells real property;
— the *Bodenverwaltung und Verwertungs GmbH* (BVVG) is the official contact for investors seeking to acquire farmland.

Those who wish to build a factory should contact local authorities, which grant permission on the basis of various criteria, in particular zoning and environmental impact. Permits are granted or denied within several weeks to several months, depending on the time of year that the request is filed, the complexity of the project and the amount of outside financing required.

Principal legal forms

It is possible to conduct business in Germany by establishing a representative office, a branch office or a subsidiary. Subsidiaries must adopt one of the country's existing legal forms.

The limited-liability company (Gesellschaft mit beschrankter Haftung – GmbH) is the most common legal form for foreign subsidiaries established by companies that wish to limit their risks to the amount of capital invested, and that have no intention of effecting a public offering. There is a great deal of flexibility in terms of capital ownership, management and the duties of the partners involved. Small- and medium-sized businesses do not generally choose the joint-stock corporation form (*Aktiengesellschaft* (AG)), since it is administratively more cumbersome and complex than a GmbH. A notary draws up the incorporating instrument for both an AG and a GmbH.

■ Limited-liability company

Requirements of a GmbH:

— minimum of three founding shareholders (in the case of an Einmann-GmbH, sole proprietorship is permitted);
— minimum capital of 50,000 marks (€25,564.59), half of which must be paid in at the time of incorporation;
— strict formalities at the time of incorporation (articles of incorporation and bylaws notarized).

Flexible management:

— minimum of one manager, who may be but need not be a shareholder;
— supervisory board (*Aufsichtsrat*) mandatory if the company workforce exceeds 500 (see AG below);
— annual general meeting of shareholders;
— presence of an independent auditor is mandatory when certain threshold levels are surpassed;
— shareholders' liability is limited to the capital invested;
— for tax and social security purposes, non-majority owner-managers are considered employees.

■ Corporation

Requirements of an AG:

— minimum of five founding shareholders (in the case of an Einmann-Aktiengesellschaft, sole proprietorship is permitted);
— minimum capital requirement of 100,000 marks (€51,129.19), half of which must be paid in at the time of incorporation;
— strict formalities at the time of incorporation (articles of incorporation and bylaws notarized).

Fairly cumbersome management:

— board of management (*Vorstand*) with at least two members, who must be natural persons, and who may be but need not be shareholders;

— supervisory board (*Aufsichtsrat*) with at least three members or more, depending on capital, and representatives of the shareholders and company employees;
— annual general meeting of shareholders;
— shareholders' liability limited to the capital invested;
— presence of one or more independent auditors elected by the annual shareholders' meeting to audit the financial statements.

Other legal forms

■ General commercial partnership (*Offene Handelsgesellschaft – OHG*)

A general commercial partnership is not a corporate entity, but has certain legal entitlements and is registered with the corporate and trade register. The partners may be individuals or corporate entities, and their liability is joint and several with respect to the entity's obligations and debts.

■ Limited commercial partnership (*Kommanditgeselleschaft – KG*)

A limited commercial partnership has no legal status, but it does have certain legal entitlements and is registered with the corporate and trade register. Active partners are personally liable for the debts of the entity. The limited sleeping partners' liability is limited to the capital invested.

■ GmbH & Co-KG

This is a type of KG in which the active partner is a GmbH. Family-owned concerns of a certain size often adopt this legal form.

Administrative procedures

The following formalities must be accomplished to establish a GmbH:

The articles of incorporation and bylaws must be drafted by a notary, and must include the following mandatory items: corporate name, business purpose, registered office, amount of capital (*Stammkapital*) and each member's contribution.

■ Choosing the corporate name

A patent search must be undertaken with the district court (*Amstgericht*) under whose jurisdiction the company is incorporated. The application must be approved by the Chamber of Commerce and Industry, and then registered by the district court.

■ Signing the articles of incorporation and bylaws

The official appointment of management and the signing of the company's articles of incorporation and bylaws take place before a public notary. Partners may be represented by a proxy-holder (*Prokurist*), provided that the latter has obtained a notarized instrument granting power of attorney.

■ Paying in of capital

Only half of the minimum capital, or 25,000 marks (12,782.29 euros), must be paid in. In-kind contributions are permitted, provided they have been valued.

■ Paying taxes

Certification by tax authorities that the investor has no outstanding unpaid taxes is required.

■ Filing the business registration form

The business registration form is signed by the manager(s) and filed with the corporate and trade register (*Handelsregister*). Several documents must be submitted with it, including the company bylaws and articles of incorporation, a list of partners and the capital amounts they have contributed, proxy or power of attorney instruments for management representatives, a certificate of minimum paid-in capital, and certification by tax authorities that no unpaid taxes are due.

Company founders acting in the name of the company to be incorporated are personally liable for such acts. From the time it is registered, the company has corporate personality or status.

■ Publication

Announcement is made in the official gazette (*Bundesanzeiger*) and in another legal bulletin.

■ Principal organization/incorporation costs

For a GmbH with initial capital of 50,000 marks (€25,564.59), incorporation costs come to around 1,700 marks (€869.20) and include:

— filing and registration fees with the corporate and trade register;
— announcement costs for publication of the incorporation instrument in the Official Gazette;
— notary fees.

Legal expense fees may be added to these amounts. They are negotiated between client and solicitor, and vary depending on the nature and complexity of services rendered.

Human resources/labour law

■ Employment contract

Permanent

A written contract signed between the employer and the employee, containing a required minimum of information on job requirements and working conditions.

Fixed-term

Allowable under certain legally specified conditions.
Maximum term: 24 months.

■ Length of the working week

The average working week comprises 38 hours, pursuant to national collective bargaining agreements.

Some employees are entitled to work a 35-hour week.

■ Overtime regulations

A maximum of two hours per day, for a total of 30 days a year. The amount of the premium depends on the contract.

■ Annual vacation period

A minimum of 24 workable days per year.

■ Paid leave and public holidays

From nine to 14 days depending on the *Länder*.

■ Wages

There is no statutory guaranteed minimum wage.

Wages are fixed by union contracts.

In the east German *Länder*, pay levels have gone from 30 to 90 per cent of wages paid in west Germany in eight years.

■ Social security

Health and maternity, disability, old age, unemployment, accidents on the job or commuting to or from work, occupational illness and family allowance benefits are provided. This coverage is not provided by a single insurance organization, but rather by several different ones – public and private, regional and trade or industry organizations.

Although no mandatory supplemental retirement scheme exists, voluntary company pension plans are offered by most large German companies.

■ Mandatory social security contributions

Social security contributions represent around 41 per cent of wages and are equally borne by the employer and the employee.

Workers' compensation insurance is fully provided for by the employer.

German wage costs exceed the European Union average by about 20 per cent.

■ Employing foreigners

Nationals of the European Union do not need permits to work in Germany. However, they must obtain a European Union national residence permit from the foreigners' office of German municipal governments (*Ausländerbehörde*). Anyone who resides in Germany for more than three months is generally granted a five-year permit, but these permits may be granted for shorter periods. Non-EU nationals must, in addition to the residence permit, apply for a work permit (*Arbeitserlaubnis*), which is delivered by the Labour Office (*Arbeitsamt*).

Paying taxes

■ Corporate income tax (*Körperschaftsteuer*)

Distributed profits: 30 per cent + solidarity surcharge of 5.5 per cent (ie 31.65 per cent).

Retained profits: 45 per cent + solidarity surcharge of 5.5 per cent (ie 47.47 per cent)

■ Personal taxes (*Einkommensteuer*)

Progressive tax rate from 0 per cent, and then from 25.9 per cent to 53 per cent.

+ a 5.5 per cent solidarity surcharge.

The minimum tax rate on personal income is expected to drop to 23.9 per cent on 1 January 1999, and to 22.9 per cent on 1 January 2000, while the maximum rate will fall to 51 per cent.

As of 1 January 2002, the respective rates should be 19.9 per cent and 48.5 per cent.

■ Religious worship tax

Levied on individuals who are members of a recognized church.

Tax rate between 4 and 7 per cent of personal income tax.

■ Value-added tax (*Umsatzsteuer*)

Reduced rate (food, books, handicrafts, etc): 7 per cent.

Standard rate: 16 per cent.

■ Municipal trade income tax (*Gewerbeerstragsteuer*)

This tax is levied on business income and capital, and is an allowable deduction from the corporate taxable income base. The basic tax rate is 5 per cent, multiplied by a local coefficient that varies from 300 to 515 per cent, resulting in an effective tax rate of between 15 and 25.75 per cent.

■ Real estate tax (*Grundsteuer*)

Average local rate: 0.35 per cent multiplied by a local coefficient that varies from 200 to 550 per cent.

Deductible from the taxable income base.

Investment incentives

Germany is divided into 16 provinces (*Länd*). The major investment incentives concern the five new provinces of the former East Germany: Brandenburg, Mecklenburg-Vorpommern, Saxony, Saxony-Anhalt and Thuringia as well as economically troubled regions such as the Ruhr and the Sarre districts. These incentives are awarded by the Federal, the *Länder* and municipal governments.

The *Deutsche Ausgleichsbank* (DtA) and the *Kreditanstalt für Wiederaufbau* (KfW), which manage the funds provided by the European Recovery Programme (ERP), together form the backbone of the financing system. Investors should not, however, apply directly to the DtA or the KfW. Applications must be submitted via the investor's local bank.

■ Subsidies

Capital goods subsidies/Equipment grants

These non-taxable subsidies are granted by right when equipment is acquired (or self-produced) for the purpose of being used within the former East Germany. These goods must be new tangible assets that are among the depreciable assets of the company. The equipment must be used in one of the new *Länder* for a period of at least three years, and personal use is limited to 10 per cent. The grant amounts to from 5 to 10 per cent of the investment, depending on the date the investment was made.

Investments made in West Berlin no longer qualify for these subsidies, while those made in East Berlin continue to be eligible. These *Investitionszulagen* may be aggregated with structure subsidies.

Structural aid

These grants are not automatically awarded, and are considered to be taxable corporate income. The *Investitionszuschüsse* are grants intended for businesses that participate in efforts to improve regional economic structures by creating or protecting jobs.

Businesses in the following sectors are not eligible for these grants: transport, dock handling, distribution, construction, real estate development, automobile dealership, agriculture, food, energy and water supply. The following types of investments do not qualify: land acquisition, the purchase of used goods, automobiles, aircraft, ships and boats and replacement purchases.

Grant amounts:

— business start-ups: up to 23% of the investment outlay;
— expansion of production facilities: up to 20% of the investment outlay;
— improvements or restructurings: up to 15%.

■ Research and development grants and subsidies

Small businesses in the high-tech field may qualify for subsidies that cover up to 75 per cent of their costs, up to a ceiling of 45,000 marks (€23,008.13), subject to the following conditions:

— the company must be located in east Germany;
— the company must have been in operation for less than two years;
— the company must employ fewer than 10 workers;
— the company founder must hold an equity stake of at least 51%.

Investment in production facility improvements can qualify for up to 80 per cent coverage of their outlay, up to a ceiling of 800,000 marks (€409,033.50). The ceiling is 1 million marks (€511,291.88) for businesses involved in production or marketing. Applications should be filed with the Ministry for Research and Technology, and are processed within six months.

■ Miscellaneous allowances and bonuses

Assistance may be granted by the Federal, the *Länder* or municipal authorities. These non-refundable allowances may not, added together, exceed 30 per cent of the investment outlay. They primarily concern projects involving research, the tourist industry and international co-operation.

For the most part, allowances available in the provinces of the former East Germany concern existing businesses, and include incentives for the development of technologies and non-polluting industrial processes, 'green' or ecological tourism, alternative energy sources and rationalization grants to small- and mid-sized businesses.

Those starting new businesses should contact their local municipal authorities and chamber of commerce to find out about obtaining:

— free land and premises;
— exemptions from real estate taxes;
— interest-rate buydown loans and guarantees on up to 80% of the loan;
— coverage of consulting fees and training costs, etc.

Potential investors can obtain information from economic development offices (*Wirtschaftsförderungsgessellschaft*) located in every region.

■ Preferential loans and guarantees

Loans for equity capital invested

Those setting up a business are entitled to a loan for investment in the new *Länder* when their invested capital amounts to at least 15 per cent of the total investment outlay. Terms and conditions:

— the loan is granted for a period of 20 years, with a ten-year grace period possible;
— up to a ceiling of between 700,000 and 2 million marks (357,904.31 euros to €1,022,583.70);
— interest rate: 0% for the first three years, reduced repayments up to the seventh year;
— nominal rate between the seventh and tenth year, market rate over the following 10 years;
— early repayment possible.

ERP loans

ERP (European Recovery Programme) investment loans are designed to encourage business start-ups, takeovers or upgrades throughout Germany in all economic sectors, including the professions. Companies with annual revenues of less than 100 million marks (€51,129,188.12) are eligible for ERP loans, although the maximum is increased to 500 million marks (€255,645,940.60) if the investment project in question concerns environmental protection.

Foreign businesses are eligible for this type of loan provided that they set up a stand-alone structure, or if they acquire an equity interest in a company already set up in one of the new *Länder*.

ERP investment loans for 20-year periods are available in east Germany, and for 15-year periods in west Germany. Rates are 4.5 per cent over the first 10 years. The loan may not exceed 2 million marks or 50 per cent of the total investment outlay. A three-year grace period is possible.

DtA loans

Existenzgründung-Programm

The *Deutsche Ausgleichsbank* (DtA) provides medium and long-term loans (up to 10 years) at a preferential rate and with a three-year grace period for investments in east or west Germany.

These loans are available to natural persons, those in the professions and small and medium-sized firms that seek to establish a business or acquire an existing firm in the new *Länder*.

The loan may cover up to 75 per cent of the total investment. Rates are 7 per cent in east Germany and 7.5 per cent in west Germany, for a 10-year term and a three-year grace period.

KFW loans

Kreditanstalt für Wiederaufbau (KFW) provides SMEs long-term loans at preferential rates for construction projects, outlays for machines and equipment and also for business takeovers. *KFW MittelstandsProgramm* provides investment credits to small and medium-sized firms in east and west Germany.

The maximum loan amount is 10 million marks for a 10-year term, and a 20-year term is available in special cases. Repayment may be deferred for two or three years. Interest rates on KFW loans are slightly lower in the five new *Länder*.

These loans may be accumulated with ERP loans, provided that the total loan package does not exceed two-thirds of the investment.

Bank loan guarantees

Special organizations have been set up to assist companies that are unable to produce the collateral or security required to obtain conventional bank loans or preferential loans. Interested investors should contact:

— the Berliner Industriebank;
— the Bürgschaftsbanken
— the Deutsche-Ausgleichsbank;
— the Treuarbeit AG.

Useful addresses in Germany

Foreign Investor Information Centre
Scharnhorst Strasse 36
10115 Berlin
Tel.: (49) 30 2014 7755

■ Financial organizations

Berliner Industriebank AG
Landeckerstrasse 2–3
W-14119 Berlin 33
Tel.: (49) 30 82 00 30

Deutsche Ausgleichsbank (DtA)
Ludwig Enzhardplatz 1–3
D-5317 Bonn
Tel.: (49) 228 83 10

Kreditanstalt für Wiederaufbau (KFW)
Palmengartenstrasse 5–9
D-60325 Frankfurt/Main
Tel.: (49) 30 82 00 30

■ Local development organizations

Wirtschaftsfürderung Berlin
Liebermannstrasse 76
13088 Berlin
Tel.: (49) 30 399 800

■ Ministries

Economics Ministry
Bundesministerium für Wirtschaft
Schanhorstrasse 36
10115 Berlin
Tel.: (49) 30 20 149

Employment and Industrial Relations Ministry
Bundesministium für Arbeit and Sozialordnung
Jaegenstrasse 9
10117 Berlin
Tel. (49) 30 20 140

Finance Ministry
Bundesministerium der Finanzen
Wilhelmstrasse 97
10117 Berlin
Tel.: (49) 30 22 42 02

Ministry for Research and Technology
Bundesministerium für Forschung und Technologie
Glinkastrasse 18–24
10117 Berlin
Tel.: (49) 30 285 400

La Fonte Ardennaise

'Moving from a representative office to a subsidiary would obviously be a step on the road to independence…'

Laurent Humbert, LFA Cologne

In 1958, La Fonte Ardennaise (LFA) had a workforce of 70 and produced 100 tons of cast iron per month in Vivier-au-Court near Sedan. By 1997, the numbers had swelled to 1,000 employees and 3,500 tons of cast iron per month, and annual revenues stood at 450 million francs.

LFA uses the Disamatic process (a high-duty continuously cast bar system without flask molding) to produce high-precision casting for machine-tools, gear boxes and valves and fittings. The company also supplies parts for the new Opel Astra, high-tech equipment for rail companies and chimney inserts and table legs for bistro-style tables. In addition, it has a subsidiary (Fondatex) which designs and builds works of art that have become collectors items.

This family-run business is at the head of an industrial market that has grown as the number of foundries in Europe has declined. It earns more than 30 per cent of its revenues in the export market: Germany is far and away the leading customer in Europe, placing 60 per cent of all orders, followed by the Benelux countries, which account for 25 per cent of the European market, and Switzerland, Sweden and Finland, which together total 15 per cent. LFA initially set up a sales force in Germany in 1986, and followed up in 1993 with a representative office in Cologne. Laurent Humbert, a 28-year-old sales engineer specializing in the German market, runs the office.

'Having a permanent structure makes us more credible in the eyes of our German partners. It shows that we intend to stick around and allows us to contact prospects and take care of after-sales service. Invoicing and delivery are handled by our parent company. Our two-person sales team, which includes me, earned revenues of 78 million francs in 1997 and we are forecasting nearly 100 million in 1998. We're exploring the possibility of setting up a subsidiary that would take the GmbH form. This would obviously be a step on the road to independence. But we aren't sure it would be in our interest financially, in terms of both taxes and social charges.'

Notes

7

Setting Up a Business in Greece

MACEDONIA

BULGARIA

TURKEY

ALBANIA

Serrai

Drama

Kilkis

Komotini

Xanth

Edhessa

Kavala

Florina

Alexandroupolis

Kastoria

Veroia

Thessaloniki

Kozani

Katerini

Poliyiros

Kariai

Grevena

Ioannina

Larisa

Kerkira

Igoumenetsa

Trikala

Kardhitsa

Volos

Aegean Sea

Arta

Karpenision

Mitilini

Preveza

Lamia

Amfissa

Mesolongion

Levadhia

Khalkis

Chios

TURKEY

Argostolion

Patrai

Samos

Corinth

Athens

Zakinthos

Navplion

Pirgos

Ionian Sea

Tripolis

Ermoupolis

Kalamata

Sparta

Rhodes

Sea of Crete

Khania

Iraklion

Mediterranean Sea

Rethimnon

Ayios Nikolaos

Key statistics

Total surface area:	131,957 square kilometres
Population:	10.5 million
GDP growth:	3.7% (1998)
Per capita GDP:	€10,126 (1998)
Public deficit/GDP ratio:	−2.4% (1998)
Public debt/GDP ratio:	106.5% (1998)
Inflation:	4.7% (1998)
Unemployment:	9.6% (1998)

Pursuing fiscal austerity with success, Greece is firmly committed to meeting the convergence criteria that will qualify it for membership in the Euro Area in 2001.

The government has implemented a programme aimed at cutting public expenditure, and is also continuing efforts to privatize in many sectors, including water supply, oil, transportation and banking.

The dismantling of several public monopolies is a source of opportunity for foreign investors. The Hellenic Centre for Investments (ELKE) offers information and advice free of charge to businesses with sizeable investment projects, and can speed up both the application review process and government approval mechanisms.

Since it joined the European Union in 1981, Greece has made ample use of European Structural Funds to upgrade its infrastructures. With the Olympic Games scheduled for Greece in 2004, new markets are expected to materialize.

The United States is the largest source of foreign investment, followed by Germany and France. Greece is a stepping stone for companies with manufacturing plans in Albania, Romania or Bulgaria, where labour costs are relatively low.

Recent foreign investors in Greece include TVX Gold (Canada); Aramco (Saudi Arabia); Promodes (France), which established a chain of Continent Hellas supermarkets; Grands Travaux de Marseille and GTM International (France) to build the Rio-Antinio bridge; Transroute (France); and Hochtief (Germany), which is investing in airport and land transport infrastructure projects.

Regulations governing foreign investment

Foreign investment in Greece is freely permitted, requiring only that a statement be filed with the Ministry of National Economy. The local bank through which funds are being transferred to Greece usually files this statement on the investor's behalf. Capital linked to the direct investment may be freely repatriated.

Investments in certain sectors are subject to special controls. They include banking, telecommunications and defence. In addition, administrative approvals may be required for manufacturing sites and activities that pose a pollution risk. Investment projects that require more than 3 billion drachmas (€9,230,769.23), or 1 billion drachmas (€3,076,923.08) if half of the equity capital is foreign, must be submitted to ELKE. ELKE reviews projects to ensure that they meet all regulatory requirements and files a report on the viability of the project. ELKE's role is to make recommendations only; it does not grant investment approval, licences or subsidies.

Principal legal forms

It is possible to do business in Greece by establishing a representative office, a branch office or a subsidiary. Subsidiaries adopt one of the country's existing legal forms. The AE (corporation) is the legal form most widely used for foreign investment in Greece.

■ Limited-liability company (EPE – Eteria Periorismenis Efthynis)

Requirements of an EPE:

— minimum of two founding shareholders (except for sole proprietorships);
— minimum capital of 6 million drachmas (€18,461.54), immediately paid in;
— strict formalities at the time of incorporation (notarized instrument).

Flexible management:

— one or more managing directors, individuals or corporate entities, may be but need not be shareholders;
— annual general meeting;

— depending on the size of the EPE, the presence of an independent auditor may be required;
— shareholders' liability is limited to the capital invested.

■ Corporation (AE – Anonymos Eteria)

Requirements of an AE:

— minimum of two founding shareholders;
— minimum capital of 20 million drachmas (61,538.46 euros), immediately paid in;
— strict and relatively costly formalities at the time of incorporation (notarized instrument).

Relatively rigid management:

— board of directors with at least three members;
— annual general meeting of shareholders;
— the presence of two independent auditors is mandatory;
— shareholders' liability is limited to the capital invested.

Other legal forms

■ General commercial partnership (OE — Omorithmos Eteria)

Requirements of an OE:

— minimum of two partners;
— no minimum capital requirement;
— partners' liability is joint and several and unlimited;
— partners are taxed on their income for half of the profits.

■ Limited partnership (EE – Eterorithmos Eteria)

— Minimum of two partners:
— active partners have joint and several and unlimited liability;
— limited sleeping partners' liability is limited to the capital invested.

■ Undeclared partnership (Afanis Eteria)

Used to form joint ventures (*Kinopraxia*), construction consortia or major industrial projects, as well as to start a business with a Greek partner.

■ Branch of an offshore company

— special legal form designed to encourage the establishment of foreign firms that wish to use Greece as a base of operations from which to develop international business. Only companies that do not do business on Greek soil may adopt this form;
— prior approval of the Ministry of National Economy is required;
— a bank guarantee must be deposited;
— tax, customs and accounting advantages: exemption from corporate income tax, partial exemption from personal income tax for foreign employees, no statutory auditors.

Administrative procedures

The following formalities must be accomplished to establish an EPE or an AE.

■ Drawing up the articles of incorporation

The articles of incorporation and bylaws must be executed in the presence of a notary public, and must include the following information: corporate name, business purpose, registered office, life of the company, share capital and its division into shares, number of shares subscribed and par value, number of directors, powers of the boards, termination and liquidation.

■ Signing the contract of incorporation

The contract of incorporation includes the incorporating instrument and company bylaws and articles of incorporation. It must be drawn up by a solicitor or a notary public and signed by the shareholders in the presence of the former.

■ Filing the written deed and registration

The instrument certifying the formation of an EPE must be filed with the court of first instance in the district of the company's registered office. For an AE, the instrument is submitted to the approval of the regional prefect. Once approved, the company is considered to be registered in the register of corporations.

■ Publishing

A summary of the articles of incorporation (EPE) or the ministerial decree (AE) is published in the official gazette.

■ Principal organization/incorporation costs

For both the EPE and the AE, incorporation costs generally total between 4 per cent and 8 per cent of capital, depending on the amount invested. However, incorporation costs may be as high as 10 per cent for an AE. To these amounts may be added legal expense fees, which vary depending on the nature and complexity of services rendered and which are negotiated between client and solicitor.

■ Processing delays

One month for an EPE, two months for an AE.

Human resources/labour law

■ Employment contract

Permanent

A written contract signed between the employer and the employee, containing a required minimum of information on job requirements and working conditions.

Fixed-term

There are no restrictions on the term of a temporary employment contract, and such contracts may be renewed twice.

■ Length of the working week

Fixed at between 38 and 40 hours by many collective bargaining agreements.

■ Overtime regulations

— vary from one sector to the other – a maximum of 30 hours a year in industry and 120 hours a year in commerce;
— premium of 25% over the regular hourly wage for overtime, rising to 75% on Sundays and legal holidays.

■ Annual vacation period

Twenty-four working days.

■ Paid holiday leave

Thirteen days.

■ Wages

— minimum wages set in collective bargaining agreements; annual summer vacation bonus equal to half a month's salary;
— year-end bonus equal to one month's salary;
— Easter bonus equal to half a month's salary;
— 14 months' salary in all.

■ Social security

Wage earners in Greece are insured through a primary social insurance fund (*IKA*) and are also enrolled in a supplemental retirement program (*TEAM*).

Insured risks include sickness, maternity, old age, disability, survivor benefits, family allowances, on-the-job accidents and occupational diseases, and unemployment.

■ Mandatory social security contributions

Employer contributions: around 27 per cent of gross salary.

Employee contributions: around 15 per cent of gross salary.

■ Employing foreigners

Non-EU nationals must obtain both residence and work permits, delivered by the Ministry of Labour. The work permit is granted for a specific job with a specific employer for a defined period of time. It may be renewed. The employer must be able to demonstrate that the employee in question possesses skills that are not available in the local market. Foreign companies that invest in Greece generally have an easier time obtaining permission to hire foreign management level personnel.

Paying taxes

■ Tax on registered capital

One per cent of the capital contribution at the time of incorporation and when capital increases are effected.

■ Corporate income tax

The tax rate for corporations (AE) is 40%.
The tax rate for listed companies is 35%.
The tax rate for limited-liability companies (EPE) is 35%.

■ Personal taxes

The personal income tax is progressive, with six brackets from 0 per cent, 5 per cent to 45 per cent.

■ Value-added tax

Reduced rates of 4 per cent and 8 per cent on essentials.
Standard rate: 18 per cent.

■ Real estate taxes

Corporate entities that own real property are taxed at a rate of 0.7 per cent on the assessed value in excess of 60 million drachmas (€184,615.38).

Some business activities are exempt from this tax.

Investment incentives

■ Development incentives

Foreign investors benefit from the same entitlement to investment incentives as Greek nationals. There are basic types of incentives: grants, low-interest rate loans and tax breaks. They vary from one region to another depending on the level of development.

Law 2601/98 amended the system of government investment aid. Outright grants have been reduced and access to them restricted. In addition, preference is given to business start-ups that create jobs. To qualify, investment projects must contribute to regional development, job creation, making businesses more competitive, restructuring sectors or production branches, increasing commercial and investment opportunities in Greek and international markets and protecting the environment.

Greece is divided into five geographic zones: A, B, C, D and Thrace. The first zone, which encompasses the area in and around Athens and Thessaloniki, is ineligible and the latter has been granted most-favoured status. The bulk of available incentives target investments made in the 'undeveloped and remote' regions, ie those in zones C and D.

Several types of aid are available: grants that vary in amount depending on the type of investment and location, interest subsidization for the financing of new equipment and tax breaks on all or a portion of investment outlays. Businesses that have been in operation for less than five years may apply for all these incentives, while others are entitled to the latter two only.

Grants are awarded to offset the cost of purchasing equipment and machinery, research into innovative products or processes, the use of new technologies, patents and programmes aimed at improving product quality. Special grants are available for investments in manufacturing or tourism that exceed 25 billion drachmas (€76,923,076.92) and that create more than 300 jobs. Incentives have also been created to promote new forms of recreation and tourism such as thermal and sea spas and winter resorts.

■ Where to apply

Applications for grants and aid are made to a variety of organizations, depending on the type and amount of the investment project. The Hellenic Centre for Investments (ELKE) handles investments that exceed 3 billion drachmas (1 billion drachmas if half of the company's equity capital is foreign). The Ministry of National Economy processes applications for aid on investments that exceed 500 million drachmas (€1,538,461.54). The Private Investment Office assesses project viability and public interest and determines what incentives will be offered. In other cases, investors should contact the relevant regional development office of the Ministry of National Economy.

The Ministry of Agriculture handles projects aimed at enhancing farming facilities and improving methods of storage, preservation, packaging and standardization of agricultural products.

The Hellenic Industrial Development Bank (ETVA) intervenes in certain zones, in particular 24 industrial sites where investors are entitled to preferential prices on the purchase of land, as well as preferential interest rates and tax breaks.

The EOMMEH, the main organization for the promotion of small and medium-sized firms, handles projects that require investments of up to 120 million drachmas (€369,230.77). It offers consulting services, grants and interest subsidies and training programmes. It is also a designated Euro-Info-Centre, providing information on European Community incentives.

Hiring subsidies

Hiring subsidies seek to promote the employment of the following priority groups: young unemployed people between the ages of 18 and 25, unemployed workers between the ages of 26 and 64 who have obtained degrees, women who are looking for work and workers in occupations or sectors that have been particularly affected by unemployment. In addition, financial aid is available to encourage self-employment among the unemployed.

Firms that create skilled full-time positions are entitled to grants that vary depending on the starting salary offer. To qualify, the employer must not have laid off workers in the preceding six months and must agree not to terminate the employment contract for at least four months after the end of the subsidized period.

Training grants are also available, targeting young people between the ages of 15 and 18. Training generally lasts four to six months. Accelerated training centres (KETEK) have been set up for the unemployed between the ages of 16 and 46. In addition, employers that provide direct training on the job are offered financial aid in the form of wage subsidies that cover one-third of the salary for 400 hours of work and training.

Useful addresses in Greece

Athens Chamber of Commerce and Industry
7–9 Akadimias Street
10671 Athens
Tel.: (30 1) 36 02 411

Bank of Greece
Central Bank
31 rue Panepistimiou
10250 Athens
Tel.: (30 1) 32 01 111

Employment Ministry
40 Piraeus Street
10437 Athens
Tel.: (30 1) 52 33 110

Federation of Greek Industries
5 Xenofontos Street
10575 Athens
Tel.: (30 1) 32 37 325

Hellenic Centre for Investments (ELKE)
3 Mitropoleos Street
10557 Athens
Tel.: (30 1) 32 42 070

Hellenic Organization for Small and Medium-sized Enterprises and Handicraft Undertakings (EOMMEH)
16 Xenias Avenue
11528 Athens
Tel.: (30 1) 77 99 972

Ministry of National Economy
Syntagma Square
10180 Athens
Tel.: (30 1) 33 32 000

Ministry of Trade
Kaniggos Square
10181 Athens
Tel.: (30 1) 361 62 41

National Bank of Greece (ETE)
86 Eolou Street
10559 Athens
Tel.: (30 1) 32 10 411

National Investment Bank for Industrial Development (ETEVA)
12–14 Amalias Avenue
10236 Athens
Tel.: (30 1) 32 41 679

Organization for the Promotion of Greek Exports (OPE)
86–88 Marimou Antipia
16346 Athens
Tel.: (30 1) 99 15 655

NAF NAF Hellas

> Greece can serve as a model to us. Ten outlets, including four in Athens, operate as flexible franchises.
>
> Gérard Sacalis, General Manager

When they were just 20 years old, Gérard and Patrick Pariente began their wholesaling business in ready-to-wear, launching the first Naf Naf collection under their own label. 'Le Grand méchant look' made its mark internationally as being young, feminine and colourful. While subsidiaries were being set up in Spain, Germany and the Netherlands, the 100th shop was opening its doors on Avenue des Ternes in Paris.

Naf Naf was listed on the Second Marché in 1993, and a year later bought out Chevignon, thereby gaining a toehold in the menswear market. With annual sales of 1.3 billion French francs, Naf Naf earns 70 per cent of its revenues in its 165 sales outlets by betting on the wisdom of setting up megastores in prime locations. Its subsidiary, Naf Naf Distribution, supplies some 3,500 points of sale, from shops to large retail department stores and by mail order.

The group's international growth is based on a franchising strategy in North America, Southeast Asia and the Near East where, according to its managing directors, markets are too protectionist to be directly accessible.

In Europe, this small fashion empire counts eight subsidiaries, including Naf Naf Hellas in Greece, which began operating in March 1994. Its Managing Director, Gérard Sacalis, is a 32-year-old Frenchman of Greek origin. The economics and business administration graduate explains: 'I was working as a financial analyst for a Renault subsidiary when Naf Naf offered me the opportunity to set up its wholesale arm in Greece. I didn't hesitate. Within six months, we plan to increase the capital of our corporation – in which I hold a 20 per cent stake – via capitalization of reserves.

This way, we'll be in compliance with the new legislation that doubles capital requirements for corporations, and will be able to pursue our growth strategy. We are supplied by our French wholesale subsidiary and sell our products to over a hundred multi-brand stores in the country. In addition, 10 outlets, including four in Athens, operate as flexible franchises.

'Normally, we work through exclusive distribution contracts granted to local agents. If the outcome is positive, the Greek model may serve as a basis for other European countries.' After posting sales of 5 million French francs in its first year of operation, Naf Naf Hellas earned 25 million francs in 1997, and recorded net earnings of around 2 million francs. 'We are forecasting 20 per cent growth per annum in the next three years,' says Gérard Sacalis. But nothing is certain. 'The Italians and the Spanish are tough competitors in low-priced fashion for the 15 to 35 age range. Fortunately, Greeks love French fashion!'

Notes

8

Setting Up a Business in Ireland

Key statistics

Total surface area:	70,273 square kilometres
Population:	3.6 million
GDP growth:	11.9% (1998)
Per capita GDP:	19,875 euros (1998)
Public deficit/GDP ratio:	0.6% (1998)
Debt/GDP ratio:	49.4% (1998)
Inflation:	1.9% (1998)
Unemployment:	7.8% (1998)

Ever since the early 1960s, Ireland has spurred economic development by attracting foreign investment. Ireland offers foreign investors one of the best tax and financial-aid packages available in the European Union, a strategy that has paid off for this small country (3.6 million inhabitants) with few natural resources: national wealth has climbed by 25 per cent over the last five years.

Ireland has long been the darling of multinationals looking for a gateway to the Single Market, but it is also a favourite among small and medium-sized companies. Who can resist a corporate income tax rate that will remain fixed at 10 per cent until 2010, compared with the 21 per cent to 45 per cent levied in the other European countries?

This tax haven mainly benefits entrepreneurs who invest in high-tech, state-of-the-art fields such as electronics, software development and production, telemarketing, pharmaceutical and beauty-care products, financial services, call centres and multimedia, not to mention film-making and post-production.

To offset the flow of goods produced in Ireland by multinationals out of the country, the Irish government is making efforts to strengthen ties between multinationals and local suppliers.

Approximately 1,100 companies with foreign capital are present on the Emerald Isle, employing one out of two Irish workers. These companies account for 55 per cent of total production and export three-quarters of all locally manufactured goods.

The United States is the number one foreign investor in Ireland, followed in order by the United Kingdom, Japan and Germany. The 500 US companies established in Ireland post an average annual return on equity (ROE) of 25 per cent, a level not likely to be rivalled elsewhere in Europe.

Recent noteworthy investments include Dell Computers (US), American Home Products Corporation, IBM (US), Hewlett Packard (US),

Gateway 2000 (US), Eastman Kodak (US), DSC Communication (US), Netscape Communications (US), KAO (Japan), NatWest Group (UK), and Deutsches Reisebüro (Germany).

Regulations governing foreign investment

Foreign direct investment is not subject to restrictions, and no prior approvals are required. The repatriation of capital and earnings is not subject to any controls.

Financial services companies (banks, insurers) that establish operations in the Shannon and Dublin offshore centres must obtain a business licence from the Irish government. The procedure is relatively long and complicated. Certain public-sector activities (electricity, postal service, telecommunications, etc) are *de facto* though not *de jure* closed to foreign investors, although this is expected to change with the implementation of European regulations on competition in regulated sectors. In the fields of electricity, gas and telecommunications, highly regulated up to now, European directives are creating new investment opportunities.

All foreign investors interested in acquiring land must receive and usually obtain prior authorization from the Irish Land Commission. The Environmental Protection Agency and municipal councils deliver building permits.

Principal legal forms

It is possible to conduct business in Ireland by establishing a representative office, a branch office or a subsidiary. Subsidiaries must adopt one of the country's existing legal forms.

There is a great deal of similarity between corporate forms in Ireland and the United Kingdom.

The private limited company is the legal form that is best suited to the needs of small to medium-sized foreign investments.

■ Private Limited Company (Ltd)

Requirements of Ltd companies:
— at least two shareholders (it is possible to form a single member private limited company) and a maximum of 50;

— no minimum capital requirement (in practice, a minimum capital of 2 Irish pounds (€2.54) divided into two shares).

Relatively flexible management:

— a board of directors with a minimum of two directors and a secretary (who may be one of the directors), a chairman and a managing director;
— annual general meeting of shareholders;
— presence of an outside auditor charged with certifying the annual accounts;
— shareholders' liability is limited to the capital invested;
— for tax and social security purposes, directors who also exercise a specific management function are considered employees (for example: executive director).

■ Public Limited Company (PLC)

Requirements of a PLC:

— at least seven shareholders;
— fully subscribed capital of at least 30,000 Irish pounds (€38,092.14), one-quarter of which must be paid up when the company is founded;
— may invite the public to subscribe to shares and bonds;
— operates like a private limited company, although the shareholders' meeting exercises a supervisory function;
— presence of an outside auditor is required;
— shareholders' liability is limited to the capital invested;
— for tax and social security purposes, directors who also exercise a specific management function are considered employees (for example: executive director).

Other legal forms

■ Partnership

Requirements:

— no minimum capital requirement;
— similar to a joint venture;
— maximum of 20 members except for certain of the professions;
— partners' liability is joint and several and unlimited.

◼ Limited partnership

Requirements:

— no minimum capital requirement;
— at least one partner (the general partner) has unlimited liability;
— limited liability of certain partners (sleeping partners that contribute capital but play no management role in the firm).

◼ Unlimited company

Requirements:

— similar to a general commercial partnership;
— no minimum capital requirement;
— partners' liability is joint and several and unlimited;
— this legal form is generally used for transactions that do not entail a financial risk.

◼ Company limited by guarantee

Requirements:

— no minimum capital requirement;
— partners' liability is limited to the capital pledged as security;
— this legal form is generally used for non-profit activities (training and teaching, research, the arts, and sports).

Administrative procedures

The following procedures must be followed to establish a business in Ireland.

◼ Choosing the corporate name

The registered company name must be filed with the Registrar of Companies after a patent search has been conducted. The corporate name is registered at the same time that the registration certificate is delivered.

■ Drafting the articles of incorporation and bylaws

One of the founding members or a solicitor draws up the articles of incorporation and bylaws. The memorandum of association indicates the corporate name, legal form, registered office, business purpose, and the amount of authorized share capital and its division into fixed amounts. The articles of association set forth the regulations for internal company management and administration.

■ Filing signed articles of incorporation and bylaws with the Registrar of Companies

The articles of incorporation and bylaws must be filed along with:

— a statement of compliance with statutory requirements;
— a statement of nominal share capital, registered office, and the names, details, nationality and profession of the directors and the statutory secretary.

■ Delivery of the certificate of incorporation

After examining the documents, the registrar delivers the certificate of incorporation and the company comes into existence, ie it acquires a corporate personality. Processing can take three to four weeks.

■ Announcement in the Gazette

The notice of incorporation is published in the Official Irish Gazette (legal bulletin).

■ Principal organization/incorporation costs

Incorporation costs come to around 1,000 Irish pounds (€1,269.74) and vary considerably depending on the initial capital investment. They include:

— filing and registration fees with the registrar: around 150 Irish pounds;
— the 1% tax levied on registered capital;
— notary fees: about 90 Irish pounds;

— miscellaneous expenses (for printing documents, seals, etc): around 20 Irish pounds;
— solicitor's fees.

Solicitor and consulting fees may be incurred in addition to the above. The amount depends on the nature and complexity of the services rendered.

Note: Private limited companies may begin transacting business as soon as they have obtained the certificate of registration from the registrar. Public limited companies may not really do so until they have obtained a trading certificate, which is delivered when statutory capital requirements have been met.

Acquiring a 'Ready-made' Company

The investor interested in setting up a business quickly should contact a solicitor or a company registration agent. These professionals can recommend an off-the-shelf-company, ie an already formed and registered company, usually a private limited company (Ltd) that has not done business since it was founded (a 'dormant company').

The investor can effect the required administrative procedures for taking over the company immediately, and the ready-made company can begin transacting business immediately.

Acquiring a shell corporation (or dormant corporate shell) is the most common way of forming a company in Ireland. It costs about 300 Irish pounds (€380.92).

Human resources/labour law

■ Employment contract

Permanent

A written contract is signed between the employer and the employee, containing a minimum of required information on job requirements and working conditions.

Fixed-term

There are no restrictions on the number of times this type of contract can be renewed or on its total term.

■ Length of the working week

The legal maximum is 48 hours a week and nine hours a day.

Under the terms of most collective bargaining agreements, the working week is 37.5 hours in the service sector and 40 hours in the industrial sector.

■ Overtime regulations

Overtime is limited to:

— 12 hours per week;
— 36 hours per month;
— 240 hours per year.

The first two hours of overtime worked are compensated at a 25 per cent premium over basic pay, and at a 50 per cent premium beyond two hours. Sunday and holiday work are paid double-time.

■ Annual vacation period

Four weeks of paid vacation are provided for in most collective bargaining agreements.

■ Paid leave and public holidays

Eight days a year.

■ Wages

There is no statutory guaranteed minimum wage. Wages are generally determined by collective bargaining.

Compensation is negotiated between employer and employee, and may include merit bonuses (productivity, teamwork, etc).

■ Social security

Social welfare insurance (Pay Related Social Insurance – PRSI) covers sickness, maternity, disability, old age, unemployment, retirement and worker's compensation. A supplemental private pension scheme is advisable. Two voluntary health insurance schemes (Voluntary Health Insurance (VHI) and BUPA) offer additional coverage for hospitalization and certain other medical expenses.

■ Mandatory social security contributions

Employer contributions: up to 12 per cent of gross salary.

Employee contributions: up to 6.75 per cent of gross salary.

■ Employing foreigners

All foreign employees must obtain a residence permit. Nationals of the European Union do not need work permits. Employees who are not nationals of the European Union must obtain work permits from the Department of Enterprise and Employment. Work permits are easily granted to employees with skills that are unavailable locally.

Paying taxes

■ Tax on registered capital

1 per cent of invested capital.

■ Corporate income tax

Standard tax rate:

— 25% on the first 100,000 Irish pounds (€126,973.80) of taxable income;
— 28% on taxable income in excess of 100,000 Irish pounds.

Reduced rate:

— 10% in many sectors, including manufacturing, finance, insurance, information technology, etc (see section on tax incentives in this chapter).

> Note: The Irish government is planning to reduce the current corporate tax rate of 32 per cent to 12.5 per cent as of 1 January 2003. Over the next five fiscal years, the rate will drop by 4 per cent a year.

So-called close companies (companies in which at least 51 per cent of the voting rights are in the hands of at least five shareholders) are subject to a 15 per cent surtax if profits are not distributed in the 18 months following the end of the fiscal year in which they were earned.

■ Personal taxes

Two income brackets, taxed at a rate of 24 per cent and 46 per cent respectively.

■ Withholding at source on wages (Pay-As-You-Earn)

Employers withhold personal income taxes at source, calculated on the basis of the wages paid to employees. This is the Pay As You Earn (PAYE) system.

■ Municipal property tax (business rate)

— Tax levied on owners and occupants of buildings used for commercial purposes (does not apply to private residences or farm buildings).
— Deductible from taxable income.
— Tax rate determined by local authorities.

■ Value-added tax (VAT)

— Zero rate: most food items, certain prescription drugs, children's clothing.
— Reduced rate: 4 and 12.5%.
— Standard rate: 21%, applied to most products and some services.

Investment incentives

Despite recent changes, Ireland still offers foreign investors one of Europe's most attractive financial and fiscal incentive packages. Among countries in the European Union, Ireland ranks third behind Greece and Italy.

■ Grants and subsidies

Industrial Development Authority

The Industrial Development Authority (IDA), a public organization based in Dublin, has 15 overseas offices: four in Europe, six in the United States and five in Asia. This network enables the IDA to effectively promote Ireland to potential investors abroad. In 1994, the IDA's missions were divided up as follows:

— Forbairt, for companies with indigenous capital;
— IDA Ireland, for the promotion of foreign inward investment.

These two agencies operate under the auspices of Forfas, which co-ordinates investments and offers advice on general policy.

IDA Ireland provides information and advice to potential foreign investors, with a clear preference for larger companies that offer high added value, create jobs and produce goods and services that are easily exportable. The agency handles the application from start to finish, dealing with everything from site location to grant awards. It also co-ordinates all required administrative procedures.

Projects that seek funding in excess of 2.5 million Irish pounds (€3,174,345.10) are reviewed by government bodies, which generally give the green light within three months.

IDA eligibility criteria

Successful incentive applications must show that:

— financial assistance is necessary to establish or expand the business;
— the investment is commercially viable;
— the equity base is sufficient;
— a realistic business plan has been drawn up.

Investments should contribute to:

— increasing the production of goods and services for international export;

— local and national economic development;
— earning substantial revenues;
— reducing the unemployment rate in the most hard-hit areas.

Eligible sectors

— manufacturing activities (medium-sized and large companies);
— light manufacturing (fewer than 50 employees);
— international services;
— business start-ups.

Types of grants

Grants for fixed assets

These grants finance site and site development, plant construction and the purchase of new machines and equipment. Fixed asset grants cover up to 60 per cent of the investment cost in under-industrialized areas and up to 45 per cent in other areas.

Job creation grants and subsidies

These grants apply to additional hires and may cover up to 24 weeks of employee wages. Half the amount is paid on the date the new job is created, and the rest is paid a week later provided that the job is maintained.

In addition, employers who hire unemployed workers who have been out of a job for at least three years are entitled to a recruitment subsidy.

Training grants

The aim of these grants is to encourage employee training by covering up to 50 per cent of trainee wages excluding social charges for existing firms, and 100 per cent of trainee wages for new businesses. For employees sent abroad for training, the grant covers travel and accommodation expenses and wages.

Feasibility study grants

Grants may be awarded to cover market research and studies to determine the feasibility of investment projects for which other aid is sought.

Research and development grants

Approved projects are eligible for grants covering up to 50 per cent of the cost, up to a ceiling of 250,000 Irish pounds (317,434.51 euros).

R&D grants are intended to promote the design of new products manufactured locally and the use of new methods.

Technology acquisition grants

These grants, which cover up to 50 per cent of costs, are used to purchase patents, trademarks and industrial processes aimed at improving company performance.

Low-interest loans

Low-interest loans and loan guarantees may be granted to small and medium-sized companies (with a workforce of 50 or less, annual revenues of less than 5 million Irish pounds). Companies in the manufacturing, services, retail and tourist industries may qualify for loans of 20,000 to 250,000 Irish pounds (€25,394.76 to €317,434.51) granted for periods of 10 to 15 years.

■ Tax incentives

Manufacturing activities

Companies that manufacture products in Ireland for export or for sale in the domestic market are taxed at a special 10 per cent corporate tax rate. For tax purposes, manufacturing is defined as the physical, chemical or biological alteration of a product or material.

Companies established prior to June 1998 qualify for this reduced rate until 31 December 2010. For those set up after June 1998, the 10 per cent rate applies until 31 December 2002, after which it will be raised to 12.5 per cent.

The special rate has gradually extended to many non-manufacturing activities such as fish-farming, mushroom production, the repair of computer parts, ships and aircraft engines, meat and fish processing and film production.

International Financial Services Centre – IFSC

Tax incentives are offered to service sector firms located in the Customs House Docks Area in central Dublin. Eligible service-sector businesses include asset management, brokerage, insurance and reinsurance, mutual fund management, financial consulting, back office services and centralized treasury management.

Prior approval of the Industrial Development Authority (IDA) must be obtained, and the IDA employment criteria in force at the time of approval must be met within two to three years. The tax advantages include:

— the reduced corporate income tax rate of 10% until 31 December 2010;
— exemption from local property taxes for 10 years;
— a write-off of building acquisition and new equipment costs of up to 100% in the first year, including commercial premises, or a double-rent deduction;
— no withholding at source on distributed dividends;
— no withholding at source on interest paid;
— exemption from VAT;
— exemption from stamp tax on most transactions.

In all, more than 400 major international financial services institutions currently operate in the Industrial Financial Services Centre, including ABN-Amro, Citibank, Deutsche Bank and Merrill Lynch.

The Shannon Airport Zone

Companies that set up operations in aeronautics, offshore banking or insurance, or that exercise a retail activity in the Shannon Airport zone are eligible for the special 10 per cent corporate tax rate until 31 December 2005, subject to prior approval. In addition, such companies are not subject to either VAT or customs and excise taxes, and are eligible for accelerated depreciation. This tax system has been extended to international services that either lead to job creation or increase the number of air passengers and cargo at Shannon Airport. Capital and training grants are also available.

Note: As part of the IDA programme, the special corporate tax rate of 10 per cent applies to computer hardware and software manufacturers as well as firms that provide consulting or technical support in these areas. IDA tax incentives have brought a number of information technology and systems providers to Ireland, such as IBM, Hewlett Packard, Microsoft, Oracle, Novell, Corel and Sunsoft. Sixty per cent of all computer software sold in Europe is now manufactured in Ireland.

Note: Projects submitted after 22 July 1998 qualify for the 10 per cent corporate tax rate until 2002, at which time the standard rate of 12.5 per cent will apply, with the exception of a limited number of projects specifically approved by the IDA or the IFSC. At the request of the

European Commission, the Irish government has agreed to limit the number of investment projects granted the 10 per cent special rate between now and 1 January 2003, the date on which the standard 12.5 per cent rate will go into effect. For the period 1998–2003, the government has agreed to accept a maximum of 77 IDA-sponsored investment projects, and 67 IFSC projects annually for the years 1998 and 1999.

Useful addresses in Ireland

Aliens Office
Garda Siochana
Harcourt Square
Dublin 2
Tel.: (353 1) 73 22 22

Central Bank of Ireland
PO Box 559, Dame Street
Dublin 2
Tel.: (353 1) 71 66 66

Companies Registration Office
Lower Castle Yard
Dublin Castle
Dublin 2
Tel.: (353 1) 661 42 22

Department of Enterprise and Employment
Kildare Street
Dublin 2
Tel.: (353 1) 661 44 44

Department of Social, Community and Family Affairs
Information and International Unit
Aras Mhic Dhiarmada
Dublin 1
Tel.: (353 1) 874 84 44

Dublin Chamber of Commerce
7 Clare Street
Dublin 2
Tel.: (353 1) 661 28 88

Industrial Development Authority (IDA)
Wilton Park House
Wilton Place
Dublin 2
Tel.: (3531) 603 40 40

IDA has an international network of 15 agencies.

Irish Business and Employers Confederation (IBEC)
Confederation House
84 Lower Baggot Street
Dublin 2
Tel.: (353 1) 660 10 11

Patents and Trademark Office
45 Merrion Square
Dublin 2
Tel.: (353 1) 661 41 44

**Shannon Free Airport
Development Company Ltd
(SFDCO)**
Shannon
County Clare
Tel.: (061) 361 555

Udaras Na Gaeltachta
Na Forbacha
County Galway
Tel.: (353 91) 92 011

MPO

Dublin, the multimedia gateway.

The support of the local authorities was decisive.

Alban Pingeot, Managing Director of MPO

Just 40 years ago, Pierre and Monique de Proix set up a vinyl disc production company in their castle in Mayenne with two employees. Today, MPO is one of the world's leading independent producers of optical disks, and manufactures CD ROMS for use in the multimedia, IT and music industries. To cite a recent example among hundreds, MPO produced the Elton John song in memory of Princess Diana.

The company has opened eight plants, not only in France, but also in Spain, California, Texas, Canada and Thailand. Today it employs 3,000 people and earns annual revenues of 1 billion francs.

Last June, MPO announced plans to establish operations in Ireland, where half of all IT products are manufactured. 'In order to work with the industry's major powerhouses such as IBM, Microsoft, Lotus and Gateway 2000, we had to be closer to them, which was the main reason we opted for Ireland,' says the Irish subsidiary's Managing Director Alban Pingeot.

When Alban Pingeot arrived in Ireland a year and a half ago, he appreciated the support offered by the Industrial Development Authority. A project head was waiting for him when he stepped off the aeroplane and stayed by his side every step of the way, from the operational start-up to the search for a suitable plant location to putting together the legal and financial aspects of the deal.

Last year, MPO bought a ready-made Ltd company from a solicitor with capital of 2 Irish pounds for an investment of 10 million Irish pounds. The company hopes to break even this year and turn a profit by next year, taxable at a rate of 10 per cent. It has a workforce of 85, including five managers and several department heads.

'But it is becoming more and more difficult to recruit Irish IT and electronics specialists,' says Alban Pingeot. 'Salaries are too high, what with Motorola, IBM and others scouting the local market for engineers.'

The company is developing a maintenance contract to enable it to intervene directly on site without the need to contact resellers.

Notes

9

Setting Up a Business in Italy

Key statistics

Total surface area:	301,308 square kilometres
Population:	57.5 million
GDP growth:	1.4% (1998)
Per capita GDP:	18,157 euros (1998)
Public deficit/GDP ratio:	−2.7% (1998)
Public debt/GDP ratio:	118.7% (1998)
Inflation:	2.4% (1998)
Unemployment:	12.2% (1997)

With 57 million inhabitants, Italy is one of Europe's premier markets, and one of its most intensely competitive. The foreign investor needs to have a keen grasp of the rules of the business game in order to successfully negotiate within a dense network of small- and medium-sized companies that are well-entrenched in the country's industrial fabric.

Industrial growth is concentrated in six north-central regions (Lombardy, Piedmont, Veneto, Emilia-Romagna, Marches and Tuscany), while Lombardy, Latium and Liguria (where the port of Genoa is located) are very active in freight services.

Around 1,630 companies in Italy (employing 527,000 people) have a foreign majority shareholder base.

Company start-ups *ex-nihilo* account for only 7 per cent of all investments. This is primarily due to the high cost of acquiring industrial sites in the most sought-after regions such as those in northern Italy.

The major sources of foreign investment are the United States, followed by France, Germany and the United Kingdom. Target sectors for foreign investment include food processing and retailing, textiles, the automotive and machine tool industry, and insurance and banking.

The major foreign businesses present in Italy are IBM, Exxon, Unilever, Ford, Renault, Michelin, Mercedes Benz, Philips, Nestlé, and Procter and Gamble. Recent foreign investors of note include Shell (the Netherlands), Auchan (France), Fidelity Investments (US), Gaz de France (France), Mannesman (Germany), and Usinor Sacilor (France).

Regulations governing foreign investment

Foreign direct investment is not subject to controls. There are no restrictions on foreign equity in Italy, with the exception of certain sectors (publishing, telecommunications, electricity, oil, airlines and maritime shipping, etc) where prior permission is required and special regulations apply. Repatriation of capital from profits is unrestricted, subject only to tax reporting requirements. Doing business in many sectors, in particular retail trade, is subject to licensing by local authorities.

Principal legal forms

It is possible to conduct business in Italy by establishing a representative office, a branch office or a subsidiary. Subsidiaries must adopt one of the country's existing legal forms.

The SRL (limited-liability company) is the most widely used legal form; the corporation or public limited form (SpA) is better suited to larger undertakings and listed companies.

■ Limited-liability company (SRL – *Società a responsabilita limitata*)

Requirements of an SRL:

— minimum of two founding shareholders (if the SRLUS form is adopted, one founding shareholder is permitted);
— minimum share capital of 20,000,000 lire (€10,329.14), fully subscribed and 30% paid in at the time of incorporation;
— relatively cumbersome incorporation procedures (notarized instrument).

Flexible management:

— a single director, who may but need not be a shareholder, or a board of directors (*consiglio d'amministrazione*) composed of several members;
— annual general meeting of shareholders;
— the company must appoint a board of three (sometimes five) independent auditors (*collegio sindicale*), depending on certain thresholds;
— shareholders' liability is limited to the capital invested.

■ Corporation (SpA – *Società per azioni*)

Requirements of an SpA:

— minimum of two shareholders;
— minimum capital of 200 million lire (€103,291.37) fully subscribed and 30% paid in at the time of incorporation;

— relatively cumbersome and costly incorporation procedures (notarized instrument);
— a single director, who may be but need not be a shareholder, or a board of directors (*consiglio d'amministrazione*) composed of three to seven members;
— the company may be governed by an executive board (*comitato esecutivo*) and a supervisory board;
— annual general meeting of shareholders;
— the company must appoint a board of independent auditors (*collegio sindicale*);
— shareholders' liability is limited to the capital invested.

Other legal forms

■ General commercial partnership (SNC – *Società in nome collectivo*)

Requirements of an SNC:

— minimum of two partners;
— no minimum capital requirement;
— partners' liability is joint and several and unlimited;
— one or more managers run the company;
— subject to personal income tax (IRPEF);
— this form is often used for family-run businesses.

■ Limited partnership (SAS – *Società in Accomandita Semplice*)

Requirements of an SAS:

— two types of partners:
  – active partners are personally liable for the debts of the entity (only active partners are involved in company management);
  – limited sleeping partners' liability is limited to the capital invested.

■ Co-operative (SC – *Società Cooperativa*)

Requirements of an SC:

— minimum of nine shareholders;
— no minimum capital requirement;

— shareholders' liability may be limited or unlimited, as specified in the articles of incorporation;
— subject to a series of audits and approvals;
— increasingly used in certain sectors (farming, construction and civil engineering).

Administrative procedures

The following procedures must be followed to establish a business in Italy.

■ Drafting the articles of incorporation and bylaws

The articles of incorporation and bylaws are drawn up by a *commercialista* or a lawyer. The *commercialista* has no equivalent in the other European countries, and plays an economic, financial, legal and tax-consulting role. In small and medium-sized businesses, the *commercialista* often acts as an informal confidant to the boss.

The articles of incorporation and bylaws must contain the following provisions: corporate name, life of the company, business purpose, share capital and distribution of earnings, number of directors and independent auditors.

■ Organization meeting

The incorporating instrument is executed in the presence of a notary. The founders or their proxy-holders approve and sign the articles of incorporation. The names of the founders are listed on the incorporating instrument.

■ Depositing and paying in of capital

The required 30 per cent of initially paid-in share capital is deposited in cash into an Italian bank (100 per cent for a limited-liability company with a sole proprietor), and is remitted after the company has registered with the Registrar of Companies.

■ Filing relevant documents

The articles of incorporation and the incorporating instrument should be filed with the clerk of the court of jurisdiction in the region of the company's registered office.

The incorporating instruments must be supported by:

— a certificate attesting that 30% of initial share capital has been deposited with a bank;
— the partners' or shareholders' and directors' tax code number;
— a notarized list of proxy-holders if the founding members are not present.

■ Registering with the Registrar of Companies

Registration must take place within 30 to 45 days after the appropriate documents have been filed with the Court. The company comes into existence, ie acquires a corporate personality, when these documents have been filed. Between the time the articles of incorporation are signed and the company is officially registered, its directors are personally and jointly liable for all commitments made by the company.

■ Publishing the incorporating instrument

The incorporating instrument is published in an Official Gazette (*bolletino ufficiale delle società per azioni ed a responsabilità limitata*).

Principal organization/incorporation costs

For an SRL with initial capital of 20,000,000 lire (€10,329.14), incorporation costs break down as follows:

— tax on registered capital: 200,000 lire (€103.29);
— miscellaneous fees (company registration, official seals): 1.3 million lire (€671.39);
— announcement in the Official Gazette: 200,000 lire (€103.29);
— notary fees: 2.4 million lire (€1,239.50). The total comes to 4.1 million lire (€2,117.47).

For an SpA with initial capital of 200 million lire (€103,291.37), incorporation costs come to around 11 million lire (€5,681.03).

Legal expenses or *commercialista* fees of 3.5 to 4 million lire (€1,807.60 to €2,065.82) may be added to these amounts, which vary depending on the nature and complexity of services rendered and which are negotiated between client and solicitor.

Human resources/labour law

■ Employment contract

Permanent

A written contract signed between the employer and the employee, containing a required minimum of information on job requirements and working conditions.

Fixed-term

There are no restrictions on the term of this type of contract.

■ Length of the working week

Set at 40 hours under the terms of most collective bargaining agreements.

■ Overtime regulations

Overtime is limited to:

— two hours a day;
— twelve hours a week; and
— 170 hours a year.

Overtime hours worked are compensated at 30 to 75 per cent above the hourly wage.

Employers are required to contribute an additional 15 per cent to the social security system for all overtime in excess of the weekly maximum of 48 hours.

■ Annual vacation period

Twenty-two days per year.

■ Paid leave and public holidays

From 8 to 11 days per year.

■ Wages

Minimum wages are set by nationwide collective bargaining agreements.

■ Social security

The INPS (*Istituto Nazionale della Previdensa Sociale*) provides coverage for sickness and maternity, disability, death, old age and unemployment. The INAIL (*Istituto Nazionale per Assicurazione centrogli Infortuni sul Cavoro*) covers worker's compensation and occupational illnesses.

■ Mandatory social security contributions

Employer contribution: around 42 per cent of gross salary.

Employee contribution: around 8 per cent of gross salary.

■ Employing foreigners

Nationals of the European Union do not need permits to work in Italy. They must obtain a residence permit delivered by the local police headquarters. Non-EU nationals must obtain a visa from an Italian embassy, delivered upon presentation of proof that the Ministry of Labour is prepared to issue a work permit. The residence permit is delivered by the local police headquarters upon presentation of a valid work permit.

Paying taxes

◼ Corporate income taxes

The corporation tax (IRPEG – Imposta sul reddito delle persone giuridiche)

Tax rate on retained reinvested profits: 19 per cent (7 per cent for newly listed companies over the first three fiscal years starting from the date the company is listed on the stock market). Tax rate on distributed profits: 37 per cent (for co-operatives, the rate varies between 18.5 per cent and 27.75 per cent).

The regional tax on companies and professionals (IRAP – Imposta regionale sulle attivita produttive)

The IRAP has replaced several taxes: the ILOR local income tax (16.20 per cent), the ICIAP tax on business premises, the capital tax (*imposta patrimonale sulle imprese*), the municipal tax and other minor taxes. The tax rate for IRAP is 4.25 per cent on added value generated by a company, and it applies to companies, artists and professionals, non-commercial bodies and state and other public administrations. IRAP is reduced by 50 per cent of the standard rate for a period of three years for new manufacturing businesses set up in economically depressed areas.

◼ Personal taxes on natural persons (IRPEF – *Imposta sul reddito delle persone fisiche*)

Progressive rates from 18.5 per cent to 45.5 per cent (five brackets).

The rate schedule applied to earned income includes the additional regional contribution of 0.5 per cent.

◼ Withholding at source on wages

Employers withhold personal income taxes at source, calculated on the basis of the wages paid to employees.

■ Value-added tax (IVA – *Imposta sul valore aggiunto*)

Depending on the type of goods and services:
Standard rate: 20%;
Reduced rates: 4%, 10%.

■ Local property tax (ICI – *Imposta comunale sugli immobili*)

Based on the rateable value of buildings and land. The rate varies from one municipality to the next from 0.4 per cent to 0.7 per cent.

Investment incentives

Italy's investment incentive policy aims to promote development in economically troubled regions and to foster small and medium-sized businesses and job creation.

■ Regional incentives

Regional incentives have tended to favour *Mezzogiorno* in southern Italy, a region that begins in Rome and includes Sicily, Sardinia, Elba and many smaller islands. But in light of the reforms enacted in 1993, *Mezzogiorno* no longer has special status and its own incentive agency. A new organization called *Sviluppo Italia* has been set up to streamline grants and subsidies, particularly in the South. Three programmes offering various types of incentives are available to companies depending on the size of their investment project.

Investments in Mezzogiorno

Grants and subsidies are available for business start-ups and expansions, and to upgrade existing firms. To qualify for aid, projects must lead to job creation, the development of new technology and the use of local resources. In addition, the government offers subsidies, long-term low-interest rate loans, leasing facilities, research and development grants, and reductions in social contributions.

A special incentive programme is open to young entrepreneurs (between the ages of 29 and 35) who start a business, offering grants and low-interest rate loans. Small and medium-sized service firms (for example, those providing information technology and systems services) are eligible for grants that cover up to 75 per cent of their costs. Research centres with at least 25 employees are eligible for grants that cover 50 per cent of their fixed investment costs, low-interest rate loans and reductions in taxes and social charges.

Companies that set up headquarters (administrative, commercial and technical centres) in *Mezzogiorno* are eligible for the same grants as those available for setting up production units, provided that they employ a workforce of at least 15.

Investments in the North

Regional governments may also grant low-interest rate loans to small and medium-sized firms that hire new workers. Regional subsidies and attractive loans are offered to companies that build hotels and tourist facilities.

■ Hiring incentives

A 50 per cent reduction (100 per cent in *Mezzogiorno*) in the base rate for social security contribution may be obtained for newly hired workers who were previously unemployed for more than two years. A 75 per cent reduction in the base rate for social security contributions may be obtained for all newly hired workers if the employment contract is submitted to the local office of the Ministry of Labour and the Social Security Institute, provided that the employer has not laid off workers holding similar positions in the preceding 12 months. This reduction is valid for one to three years, depending on how long the newly hired worker was unemployed prior to recruitment.

Reduced social contributions are offered to employers that hire young workers (29 and under) under apprenticeship or vocational training programmes. Reduced social contributions are also available for employees hired in connection with approved on-the-job training programmes. The reduction is valid for a defined period depending on the term of the contract, the type of training, the applicant's age and, for the unemployed, the length of the jobless period.

■ Tax incentives

A few of the available tax incentives include:
— a credit on the VAT totalling 6% of the value of new machinery and equipment investment outlays;

— double depreciation on assets for the first three years;
— exemption from the tax on capital gains that are reinvested in depreciable assets;
— a 25% tax deduction on the cost of energy-saving investments.

Special tax treatment for headquarters?

With the exception of Whirlpool and IBM (for its southern European operations), few multinationals have selected Italy as their corporate headquarters. In theory, headquarters are exempt from taxes provided that they are not engaged in commercial activities and do not generate profits. In practice, business centres declare nominal profits and pay corporate and local business taxes to avoid being investigated by the Italian tax authorities.

◼ Research and development grants

Research and development funding is available through the Ministry of Universities and Scientific and Technological Research, the Ministry of Industry's General Directorate for Industrial Production, the Innovative Technology Fund (FIT) and the National Research Council (CNR). Subsidy amounts depend on several criteria including the size of the company, the technological value of the project, industrial risk and location in a disadvantaged region.

L'Istituto Mobiliare Italiano (IMI) also offers businesses funding for technology projects that is refundable only if the project succeeds. Research expenditures are eligible for special amortization. The Sabatini Act facilitates the purchase or sale of technologically sophisticated machine tools, and offers grants and low-interest rate loans to both small and medium-sized firms and larger enterprises.

Useful addresses in Italy

Association of Italian Chambers of Commerce
Via Flaminia, n. 21 int. 12/a
00196 Roma
Tel.: (39) 0 632 15 660

Assolombarda
Via Pantano 9
20122 Milano
Tel.: (39) 0 2 58 37 01
Provides advisory services for investors interested in Lombardy, one of the
most attractive regions for foreign business.

IRFIS (Mediocredito della Sicilia)
Via G Bonanno 47
Palermo
Tel.: (39) 0 91 30 03 42

Istituto Mobiliare Italiano (IMI)
Via dell' Arte 25
00144 Roma
Tel.: (39) 0 65 95 91

Istituto per la Promozione Industriale (IPI)
Tel.: (39) 0 68 09 721
This organization was previously known as the Istituto per l'Assistenza allo
Sviluppo des Mezzogiorno, and provided information on Mezzogiorno.
Today, it offers information on all declining regions.

Italian Bankers' Association (ABI)
Piazza del Gesu 49
00186 Roma
Tel.: (39) 0 676 71

Italian Chamber of Commerce and Industry
Via Meravigli 96
20 123 Milano
Tel.: (39) 0 2 85 151

Italian Trade Commission (ICE)
Viale Litz 21
00144 Roma
Tel.: (39) 0 65 99 21

Mediocredito centrale
Via Piedmonte 51
00187 Roma
Tel.: (39) 0 64 79 11

Ministry of Industry
Industrial Production Institute
Via Molise 2
00187 Roma
Tel.: (39) 0 6 470 51

Ministry of Labour
Via Flavia 6
Roma
Tel.: (39) 0 648 643 04

Ministry of the Treasury, Budget and Economic Planning
Via XX Settembre 97
00 188 Roma
Tel.: (39) 0 6 476 11
These two ministries are charged with negotiating incentives in Mezzogiorno.

Ministry of Universities and Scientific and Technological Research
Piazzale Kennedy 20
00144 Roma
Tel.: (39) 0 6 59591

National Federation of Industries
Viale dell' Astronomia 30
00144 Roma
Tel.: (39) 0 6 590 31

National Social Security Institute (INPS)
Via Ciro il Grande 21
01144 Roma
Tel.: (39) 0 6 590 544 84

Societa Finanziaria Industriale Rinascita Sardegna (SFIRS)
Via S Margherita 4
Cagliari
Tel.: (39) 0 70 .66 41 86

ADECCO SPA (Società di Fornitura di Lavoro Temporaneo)

Italians appreciate the advantages of hiring temps. . . an opportunity for skilled people looking for work.

Jérôme Caille, Managing Director

ADECCO, the result of the 1996 merger between the Swiss ADIA and the French ECCO, currently leads the world human resources market. With more than 3,000 agencies located in 48 countries, ADECCO earned revenues of 47 billion French francs last year and posted a profit of 1.24

billion French francs, a 25 per cent increase over 1996. ADECCO's development strategy has paid dividends: it is the leading provider of temporary workers in 6 of the world's 11 biggest markets (France, Germany, Canada, Australia, Switzerland and Spain).

Along with Greece, Italy was the last country in the world to permit the use of temporary workers to meet short-term personnel needs. ADECCO wasted little time, setting up a subsidiary to spearhead local operations just one month after Italy passed the Treu Act in 1997. The subsidiary currently co-ordinates the activities of 65 agencies based in Turin, Milan, Rome, Naples, Padua and Bologna.

Jérôme Caille is responsible for doing preliminary analyses of the potential of the market, which experts say is worth 5 billion French francs. He currently runs the Italian subsidiary, which has a permanent staff of 250, including around 30 people based at the Milan headquarters.

'We reached our initial goal, which was to make 6,000 temps available in 1998, and 20–30 per cent of them have been permanently hired by the companies they went to work for on short-term assignments. Our major clients include groups such as Michelin, Citroën, Renault, Danone, Nestlé, Microsoft and, naturally, Italian companies such as Pirelli, Benetton, Barilla, Fiat, Ferrero. . . and let's not forget Ferrari, surely one of our most prestigious.

'Temporary employment is to permanent employment what the mobile phone is to the fixed telephone. Italians are attracted to things that make life simpler and employers were quick to see the value of interim employment: the recruitment of people with the desired profile, personnel management and also replacements for absences. The flexibility of this kind of work makes it possible to extend the contract for up to two years via successive renewals, thereby avoiding the constraints of the traditional fixed-term contract, which can only be renewed once. The best people are eventually hired permanently.

'Temporary employment has become a real opportunity, even for those at the high end of the skills spectrum who are looking for work,' adds Jérôme Caille. 'To such an extent that we have set up a Web site, Jobs around the world (www.adecco.com), that enables people to look for work in 48 different countries.'

A must for those who are looking to expatriate. With or without educational baggage.

Notes

10

Setting Up a Business in Luxembourg

Key statistics

Total surface area:	2,586 square kilometres
Population:	424,000
GDP growth:	5.7% (1998)
Per capita GDP:	€34,670 (1998)
Public deficit/GDP ratio:	2.1% (1998)
Public debt/GDP ratio:	6.7% (1998)
Inflation:	1% (1998)
Unemployment:	2.8% (1998)

Luxembourg is firmly committed to the political and monetary construction of Europe. It is the European Union's smallest but most affluent nation, with economic growth above the EU average (it boasts the world's highest per capita GDP) and inflation and unemployment are virtually non-existent.

Once driven by the iron and steel industry, the Luxembourg economy has now diversified into the service sector. Thanks to favourable tax treatment and banking secrecy, financial services have flourished, now accounting for 60 per cent of GDP. No fewer than 230 banks and 89 insurance companies have an operating presence in Luxembourg.

To avoid being overly dependent on the financial services sector, Luxembourg actively seeks out foreign investment in high-tech industries (particularly those related to the environment), trade and communications. A media, communications and information hub, Luxembourg offers tax advantages to enterprises that produce films and television programmes there.

The primary sources of foreign investment are the United States, Japan and other EU member nations (led by Belgium, Germany and France). Since the early 1970s, more than 130 industrial enterprises have decided to establish operations in Luxembourg, creating some 11,000 new jobs.

With a workforce of 3,600, Goodyear (US) is Luxembourg's second-largest employer. Most recent foreign investment has been undertaken by companies already established in Luxembourg: Husky Injection Molding Systems (Canada), European Satellite Multimedia Services, Euronimbus (US-German joint venture) and Auchan (France). Henkel (Germany) bought out a washing powder and soap manufacturer, and the US-based chemicals company DuPont De Nemours, one of Luxembourg's top employers with a workforce of 1,300, has built a fifth production line that produces ultra-light polyester film. Finally, TDK (Japan) employs 680 people in Luxembourg, and has begun production of CDs at its Niederkerschen site.

Regulations governing foreign investment

Foreign direct investment (start-ups and acquisitions, equity investments) is not subject to any specific prior approval. Applications to engage in handicraft or trade-related activities are submitted to the approval of the Ministry of Small Businesses, while the Ministry of Economics (Industrial Division) handles requests to establish manufacturing sites. In some cases, those wishing to engage in trade-related activities or practice a particular profession must demonstrate that they have the necessary credentials. Industrial activities require a permit certifying that the plant and production processes comply with environmental standards.

The Ministry of Finance delivers authorizations pertaining to banking and financial services after the Financial Sector Oversight Commission has reviewed applications. This requirement is waived for banks that are already established in an EU member country. The Ministry of Finance also delivers insurance and reinsurance business licences after applications have been reviewed by the Insurance Commissioner. Again, this requirement is waived for insurance companies with operations in another EU member country.

Principal legal forms

It is possible to conduct business in Luxembourg by establishing a representative office, a branch office or a subsidiary. Subsidiaries must adopt one of the country's existing legal forms.

The SARL and SA forms used in Luxembourg are very similar to their French counterparts. It should be kept in mind that foreign investors stand a better chance of receiving grants and subsidies if they establish an SA rather than an SARL. In addition, the transfer of shares is more flexible for an SA.

■ Limited-liability company (SARL)

Requirements of an SARL:

— minimum of two founding shareholders (although sole proprietorship is permitted) and a maximum of 40;
— minimum share capital of LUF 500,000 (€12,394.16), fully subscribed and paid in;
— strict and relatively costly formalities at the time of incorporation (notarized instrument).

Flexible management:

— a minimum of one managing director, who must be a natural person but who need not be a shareholder;
— annual general meeting required for companies with more than 25 shareholders (if there are fewer than 25, voting by mail is permitted);
— depending on the size of the SARL, the presence of an independent auditor may be required;
— shareholders' liability is limited to the capital invested.

■ Corporation (SA)

Requirements of an SA:

— minimum of two founding shareholders;
— minimum authorized capital of LUF 1,250,000 (€30,986.69), of which 25% must be paid in at the time of incorporation;
— strict and relatively costly formalities at the time of incorporation (bylaws and articles of incorporation notarized).

Management:

— board of directors with three members minimum, who may but need not be shareholders, appointed for a maximum period of six years (for companies with a workforce of 1,000 or more: a board of directors with at least nine members, of which one-third are personnel representatives);
— annual general meeting of shareholders;
— depending on the size of the company, the presence of an independent auditor may be required;
— shareholders' liability is limited to capital invested.

Other legal forms

■ General commercial partnership (SENC)

Requirements of a SENC:

— no minimum capital requirement;
— minimum of two partners;
— partners' liability is joint and several and unlimited;
— partners are subject to personal taxes on income;
— mainly used to form small family-owned retail and handicrafts businesses.

■ Limited partnership (SECS)

Requirements of a SECS:

— no minimum capital requirement;
— minimum of two partners;
— active partners have unlimited, joint and several liability;
— limited sleeping partners' liability is limited to the capital invested.

■ Partnership limited by shares (SCA)

Requirements of an SCA are similar to a SECS, with two differences:

— limited partners' shares are freely transferable;
— the partnership is subject to corporate income tax.

■ Co-operative corporation (SC)

Requirements of an SC:

— minimum of seven partners;
— no minimum capital requirement;
— shareholders' liability may be joint and several, unlimited or limited to the capital invested, depending on the bylaws and articles of incorporation;
— frequently used in insurance, agriculture and grape growing.

Partnership

Recommended for joint professional practices and real estate management.

Administrative procedures

The following procedures must be followed to establish a business in Luxembourg.

■ Drafting the incorporating instrument

The articles of incorporation and bylaws are drawn up:

— by a notary public for both the SA and the SARL, failing which they are null and void;
— by a notary public or by private signature for the partnership or limited partnership form, at the discretion of the founders.

From the time the articles of incorporation and bylaws are executed, the company has corporate personality or status. Unlike most other EU countries, where administrative procedures take longer to accomplish, it is not necessary in Luxembourg to wait until the company is officially registered.

■ Filing the incorporating instrument

Once the incorporating instrument is executed, the notary public must file for registration within 15 days, and the founders must file within three months.

■ Announcement

The articles of incorporation and bylaws are entered with the clerk of the district court of Luxembourg or Diekirch, depending on where the company's registered office is located, within one month of drawing up the incorporating instrument and registration with the Commercial Register.

■ Registration

Companies must enter the following information on the Commercial Register: corporate name, business purpose, share capital, registered office, names of all directors and officers, and date of incorporation.

■ Publication

The articles of incorporation and bylaws are published in full in the official gazette (*Mémorial*). For general commercial and limited partnerships, this information is published in abridged form. These instruments are effective against third parties only as of publication in the *Mémorial*.

■ Principal organization/incorporation costs

For an SARL with initial capital of LUF 500,000 (€12,394.68), incorporation costs total around LUF 22,400 (€555.28), broken down as follows:

— tax on registered capital of 1%;
— registration with the Commercial Register: LUF 2,400 (€59.52);
— announcement in the *Mémorial*: LUF 10,000 (€247.89);
— notary fees: LF 5,000 (€123.95).

For an SA with initial capital of LUF 1,250,000 (€30,986.69), incorporation costs come to around LUF 40,000 (€991.57).

Legal expense fees may be added to these amounts, generally LUF 30,000 to LUF 40,000 (€743 to €991.57). Expenses are negotiated between client and solicitor, and vary depending on the nature and complexity of services rendered.

Human resources/labour law

■ Employment contract

Permanent

A written contract signed between the employer and the employee, containing a required minimum of information on job requirements and working conditions.

Fixed-term

A maximum term of two years, including renewals.

◼ Length of the working week

Legal maximum of 40 hours.
In practice, the average working week is 38/39 hours.

◼ Overtime regulations

Employers must obtain prior authorization from the government before asking employees to work overtime. Overtime work is paid at a premium of 25 per cent for wage earners and 50 per cent for salaried employees. A premium of 70 per cent is paid for work on Sundays and holidays.

◼ Annual vacation period

Twenty-five days a year.

◼ Paid leave and public holidays

Ten days a year.

◼ Wages

The minimum wage is linked to the cost of living and adjusted annually.

Industry-wide collective bargaining agreements exist.

Many companies offer a 13th month salary, depending on length of service.

◼ Social security

Health and maternity, disability and old age, work-related accidents and occupational diseases, unemployment and family allowance benefits are provided.

■ Mandatory social security contributions

Employer contribution: between 14 per cent and 20 per cent of gross salary.

Employee contribution: between 10 per cent and 13 per cent of gross salary.

■ Employing foreigners

Nationals of the European Union do not need permits to work in Luxembourg. Nationals of other foreign countries must obtain a residence permit from the Ministry of Justice and then a work permit from the Employment Administration.

Employers generally make requests for work permits. Management level employees usually have little problem obtaining them for an initial period of one year, renewable thereafter for one year, then two years and five years.

Paying taxes

■ Tax on registered capital (*Gesellschaftsteuer*)

One per cent of the capital contribution.

■ Corporate income tax (IRC – *Impôt sur le Revenu des Collectivités*)

The tax rate on taxable corporate income is as follows:

— up to LUF 400,000 (€9,915.74): 20%;
— LUF 400,000 to LUF 600,000 (€14,873.61): LUF 80,000 + 50% on the portion over LUF 400,000;
— LUF 600,000: 30% on total taxable income;

a surtax of 4% is levied on income in excess of LUF 600,000 to finance the employment fund, bringing the effective tax rate to 31.2 per cent.

■ Personal taxes (IRP)

Levied on individuals and general partnerships.

Graduated system of 18 tax brackets (from 0 per cent to a marginal rate of 10 per cent up to 47.15 per cent).

◼ Value-added tax (*Umsatzsteuer*)

The tax rate depends on the nature of the goods and services:

— Reduced rates of 3%, 6% and 12%;
— Standard rate: 15%.

◼ Municipal business tax (*Gewerbsteuer*)

— Assessed on the basis of 'economic' profit.
— The rate for Luxembourg City is 9.09 per cent.

◼ Real estate taxes (*Grundsteuer*)

Levied on real property.
Maximum rate of 3 per cent.

Investment incentives

Incentives are generally granted on a regional basis. Businesses are eligible for grants of various kinds awarded on the basis of the type of investment, the number of jobs created and export potential.

◼ Financial incentives

Grants and loans may be obtained through the *Société Nationale de Crédit à l'Investissement* (SNCI), a public bank.

SME grants

Grants covering up to 15 per cent of investment outlays are available to small businesses, defined as those with annual revenues of less than €5 million employing fewer than 50 people. The SNCI offers loans at an interest rate of 3 per cent per annum to offset the cost of opening a retail outlet, a hotel or a restaurant. In certain cases, the SNCI grants equity loans for a maximum term of 10 years.

The national and local government may also offer land and buildings to investors on attractive terms.

Innovation grants

The government promotes new product development by financing 25 to 50 per cent of approved investment costs and up to 75 per cent if the project requires fundamental research. Amounts are determined on the basis of other innovation subsidies that may be granted by the Ministry of Economics. The interest rate on loans granted under this programme is 3 per cent per annum. Requests for information should be addressed to the SNCI.

Environmental protection incentives

Subsidies of up to 25 per cent of the total outlay are available to offset the cost of environmental protection and energy saving measures. Such aid is offered to enable:

— new businesses to exceed minimum environmental protection standards;
— existing companies to comply with the new standards.

Regional incentives

Three zones have been designated (in the south, north and east) as entitled to aid, and the following cantons: Capellen, Esch sur Alzette, Wiltz, Clervaux, Grevenmacher, and Luxembourg. Maximum aid offered under regional programmes is 17.5 per cent of investment costs in the north and east and 20 per cent in the south (25 per cent for existing production units). Applications should be submitted to the Ministry of Economics.

Companies may also apply for aid from one of three European structural funds (ERDF, EAGGF, ESF), depending on where planned investments are to be made.

■ Tax incentives

Tax credit for investment

A corporate income tax credit of 12 per cent is also offered for additional investment to tangible depreciable fixed assets other than land and buildings made during the fiscal year.

The 1929 holding company: exempt from corporate income tax

The Holding Companies Act of 31 July 1929 provides for preferential tax treatment of Luxembourg-based holding companies. To qualify, the company must limit its activity to the following areas:

— the purchase, management and sale of equity interests in Luxembourg or foreign companies;
— the holding and management of equity security portfolios;
— the purchase, sale and use of trademarks and patents via the granting of licences;
— the granting of loans and advances to companies in which it holds a substantial equity interest.

Holding companies may not engage in manufacturing, commercial or service-related activities.

Legal form

While holding companies may use any of Luxembourg's corporate legal forms, most are SAs.

Taxation

— 1% tax on registered capital at the time of incorporation and on subsequent capital increases;
— annual subscription duty of 0.2% on the holding company's capital, defined as the effective value of its shares;
— no taxes on income or the proceeds of liquidation;
— no withholding at source on dividends, interest or royalties paid by the holding company.

However, double-tax treaties do not apply to holding companies. If the holding company receives dividends from foreign subsidiaries that are subject to withholding taxes, these taxes are not reduced in the country of origin and may not be credited against Luxembourg taxes.

Reduced taxes for co-ordination companies

Companies incorporated in Luxembourg whose sole purpose is to provide administrative services to other members of the same group are taxed on a fixed basis. To qualify, such companies must receive prior approval from the Luxembourg tax authorities, granted for an indefinite period.

These co-ordination centres may centralize accounting records, process electronic data and conduct market research and advertising-related activities, but they may not effect financial transactions except the payment of invoices in multiple currencies. Taxable income is equal to 5 per cent of expenses. If expenses do not exceed LUF 30 million (€743,680.57), profit is assumed to be LUF 1,500,000 (€37,184.02). Although more restrictive than Belgian co-ordination centres in terms of allowable activities, Luxembourg co-ordination companies are under no obligation to create jobs.

Reduced taxes for 'reinsurance captives'

Reinsurance captives whose activity is limited to reinsuring the risks of companies that are members of the same group may set up reserves for 'fluctuation in claims experience' to strengthen the reserves usually set up by insurers.

These reserves are tax deductible, and result in a substantial reduction in taxable income for such companies.

WHAT IS A SOPARFI?

Features

— No restrictions are placed on the type of activity that a SOPARFI (*Société de Participation Financière*) may engage in, whether commercial or financial.
— The SOPARFI is subject to the income tax on common-law corporations and is covered under double-tax treaties and the parent-subsidiary directive.
— Dividends between parent and subsidiaries (resident or foreign) are tax exempt, as are capital gains on the transfer of equity securities.

Legal form

While any of Luxembourg's corporate legal forms may be used, most are SAs.

Taxation

— initial capital tax of 1% at the time of incorporation;
— exempt from taxes on dividends and capital gains provided that certain conditions are met.

For dividends

— an equity interest equal to at least 10% of the subsidiary's capital or at least LUF 50 million (€1,239,467.60);
— the equity securities are held for an uninterrupted period of at least 12 months;
— the subsidiary must be subject to a foreign corporate income tax similar to the Luxembourg corporate income tax (IRC).

For capital gains

— the transferred equity interest must constitute at least 25% of the subsidiary's share capital or have cost at least LUF 250 million (€6,197,338.12);
— the equity securities have been held for an uninterrupted period of at least 12 months prior to the start of the accounting period of the fiscal year in which the transfer occurs;
— the subsidiary must be subject to a foreign corporate income tax similar to the Luxembourg corporate income tax (IRC).

Withholding tax on dividends paid by the SOPARFI:

Exemption from withholding tax (25 per cent), provided that the dividends are distributed to a taxable EU parent company that has held a direct equity interest of at least 25 per cent for an uninterrupted period of two years at the time of distribution.

■ Hiring subsidies

The government has set up a variety of programmes designed to promote the hiring of young workers. There are hiring grants for employers who take on workers under the age of 25 in sectors where a shortage of skilled labour exists, as well as for those who hire workers at a starting salary above the minimum wage. In addition, expenses incurred by the employer to train apprentice workers are reimbursed.

Employers that hire the long-term unemployed are eligible for grants. Those that hire job seekers under 30 or over 50 who have been out of work for more than a year are exempt from social charges.

As of 1 July 1996 and until 31 December 1999, a tax subsidy is available to industrial, commercial, handicrafts and agricultural companies, as well as to those in the professions, to encourage the hiring of those who have been out of work for at least three months. To qualify, employers must offer a permanent contract (or a fixed-term contract of at least two years) and at least 16 hours of paid work per week. The monthly tax subsidy amounts to 10 per cent of gross monthly salary, deductible as an operating expense.

The tax reduction is valid for 36 months, on the basis of the tax year in which the salary is paid. In cases where the company's taxable income is insufficient, the subsidy can be carried forward over the next 10 years.

Geographic mobility allowances and early retirement incentives are also available.

Useful addresses in Luxembourg

Chamber of Commerce
7, rue Alcide de Gaspéri
L 1615 Luxembourg-Kirchberg
Tel.: (352) 423 93 91

Chambre des Métiers
2, circuit de la Foire Internationale
L-1347 Luxembourg
Tel.: (352) 42 67 67 1

Corporate Independent Auditors' Institute
7, rue Alcide de Gaspéri
L-1615 Luxembourg-Kirchberg
Tel: (352) 43 74 84

Employment Administration
38A, rue Philippe II
L-2010 Luxembourg
Tel.: (352) 478 53 00

Industrialists' Federation
7, rue Alcide de Gaspéri
L-1615 Luxembourg-Kirchberg
Tel.: (352) 435 366

Intellectual Property Register
Ministry of Economics
19/21, boulevard Royal
L-2914 Luxembourg
Tel.: (352) 478 41 50

**Ministry of Economics
Foreign Investors' Office**
19/21, boulevard Royal
L-2914 Luxembourg
Tel.: (352) 478 41 51

Ministry of Finance
3, rue de la Congrégation
L-2931 Luxembourg
Tel.: (352) 4 78 01 10

Ministry of Foreign Affairs, Foreign Trade and Co-operation
5, rue Notre Dame
L- 2911 Luxembourg
Tel.: (352) 478 23 64

Ministry of Small Businesses
6, avenue Emile Reuter
L-2937 Luxembourg
Tel.: (352) 478 47 15

Ministry of the Environment
18, montée de la Pétrusse
L-2918 Luxembourg
Tel: (352) 40 04 10

Société Nationale de Crédit et d'Investissement (SNCI)
Centre du Saint Esprit
7, rue du Saint Esprit
L-1475 Luxembourg
Tel.: (352) 461 97 11

Tax Administration
45, boulevard Roosevelt
L-2982 Luxembourg
Tel.: (352) 460 451

Trade and Company Register
rue du Palais de Justice
L- 2010 Luxembourg
Tel.: (352) 22 18 83

MUSEAL SA

Why didn't I pursue this dream earlier?

Pierre-Antoine Laurent, Managing Director

Who, in the mad rush for last-minute gifts on 24 December, has not wished for an object with a history that stands outside time and fashion?

In Luxembourg, it is now possible to avoid the tyranny of gadget purchasing thanks to Museal, an art gallery that opened for business on November 21, 1998, in the heart of the old city.

Museal offers reproductions of works of art from the world's major museums: the MOMA (New York's Museum of Modern Art), the Victoria and Albert Museum in London, the Vatican Museum, Bogota's Gold Museum, the Louvre, the Cluny Museum, etc. Sculptures, jewellery, old games, tableware, writing accoutrements and other objects are offered for retail sale at reasonable prices. A showroom has been set up to enable businesses and retailers to pool orders.

In addition, the gallery is the exclusive representative for one of the only remaining old-fashioned engravers, Benneton Graveur, the Paris house founded in 1880.

Museal's founder, Pierre-Antoine Laurent, began a second career after having been a highly successful head of purchasing and exports for several different companies.

'My professional work was rewarding, and I was what you might call a happy manager. But I've always had a passion for beauty and I decided to do something in life that would allow me to live in an artistic milieu at last. Why didn't I pursue this dream earlier?'

In 1998, Pierre-Antoine Laurent found the ideal spot for his gallery and established an SA in which he invested 1 million French francs.

'You have to obtain a statement certifying your ability to manage and exercise a technical artistic activity, which was no problem for me given my former duties. I actually think this is a good thing to demand,' he stresses. 'I obtained a business start-up grant from the Ministry of Small Businesses. In a word, I have no worries: my business plan is on target and my initial objectives have been surpassed. The potential for growth is enormous.'

This year, Pierre-Antoine Laurent has plans to offer luxury retailers (hair salons, jewellery stores, fashion outlets, cigar stores, etc) the opportunity to purchase a corner of 20 to 50 articles for less than 5,000 French francs.

'With this corner network, we're taking the museum to the street. From now on, people won't have to go inside the Louvre to offer a gift that has a history to it.'

Notes

11

Setting Up a Business in the Netherlands

Key statistics

Total surface area:	41,526 square kilometres
Population:	15.6 million
GDP growth:	3.7% (1998)
Per capita GDP:	21,559 euros (1998)
Public deficit/GDP ratio:	–0.9% (1998)
Public debt/GDP ratio:	67.7% (1998)
Inflation:	1.9% (1998)
Unemployment:	4% (1998)

Despite its small size, the Netherlands is a veritable economic giant that is very open to foreign investment. Part of the European heartland, the country boasts a high-quality infrastructure, a genuinely international outlook and reach, and a skilled, multilingual work force. The Netherlands is also a market of 15.6 million consumers with ample purchasing power.

Other major drawing cards include favourable tax treatment for multinationals, a dynamic banking sector, and flexible corporate and business legislation.

The Netherlands Foreign Investment Agency (NFIA) plays an active role in attracting foreign investors to the country, and has convinced scores of US and Japanese corporations to locate their European headquarters in the Netherlands.

Sectors that have been extensively promoted by public officials include the automotive, chemicals, biotechnology, electronics, information systems and technologies, and food products industries. The privatization of certain key sectors (energy and telecommunications, for example) has opened up new opportunities.

More than 6,500 foreign businesses have established a presence in the Netherlands. Amsterdam and Rotterdam receive the highest number of projects, but the other provinces also attract investors, especially in the south.

By country, the biggest investors in the Netherlands are the United States, Japan, the United Kingdom, Germany and France.

Recent investments worth noting include: Western Digital (US), Bristol Technology (US), Iomega (US), Tilloston Healthcare (US), Sony Music (Japan), and Europe Precision Molding (Japan), a Mitsubishi subsidiary that is building a factory to manufacture plastic packaging for compact discs.

Regulations governing foreign investment

Foreign direct investment is not generally subject to any prior government approval mechanism in the Netherlands. For statistical monitoring purposes only, transactions involving amounts in excess of 25,000 guilders must be reported to the balance of payments department of the Dutch Central Bank. Dividends, profits and proceeds from the liquidation of a business may be freely repatriated, provided that accredited intermediaries (banks, brokers, notaries, etc) effect the transfer.

Investment in certain sectors such as banking, insurance and telecommunications is subject to prior approval. In addition, the Environmental Management act requires that environmental-protection permits be obtained prior to opening factories, laboratories, garages, etc.

Principal legal forms

It is possible to conduct business in the Netherlands by establishing a representative office, a branch office or a subsidiary. Subsidiaries must adopt one of the country's existing legal forms.

Most foreign firms that set up operations in the Netherlands choose the closed limited (*Besloten Vennootschap* (BV)) form. Investors that plan to invite the public to subscribe to shares or bonds generally opt to form a corporation (*Naamloze Vennootschap* (NV)).

■ Closed limited company (BV – Besloten Vennootschap met beperkte aansprakelijkheid)

Requirements of a BV:

— minimum of two founding shareholders, individuals or corporate entities (one in the case of a single-owner BV);
— minimum capital of 40,000 guilders (€18,151.20), of which 20% must be subscribed and 25% paid in on incorporation, with a minimum of 40,000 guilders;
— strict formalities at the time of incorporation (notarized instrument).

Relatively flexible management:

— one or more managing directors appointed to a managing board; they may be but need not be shareholders;
— annual general meeting of shareholders;

— supervisory board mandatory for large BV;
— depending on the size of the BV, the presence of an independent auditor may be required;
— shareholders' liability limited to the capital invested.
— for tax and social security purposes, managing directors who hold an employment contract are considered employees, except for the majority shareholder-managing director.

▇ Corporation (NV – Naamloze Vennootschap)

Requirements of an NV:

— one shareholder is required;
— minimum authorized capital of 100,000 guilders (€45,378.23), of which 20% must be subscribed and 25% paid in on incorporation, with a minimum of 100,000 guilders;
— strict formalities at the time of incorporation (notarized instrument).

Relatively flexible management:

— one or more managing directors appointed to a managing board; they may be but need not be shareholders;
— annual general meeting of shareholders;
— supervisory board mandatory for large NV;
— depending on the size of the NV, the presence of an independent auditor may be required;
— shareholders' liability limited to the capital invested.
— for tax and social security purposes, managing directors who hold an employment contract are considered employees, except for the majority shareholder-managing director.

Note: Regardless of the legal form, companies that have more than 22.5 million guilders (€453,780.21) in capital, and a workforce that exceeds 100 or that have a works council (two of the three criteria) must have a supervisory board to oversee company management. Companies fulfilling these conditions must adopt a special form of organization called the *Structuurvennootschap* (SV).

Other legal forms

▇ General commercial partnership (VOF – Vennootschap Onder Firma)

Requirements of a VOF:

— minimum of two partners;
— partners' liability is joint and several and unlimited;
— for tax reasons, used by large corporations to form joint ventures;
— also used to form small family-owned businesses.

■ Limited commercial partnership (CV – Commanditaire Vennootschap)

Requirements of a CV:

There are two types of partners:

— active partners have unlimited liability;
— limited sleeping partners' liability is limited to the capital invested.

■ Partnership (Maatschap)

Requirements:

— does not enjoy corporate status;
— used by professionals in joint practice.

■ Co-operative corporation (Coöperatie)

This legal form is mainly used in the agricultural sector.

Administrative procedures

The following formalities must be accomplished to establish a BV or an NV.

■ Drafting the articles of incorporation and bylaws

They are included in the notarized incorporating instrument and must contain the following information: corporate name, business purpose, registered office, amount of capital and its division into shares, number and nominal value of shares, names and details of founding members.

◼ The no-objection statement

The incorporating instrument must be filed with the Ministry of Justice, which verifies that all statutory requirements have been met and delivers a no-objection statement within two to four months. In the interim, the founding members may begin doing business, provided that third parties are informed that the company is in formation (*In Oprichting*). Throughout this period, company managers are held personally liable for all corporate acts and obligations.

◼ Registering the company with the Trade Register (Handelsregister)

Company managers must file with the trade register of the local chamber of commerce in the region in which the statutory registered office is located.

◼ Paying the tax on registered capital

The 1 per cent tax on registered capital must be paid within one month of paying in of capital.

◼ Announcement

The secretary of the chamber of commerce ensures that the notice of incorporation is published in the official gazette (*Staatscourant*).

◼ Principal incorporation/organization costs

In addition to the aforementioned 1 per cent tax on registered capital, costs include official publication and notary fees and chamber of commerce registration fees. For a BV with capital of 40,000 guilders (€18,151.20), incorporation costs come to around 5,000 guilders (€2,268.90), including notary fees.

Legal expenses are negotiated between client and solicitor, and vary depending on the nature and complexity of services rendered.

Human resources/labour law

■ Employment contract

Permanent

A written contract signed between the employer and the employee, containing a required minimum of information on job requirements and working conditions.

Fixed-term

May be renewed three times.

Transforms into a permanent contract after the second renewal if the total duration of the two fixed-term contracts exceeds three years.

■ Length of the working week

Thirty-eight to 40 hours, depending on the terms of special regulations of nationwide collective bargaining agreements.

■ Overtime regulations

Restrictions on working time:

— 12 hours a day;
— 60 hours a week;
— 624 hours over 13 weeks.

Premium of 25 per cent over the regular hourly wage for the first two hours of overtime, 50 per cent thereafter, 75 per cent on Saturdays and 100 per cent on Sundays and holidays.

■ Annual vacation period

Four weeks a year.

In practice, trade unions have been able to negotiate one to two weeks' additional time off for many workers.

■ Paid leave and holidays

Nine days per year.

■ Wages

Statutory minimum wage and minimum annual vacation allowance of 8 per cent of gross annual minimum wage.

Wages and annual increases are often set in collective bargaining agreements in many sectors and for different personnel categories.

■ Social security

Sickness and maternity, work-related accidents and disability, old age, supplemental retirement, unemployment and family allowance benefits are provided.

■ Mandatory social security contributions

Employer contributions: 18 per cent of gross salary.

Employee contributions: 35 per cent of gross salary.

■ Employing foreigners

Nationals of the European Union do not need permits to work in the Netherlands, but they must obtain a residence permit. Employers of non-EU nationals must apply for a work permit with the Labour Office. The work permit is granted for a specific job and for a maximum of one year. It can be renewed. The residence permit is granted once the work permit has been obtained. It is very difficult for foreign unskilled workers from outside the European Union to obtain permission to work in the Netherlands.

Paying taxes

■ Tax on registered capital (Belasting van rechtsverkeer)

One per cent.

■ Corporation tax (Vennootschapsbelasting)

The corporate tax rate is 35 per cent, whether or not profits are distributed.

■ Personal taxes (Inkomstenbelasting)

The personal income tax is progressive, up to a maximum rate of 60 per cent.

■ Withholding at the source on wages (Loonbelasting)

Employers withhold personal income taxes at source, calculated on the basis of the wages paid to employees.

■ Value-added tax (BTW – Belasting Toegevoegde Waarde)

Depending on the nature of goods and services:

Reduced rate: 6%;
Standard rate: 17.5%.

■ Real estate taxes (Gemeentelijke belasting op onroerend goed)

Levied on buildings and land. The rate varies from one municipality to the next.

Note: To offset the high maximum tax rate on personal income, foreign managers posted in the Netherlands are generally granted a 35 per cent non-taxable allowance deduction for the first five years of residence, renewable once for another five years.

Investment incentives

A variety of incentives are available to promote business start-ups, expansion and hiring. Interested investors may contact the Netherlands Foreign Investment Agency (NFIA), a division of the Ministry of Economic Affairs located in The Hague, or regional government organizations.

■ Community grants

Three areas are currently eligible for assistance in the form of European structural funds: the North (Flevoland, Overijssel, Friesland, Groningen-Denthe), Limbourg and Zelande. The European Union has focused support on the North, the deserted Zelande area (which is mainly comprised of small islands that are covered by the sea), and the Limbourg border area.

■ Regional investment programmes (IPR)

Businesses that set up operations in economically fragile regions of the Netherlands (Groningue, Friesland, Limbourg, Drenthe, Flevoland and certain business parks on the outskirts of large cities) are eligible for assistance in the form of grants, low interest rate loans, equity interests, financial consulting services, etc.

Depending on the area and the nature of the project (business start-up, first five years of development, expansion of an existing firm), grants cover from 10 to 20 per cent of investment costs. If they exceed 5 million guilders (€2,268,901) 50 per cent of investment costs can be written off in the first year of operation.

Applications should be sent to the local regional development agency: *Northern Development Corp* (NOM) in the North, *Limbourg Investment and Development Corp* (LIOF) or the *Overijssel Development Corp* (OOM).

Projects that call for outlays in excess of 10 million guilders (€4,537,802.10) are submitted to the prior approval of the Ministry of Economic Affairs. For those that require more than 30 million guilders (€13,613,406), terms and conditions are negotiated with the Ministry.

■ Headquarters for large corporations

Groups that choose the Netherlands as their regional headquarters for the sole purpose of co-ordinating their business activities and make no profit may negotiate for favourable tax treatment with the Dutch tax authorities prior to setting up.

■ The greenfield investment ruling

Foreign investors considering establishing operations in the Netherlands can request an advance tax ruling determined on the basis of the information supplied. This ruling is considered binding on the tax authorities for a defined period (generally four years). In practice, although this ruling generally entails a reduction in taxable income, investors that seek it are more concerned with the tax security it offers than with the favourable treatment that may be granted.

Chief among these rulings is the so-called 'greenfield investment ruling', for which only foreign businesses investing in the Netherlands for the first time are eligible. If the investment creates jobs, tax authorities will define taxable income and grant a certain number of fiscal advantages pertaining to royalties, depreciation, VAT and customs and excise duties.

Dutch holding companies

The participation exemption from dividends and capital gains taxes

Requirements:
— The Dutch holding company is exempt from taxes on dividends received from subsidiaries and on capital gains on the sale of equity participations.
— Foreign investors can obtain an advance ruling to ensure that the tax authorities will grant this advantage.
— Legal form:
— BV or NV incorporated in the Netherlands.

Taxation:
— Initial capital tax of 1 per cent of the initial capital at the time of incorporation.

Advantages:
— Dividends received by the holding company are exempt from taxation, as are capital gains, provided that:
— the holding company has a capital stake of at least 5% in the subsidiary paying the dividends;

— shares are held without interruption starting from the opening of the fiscal year.

For equity interest in the profits of a foreign company, two additional conditions must be met:

— the foreign subsidiary must be subject to corporate income tax in the country in which it is established;

— the shares held in the foreign company must not be held in an investment portfolio.

In addition, the Dutch holding company must do business in the Netherlands or provide services that are essential to the group to which it belongs (corporate offices, tax or investment management, etc).

Drawback:

The Dutch holding company may not deduct from taxable income the costs related to its equity interests.

◼ Multinational financial services companies

In recent years, financial services subsidiaries of multinationals have been leaving the Netherlands to set up in countries that offer more attractive tax treatment such as Belgium and Ireland. In an attempt to reverse this trend, the Dutch government has adopted a tax system designed to attract the investment and financing arms of multinational groups.

Dutch subsidiaries that manage the financing and short-term investments of one or more multinational groups may set up tax-free contingency reserves of up to 80 per cent of the profits generated by such activities. The result is that the effective rate of corporate income taxation falls from 35 per cent to only 7 per cent.

To qualify, the following requirements must be met:

— the financing company must do all its business from the Netherlands;

— the beneficiaries of these financing transactions must be multinationals, ie they must have an operating presence in four countries (where they earn 5% of their revenues) or on two continents (where they earn 10% of their revenues);

— like their foreign-based counterparts, groups that are domiciled in the Netherlands may benefit from the financing activities of the companies, provided that the ratio of loans flowing into the Netherlands does not exceed 10%.

When a contingency for which the reserve has been set up occurs, that portion of the reserve corresponding to the loss must be allocated to cover it. In some cases, this sum may be tax exempt or may qualify for a 10 per cent tax reduction. In other cases, the portion of the reserve that has been used to cover the contingency is taxed at the standard 35 per cent rate.

Companies incorporated in the Netherlands that have an equity interest in a foreign subsidiary that exercises a financial activity are no longer exempted from paying taxes on dividends received from these subsidiaries or on capital gains if these financial subsidiaries are considered 'passive'. To be considered 'active', half of their revenues must be derived from group financing activities, their activities must be more than 20 per cent financed by lenders from outside the group and they must have their own directors, officers and personnel.

■ New technology grants

The Executive Agency of the Ministry of Economic Affairs (*SENTER*) is charged with providing information and grants and loans to companies operating in the new technology sector. Grants are offered for projects covering such fields as biotechnology and medicine, new materials and information technology and systems.

Grants fund up to 37.5 per cent of project costs, up to ceilings depending on the type of project. Eligible costs include feasibility studies, research and development, and the production of prototypes.

■ Environmental protection and renewable energy grants

There are a number of grant programmes that support environmental improvement projects. The Ministry of the Economic Affairs and the Ministry of Education have implemented a subsidy to promote 'green' research and development. Projects are selected through competitive bidding.

Grants are available to businesses with projects aimed at developing new technologies for reducing pollution. These types of grants are issued by NOVEM, an organization based in Utrecht.

■ Hiring and training subsidies

Companies that hire job seekers who have been unemployed for at least two years are entitled to:

— a four-year exemption from the employer's mandatory social security contribution;

— a training grant for each newly hired worker, ranging from 3,000 to 15,000 guilders (€1,361.34 to €6,806.70);

— a grant of from 7,500 to 15,000 guilders (€3,403.35 to €6,806.70) for every unemployed worker hired under an apprentice contract.

Employers are entitled to a grant of 800 guilders (€363.02) a quarter for every worker aged 23 or older hired at minimum wage. Companies that pay new staff a starting wage that is 115 per cent of the minimum wage qualify for tax and social security deductions.

A tax benefit is offered to companies that hire research and development personnel, in the form of a deduction from the monthly tax withheld at source on wages.

Each full-time job created in the province of Flevoland entitles the employer to a grant of 10,000 guilders (€4,537.80). In the city of Lelystad, a grant of 25,000 guilders (€11,344.50) per job created is awarded.

Education and training subsidies are available covering up to 50 per cent of training costs, including wages, if it is deemed that such training is required to maintain the worker's job. The Labour Office reviews applications.

Employers may deduct 20 per cent of training costs (or 40 per cent of the first 60,000 guilders (€27,226.81) if total annual expenditures do not exceed 250,000 guilders (€113,445.05)), and an additional 40 per cent for employees over the age of 40, up to a maximum total deduction of 5 million guilders (€2,268,901).

■ Export incentives

Exporting firms may apply for low-interest rate loans from the EFF (Export Financing Facility) to finance competitive bids on international projects.

Companies that do business with developing countries may apply to the ORET (*Ontwikkelings Relevanten Transport Actions*) for government-financed loans with interest rates of between 2.5 per cent and 3.5 per cent that cover up to 40 per cent of the investment.

Useful addresses in the Netherlands

Amsterdam Chamber of Commerce
De Ruyterkade 5
1013 AA Amsterdam
Tel.: (31 20) 523 66 00

Flevoland Chamber of Commerce
Business Link Flevoland
De Schans 19–09
8231 KA Lelystad-BP 123
8200 AC Lelystad
Tel.: (31 320) 28 62 86

The Hague Chamber of Commerce
Alexander Gogelweg 16
2517 JH The Hague
Tel.: (31 70) 379 57 95

Netherlands Foreign Investment Agency (NFIA)
Bezuidenhoutseweg 2
PO Box 20101
2500 EC, The Hague
Tel.: (31 70) 379 88 18

Dutch Central Bank
De Nederlandsche Bank NV
Westeinde 1
1000 AB Amsterdam
Tel.: (31 20) 524 91 11

Instituut voor het Midden-en Kleinbeddrijf
Planetenweg 115
Postbus 3140
KC HOODDORP
Tel.: (31 23) 568 18 00

Ministry of Finance
Ministerie van Financën
Korte Voorhout 7
Postbus 20201
2500 EE The Hague
Tel.: (31 70) 376 77 67

Ministry of Labour and Social Affairs
Ministerie van Sociale Zacken en Werkgelegenheid
Zeestraat, 73
Postbus 20801
2500 EV The Hague
Tel.: (31 70) 371 59 11

Netherlands Industrial Property Office
PO Box 5820
2280 HV
Rijswijh
Tel.: (31 70) 398 66 55

SENTER
Unit S&O
Postbox 30732
2500 GS, The Hague
Tel.: (31 70) 361 03 10

Network of Dutch Innovation Centres
Innovatie Centra Netwerk Nederland
Kongracht 61–62
Postbus 20104
2500 EC The Hague
Tel.: (31 70) 356 76 76

Décathlon Nederland

Finding available land for our 'Parc de la Forme' concept is a real challenge. . .

Philippe Durand, Managing Director

After making its mark in the recreation market in France, Décathlon is determined to win over the Dutch. It plans to open some 20 outlets in the coming year. Décathlon, which leads the French sports apparel market, entrusted this greenfield project to 40-year-old Philippe Durand. A fitting challenge for this all-round sports enthusiast whose favourite pastimes are sailing and skiing. Despite his sporting nature, Philippe managed to hit the books as well, earning advanced degrees in sociology and statistical demographics before starting out as department supervisor at one of the Décathlon outlets in Toulon.

'Then I was appointed Store Manager in Pau, and after that Southwest Regional Manager. But from the outset, I expressed a desire to expatriate,' he says. 'I realized right away that I would feel more disoriented here than I would have if I had been expatriated to a southern European country like Spain. I started taking Dutch lessons, which was absolutely essential, and I started scouting around for a suitable location. The Dutch way of life is very different from the French. People stop working at 5 o'clock in the evening, and they spend a lot of their after-hours time on leisure activities, especially sports.'

From his office in Rotterdam, Philippe Durand can capitalize on the experience of his counterparts who have launched, respectively, three outlets in Germany, 20 in Spain, eight in Italy, three in Belgium and most recently in the UK. But every country has its own culture, and there is no one model that can be extrapolated throughout Europe.

With a total of 220 retail outlets, Décathlon posts annual sales of 12 billion French francs, of which only 10 per cent are outside France. After having staked out the French market, Décathlon is determined to step up its international expansion – in terms of both production and sales. While 65 per cent of its articles are produced in Europe, it also has units in the United States, Argentina, Brazil and Asia. And business is good. The group has become the master of the art of manufacturing bicycles, hiking boots and backpacks under its own brand name.

'When I got here, I contacted the Netherlands Foreign Investment Agency (NFIA) and began working with a private consultant who knew municipal decision-makers, circuits and opportunities. In addition to the retail outlets, I also have to set up the Parc de la Forme, a sort of Décathlonland for people who want to buy sports gear but also try it out and – why not – hook up with golf, basketball or hockey partners.'

'Finding available land for this concept is a real challenge. Outlying retail outlets are virtually non-existent in this small, relatively densely populated country with 15 million inhabitants. Plus, you're not encouraged to use your car to go shopping, due to overcrowding on the motorways. IKEA encountered this problem before we did, but managed to set up eight outlets in 20 years. Décathlon's idea is to establish outlets around Amsterdam, Eindhoven and Rotterdam. The first site is scheduled to open in Amsterdam in the spring of 2000. Half of the store's 100 or so employees will be women, who will certainly appreciate the part-time formulae that are widely practised here.'

There is no doubt that we'll soon be seeing Dutch citizens on Décathlon bicycles. After just a few spins, the bike market will be won over.

Notes

12

Setting Up a Business in Portugal

Key statistics

Total surface area:	91,905 square kilometres
Population:	9.9 million
GDP growth:	4% (1998)
Per capita GDP:	9,441 euros (1998)
Public deficit/GDP ratio:	−2.3% (1998)
Public debt/GDP ratio:	57.8% (1998)
Inflation:	2.8% (1998)
Unemployment:	4.9% (1998)

Portugal has attracted a number of foreign investors since it joined the European Union. The liberalization of several sectors of the economy, low-priced labour, economic ties with Africa and South America, and Expo '98 have all played a key role in this investment boom.

Today's high-growth sectors include telecommunications, information systems and technology and the services industry (banking and insurance). Since legislation easing regulations governing the opening of retail shopping complexes was passed in 1997, they have started to flourish.

Portuguese businesses are actively seeking out partners that can provide them with new technologies, particularly in the civil building trade and in industrial manufacturing.

The primary aim of these partnerships is to develop joint ventures poised to attack emerging markets in Brazil, Angola, Mozambique, Guinea and Cape Verde.

The most spectacular investment has to be that of Ford and Volkswagen in a production unit near Lisbon, which accounts for 3 per cent of the country's total output.

More than 66 per cent of total investments are European, in particular from the United Kingdom, Spain, Germany and France. The greater Lisbon area attracts 70 per cent of all establishments, while the north attracts 12 per cent and the centre of the country 10 per cent.

British Petroleum, Siemens (Germany), Pioneer Electronics (Japan), Chrysler, Texas Instruments (US), Lear (US), Ford (US), Samsung (Korea) and Normetro (a joint venture between the German Daimler Benz and the Swedish Asea Brown Boveri) have all invested in Portugal.

Regulations governing foreign investment

Foreign direct investment is not restricted. For statistical monitoring purposes, such investments must be registered within 30 days, subject to fines for failure to comply with:

— the ICEP (Portuguese Trade, Tourism and Investment Institute); or
— the regional planning and finance secretariat (for Madeira and the Azores).

Investments that are subject to the prior approval of the ICEP include those considered to pose a threat to public safety or security as well as in the defence sector.

The government may sign investment contracts when projects are considered to be of public interest, or if they are deemed to have an impact on the Portuguese economy or contribute to the development of disadvantaged regions.

Principal legal forms

It is possible to do business in Portugal by establishing a representative office, a branch office or a subsidiary. Subsidiaries must adopt one of the country's existing legal forms.

The limited-liability company, the legal form most widely used by investors in Portugal, is particularly adapted to small and medium-sized undertakings, while large concerns usually opt to form a corporation.

■ Limited-liability company (Lda – *Sociedade por quotas de responsabilidade limitada*)

Requirements of an Lda:

— minimum of two founding shareholders (sole proprietorship is permitted);
— minimum capital of €5000, fully subscribed and 50% paid in at the time of incorporation;
— strict formalities at the time of incorporation (notarized instrument).

Flexible management:

— minimum of one manager, need not be a shareholder but must be a resident of Portugal;

— supervisory board required in certain cases;
— annual general meeting;
— presence of a statutory auditor (*revisor oficial de contas*) is mandatory when certain thresholds are reached;
— shareholders' liability is limited to the capital invested.

■ Corporation (SA – *Sociedade anonima de responsabilidade limitada*)

Requirements of an SA:

— minimum of five shareholders, no nationality or residence requirements;
— minimum share capital of €50,000, fully subscribed and 30% paid in at the time of incorporation;
— strict formalities at the time of incorporation (notarized instrument).

Management:

— companies with share capital of less than €200,000:
— one or more managing directors and a statutory auditor (*revisor oficial de contas*);
— companies with share capital of more than €200,000:
— either a board of directors (*conselho de administraçao*) with at least three members who must be individuals;
— or an executive board (*direççao*) with three to five members (must be natural persons);
— plus a supervisory board (*conselho geral*) composed of 3 to 15 shareholders (who must be natural persons) and a statutory auditor;
— shareholders' liability limited to capital invested.

Other legal forms

■ General commercial partnership (*Sociedade em nome colectivo*)

Requirements:

— minimum of two partners;
— partners' liability is joint and several and unlimited.
— consent of all partners required for the transfer of shares.

■ Limited commercial partnership (*Sociedade em comandita simple*)

Requirements:

— Two types of partners:
— active partners have unlimited liability;
— limited sleeping partners' liability is limited to the capital invested.

Administrative procedures

The following formalities must be accomplished to establish a company.

■ Corporate name

Prior approval of the *Registo Nacional de Pessoas Colectivas* (RNPC) is required for the use of the corporate name.

■ Drawing up the articles of incorporation

The articles of incorporation and bylaws must be drawn up by a notary public and executed in his presence by the founding members. They must include the following information: legal form, corporate name, business purpose, registered office, start-up date, number of founding members, share capital and its division into shares.

■ Registering the company with the Trade Register

Within 90 days of drawing up the articles of incorporation and bylaws, the founders must register with the Trade Register (*Conservatoria do registo comercial*) of the region in which the statutory registered office is located. The company comes into existence when the articles of incorporation and bylaws are signed, but does not acquire a corporate personality until it is registered.

■ Publication

The articles of incorporation and bylaws are published in both a legal bulletin and the official gazette (*Diàrio da Republica*). They are then filed with the Trade Register. The National Register of Juridical Persons (CNPM) delivers the company's permanent identification card.

Note: Business Formalities Centres were set up in 1997 to enable investors to accomplish all required start-up procedures in one place.

■ Principal organization/incorporation costs

To establish a *Sociedade Anonima* with share capital of €50,000, incorporation costs (including the notarized instrument) come to around 350,000 escudos (€1,745.79). Additional legal fees of 300,000 to 500,000 escudos (€1,496.39 to €2,493.99) may be incurred. They are negotiated between client and solicitor, and vary depending on the nature and complexity of services rendered.

Human resources/labour law

■ Employment contract

Permanent

A written contract between the employer and the employee, containing a required minimum of information on job requirements and working conditions.

Fixed-term

Minimum term of six months, maximum term of three years. May be renewed twice.

■ Length of the working week

Legally set at 40 hours.

Most collective bargaining agreements set the working week at between 35 and 40 hours.

■ Overtime regulations

Restrictions on overtime:

— 2 hours a day;
— 200 hours a year.

Premium of 50 per cent over the regular hourly wage for the first hour of overtime, 75 per cent thereafter, and 100 per cent on obligatory weekly rest days and on legal holidays.

■ Annual vacation period

Thirty days a year.

■ Paid leave and public holidays

Thirteen days a year.

■ Wages

Statutory minimum wage.

Wages are often set in collective bargaining agreements in many sectors. They are generally paid in 14 instalments over the year.

■ Social security

Sickness and maternity, disability, old age, unemployment and family allowance benefits are provided. Since work-related accidents are not covered by Social Security, employers are required to take out a policy with a private insurer.

■ Mandatory social security contributions

Employer contribution: around 24.5 per cent of gross salary.

Employee contribution: around 11 per cent of gross salary.

■ Employing foreigners

All foreigners who reside in Portugal must obtain a residence permit, valid for one year and renewable thereafter for one-year periods. Non-EU nationals must, in addition, apply for a work permit from the Ministry of Employment and Social Security.

Companies may only hire non-EU nationals if the investment project is a family concern whose total workforce is no more than five. In other cases, Portuguese firms may hire non-EU nationals if at least 90 per cent of the company's workforce is comprised of Portuguese or EU citizens. Exceptions are granted in the public interest or if there is a lack of relevant specialists.

Employment contracts with foreign workers must be registered with the Ministry of Employment, and must contain the following information: the contractual obligations of the employer and the employee, the starting date and term of the contract, professional qualifications, job title, salary and method of payment.

Paying taxes

■ Corporate income tax (IRC – *Imposto sobre o rendimento das pessoas colectivas*)

— Corporate tax rate of 34 per cent + variable municipal tax (*Derrama*) of 0 per cent to 10 per cent.
— A reduced rate of 20 per cent applies to companies whose principal activity is not commercial, industrial or farm-related.
— A reduced rate of 27.5 per cent applies to real estate investment companies.
— Branch offices: 25 per cent + variable municipal tax of 27.5 per cent maximum.

■ Personal taxes (IRS – *Imposto sobre o rendimento das pessoas singulares*)

Progressive tax rate of 15 per cent to 40 per cent (four brackets).

■ Value-added tax (IVA – *Imposto sobre o valor acrescentado*)

Depending on the nature of the goods and services, the applicable rates are as follows:

— Zero rate;
— Reduced rate (food staples): 5%, 12%;
— Standard rate: 17%.

In Madeira and the Azores, the applicable rates are 4 per cent, 8 per cent and 13 per cent, respectively.

■ Municipal contribution (*Contribuiçào autàrquica*)

Assessed on the value of real estate assets:

— 0.8% to 1% on urban real estate assets;
— 0.7% to 1.3% on rural real estate assets.

■ Real estate taxes (*Contribuiçào predial*)

— Rural property: 14% on average;
— Urban property: 18% on average.

Investment incentives

■ Financial incentives

Given that its per capita GDP is 75 per cent below the European Union average, Portugal is a major beneficiary of European structural funds. The backbone of the Portuguese incentive system is European level funds such as the European Social Fund (ESF), the European Regional Development Fund (ERDF), the European Agricultural Guarantee Fund (EAGGF) and the Cohesion Fund.

Portugal also offers a wide array of financial advantages designed to step up the modernization of various economic sectors (manufacturing, tourism, agriculture, etc) and promote development in disadvantaged areas of the country. The Portuguese Trade, Tourism and Investment Institute (ICEP) has been set up to orient, advise and inform foreign investors on opportunities in Portugal.

■ For small and medium-sized firms, the IAPMEI

The Small and Medium-sized Enterprises and Investment Institute (IAPMEI) manages the PEDIP II package. In addition, it offers small and medium-sized firms:

— technical information and training;
— inter-business co-operation and alignment opportunities;

— support for new businesses;
— financial assistance to support the development of SMEs;
— foreign assignments.

Above all, the IAPMEI reviews applications for grants, especially in the manufacturing sector.

Helping SMEs

SAJE (Incentive programme for young entrepreneurs) finances investments made by companies run by young entrepreneurs aged 18 to 35, with emphasis on the following sectors: manufacturing and retail, tourism, culture, handicrafts and the environment. Grants are available covering up to 75 per cent of approved investment costs.

RIME (Incentive programme for micro-businesses) promotes the establishment and upgrading of micro-businesses (those employing fewer than 10 people) and small firms (with a workforce of 10 to 40) by subsidizing financing needs and job creation.

PROCOM aims to encourage innovation, inter-industry co-operation and retail development. It offers aid in the form of grants, interest rate subsidies and attractive leasing arrangements for some types of equipment rentals.

■ Industrial incentives

On the strength of PEDIP I, the first strategic programme aimed at revitalizing and modernizing Portuguese industry, a more diversified and sophisticated successor programme has been launched. PEDIP II includes five distinct incentive areas:

— SINDEPEDIP offers direct support to industrial firms that wish to modernize, develop, and implement environmental improvement measures and seeks to attract foreign investors through its Strategic Projects under a Contractual Regime measure.
— SINFRAPEDIP offers support to enterprises that introduce new technologies.
— SINFEPEDIP promotes increased reliance on financial engineering techniques in industry (venture capital, mergers and acquisitions and investment funds).
— SINAIPEDIP fosters industry associations.
— SINETPEDIP supports technical schools and institutes.

PEDIP II is not only interested in investment projects, but also in the companies that devise them.

The Portuguese firm or the joint venture set up with a foreign company must demonstrate the feasibility of the project to the IAPMEI, which can lend assistance in the early phases of the project by providing grants that cover feasibility studies. The standard application form is in Portuguese, and candidates should expect a two-month wait.

Industrial investments are eligible for interest-free loans of up to 500 million escudos (€2,493,989.49) per company, for a two- to seven-year term. Zero-interest loans in connection with investment projects whose cost exceeds 2.5 billion escudos (12,469,947.43 euros) are negotiated on a case-by-case basis. For non-industrial investments, financial aid is available covering up to 65 per cent of the cost. Grants for employee training costs, evaluated separately, cover up to 90 per cent of direct expenditures and 50 per cent of the cost of training materials.

■ Promoting tourism

The Portuguese government is particularly interested in developing the tourist industry.

SIFIT III, the financial incentive programme for tourism investments, offers funding that covers from 15 to 50 per cent of total outlays for tourism projects, particularly in disadvantaged regions.

The programme targets investments in hotel complexes and upscale recreational facilities.

Priority is also accorded to 'green' or environmentally friendly projects.

To be eligible for funding, a minimum investment of 100 million escudos (€498,797.90) is required. The maximum cash grant available is 250 million escudos (€1,246,994.74), rising to 500 million escudos (€249,989.49) in special cases (such as projects to build marinas).

Most of these grants must be repaid over 10 years, with a three-year grace period.

Smaller tourism investments requiring outlays between 20 and 100 million escudos (€99,759.58 and €498,797.90) may be eligible for SIR (regional incentive programme) funding. The Tourism Fund issues recommendations on projects and grants subsidies.

Textile incentives

The RETEX programme is designed to encourage improvements in the productivity, marketing and management of textile firms.

Only certain regions are eligible for financial aid, which is provided in the form of grants, venture capital and interest-rate subsidies.

■ Agriculture and fishing incentives

IFADAP (Financial Institute for the Development of Agriculture and Fishing) offers financial aid under the agriculture-specific PEDAP programme.

Grants are aimed at promoting investments made to improve productivity and investments made to improve the processing and marketing of agricultural and fishing products.

The PROPESCA programme supports efforts to improve the marketing and packaging of agricultural and seafood products through grants and interest-rate subsidies that can cover from 60 to 100 per cent of the investment.

■ Job creation and professional training

IEFP, the Institute for Employment and Professional Training, finances programmes aimed at promoting the professional integration of young people and the unemployed.

Financial aid is also granted for vocational training aimed at helping manual workers adjust to technological change and reducing regional inequalities in the job market.

■ Regional incentives

SIR, the regional incentive system, focuses aid on less developed regions in the aim of diversifying production and creating jobs. The system covers most of the non-coastal regions of the country, Alentejo and a portion of the Algarve. SIR awards cash investment grants of up to 50 million escudos (€249,398.94).

For more costly investment programmes, SIR provides grant and loan subsidy packages. Cash grants cover from 30 to 50 per cent of total investment outlays, while loans for up to 60 per cent of the investment are repayable in three to six years with a one- to three-year grace period.

In addition, subsidies are offered to cover feasibility studies, with the amount determined on the basis of the region and the quality of the proposal.

Requests for information may be obtained from the General Office of Regional Investment or the IAPMEI.

■ Tax incentives

Investors with innovative projects, or projects that contribute to modernizing the Portuguese economy, can negotiate directly with the Portuguese government for special tax and real estate advantages when their investment requires an outlay of 5 billion escudos (€24,939,894.85) or more.

Tax credits for investment

From 31 December, 2010, investments in production facilities that require an outlay of 1 billion escudos or more €4,987,979) may qualify for tax incentives provided that they are deemed to: be in the national economic interest; reduce regional inequalities; create jobs; contribute to technological and scientific innovation. After concluding a contract with the government, investors are entitled to a corporate income tax credit (IRC) and to a reduction in local tax (Sisa) and the stamp tax.

Tax breaks for micro-businesses and SMEs

To strengthen the cash flow of small and medium-sized firms and stimulate productive investment, some businesses are eligible for a deduction in taxable income of up to 30 per cent of an amount equal to 10 per cent of the additional investment compared to the prior year made in 1998, 1999 and 2000. In addition, registration and notary fees in connection with capital increases effected between 1 January 1998 and 31 December 2000 are waived.

Micro-businesses and small firms are eligible for employment subsidies, a 20 per cent reduction in the corporate income tax for the years 1999 to 2001 (a 15 per cent reduction for those operating in certain regions of Portugal), exemption from the SISA (tax on the transfer of property rights for consideration) on business premises and the first residence purchased by entrepreneurs under the age of 35.

Free zones

Tax incentives are offered to businesses that establish operations in Madeira and the Azores. In Madeira, foreign investment projects are reviewed by the regional authorities, in particular the Madeira Development Society (SDM), which won the right to develop and manage the free area until 2017.

Eligible projects include the following sectors: manufacturing, financial services, international services and navigation under the Portuguese flag.

The Offshore Centre allows banks, financial institutions, investment funds and insurance companies to effect routine financial transactions as well as mutual fund management, bond issues, insurance and financial leasing. Other offshore services include dealing, consulting, invoicing and the management of industrial property rights.

The following tax advantages may be granted:

— exemption from the transfer tax due on the acquisition of real estate for use in the business;
— exemption from the corporation tax (IRC) until 31 December 2011;
— exemption from withholding at source on dividends, interest and royalties;
— exemption from taxes due on capital gains realized on the sale of long-term assets;
— exemption from the capital tax due at the time of incorporation and levied on subsequent capital increases;
— exemption from local taxes;
— exemption from the stamp tax.

Useful addresses in Portugal

Commercial Register
Registo do Comercio
rua Nova do Almada, 35
1200 Lisbon
Tel.: (351 1) 1 36 15 56

Foreign Office
Servico de Estrangeros
avenida A Augusto de Aguiar 20-R/C
1000 Lisbon
Tel.: (351 1) 314 31 12

GACE (a unit of the IAPMEI that provides assistance in establishing new businesses)
rua Rodrigo da Fonseca, 73
1297 Lisbon
Tel.: (351 1) 386 43 33

General Department of Regional Investment
Direccao-Geral do Desenvolvimento
avenida D Carlos I, 126–70
1200 Lisbon
Tel.: (351 1) 396 81 69

Institute for Employment and Professional Training (IEFP)
Instituto de Emprego e Formacao Profissional
rua das Picoas, 14
1050 Lisbon
Tel.: (351 1) 356 38 01

Madeira Development Society (SDM)
Sociedade de Desenvolvimento da Madeira
rua Imperatriz Dona Amelia
PO Box 4164 Madeira
Tel.: (351 1) 91 25 466

Ministry of Employment and Social Security
Ministerio Emprego e da Segurança Social
rua Rodrigo da Fonseca, 55
1200 Lisbon
Tel.: (351 1) 352 50 21

Ministry of Finance
Ministerio da Finanças
avenida Infante D. Henrique, 1B
1100 Lisbon
Tel.: (351 1) 886 91 46

National Tourism Fund
(Fundo de Turismo)
avenida Antonio Augusto de Aguiar, 122–11
1050 Lisbon
Tel.: (351 1) 352 62 34

Official Gazette
Diaro da Republica
rua D Francisco Manuel de Melo, 5
1000 Lisbon
Tel.: (351 1) 69 34 14

PEDIP
rua Rodrigues de Sampaio, 13
1100 Lisbon
Tel.: (351 1) 315 55 48

Porto Industrial Association
avenida da Boavista 2761
4100 Porto
Tel.: (351) 2 617 68 40

Portuguese Chamber of Commerce and Industry
rua das Portas de Santos Antao, 89
1134 Lisbon
Tel.: (351 1) 32 71 79

Portuguese Industry Confederation
Confederaçao da Industria Portuguesa
avenida 5 de Outubro
1000 Lisbon
Tel.: (351 1) 54 74 54

Portuguese Trade, Tourism and Investment Institute (ICEP)
avenida 5 de Outubro 101–03
1000 Lisbon
Tel.: (351 1) 793 01 03

RNPC
Registo Nacional de Pessoas Colectivas
Praça Silvestre Pinheiro Ferreira, 1 C
1500 Lisbon
Tel: (351 1) 774 12 75

Small and Medium-sized Enterprises and Investment Institute
Instituto de Apoio as Pequenas e Medias Empresas e Investimento (IAPMEI)
rua Rodrigo de Fonseca, 73
1297 Lisbon
Tel.: (351 1) 386 43 33

Bazin Portugal

Real estate investments offer a better return in Portugal than in France at the moment, particularly due to more advantageous tax treatment.

Eric de Chabot-Tramecourt, Managing Director of Bazin Portugal.

'Ever since I finished school, I'd always wanted to set up my own business,' says Eric de Chabot-Tramecourt, who now runs Bazin Portugal, a company specialized in commercial real estate management (office space and industrial plants). That said, a career abroad needs to be carefully thought out, and this 37-year-old businessman already had ample experience of both Portugal and property appraisal and management.

With degrees from both the Ecole Supérieure de Commerce de Nantes and Ohio State University, Eric and an agricultural engineer friend set up Secoia Lda to manage 5,000 hectares of land and forest in southern Portugal. Their timing could not have been better: Portugal joined the European Community three months later and foreign investors were on the prowl for opportunities. Secoia began building up business in both real estate transactions and the import/export of food products.

'I actually met Patrice and Benoît Bazin when I played the role of interpreter during negotiations. They're the current executive directors of the Bazin Group, whose roots go back to 1770. They asked me if I was interested in setting up a subsidiary in Lisbon and that's how, in 1994, we started Bazin Portugal as an Lda – the Portuguese equivalent of a private limited company.

'To get the ball rolling, I started marketing and was able to convince real estate developers to let us handle their new buildings. We currently manage 100,000 square metres of office space in the greater Lisbon area. Overall, we manage 15 sites – 2,000 lots for 175 co-owners. Our clients are private investors, both retail and corporate, and institutional investors such as the Portuguese Caisse Générale des Dépôts, the pension fund of the Bank of Portugal, the real estate fund of the BPI, etc.

'Real estate investments offer a better return in Portugal than in France at the moment, particularly due to more advantageous tax treatment. With the arrival of the Euro Area, of which Portugal is an early member, it is likely that demand on the part of investors will grow. The early indicators are already visible.

'We also manage an industrial automotive zone called Autoeuropa, where Ford and Volkswagen are building the Galaxy and the Sharan, and where auto parts makers such as Sommer Allibert, Bentler, Vanpro, PPG, Tenneco and others are present.

'Bazin Portugal earns 85 per cent of its revenues from the management of building resources and public spaces (walls, lifts, air conditioning, smoke detectors, security, etc). When investors, whether foreign or not, rent out their real estate holdings, Bazin Portugal also takes care of the leases that they have contracted as part of leasehold management mandates.

'In addition, real estate appraisers are also involved in design studies, which often lead to new deals. We conducted a design study in November 1995 on security and condominium fees for a 45-hectare residential project to build 92 luxury villas at Estoril with sports facilities (swimming pool and tennis courts) and a clubhouse. The developer has just informed us that we've been selected to 'manage the property', explains Eric de Chabot-Tramecourt. This is really good news, which only confirms the importance of constant prospects and maintaining contacts over time.

'I often use a scooter to get around to avoid traffic jams in Lisbon. Life in Portugal has its positive aspects. Almost every weekend, I take my wife and five children to Caparica Beach, where there are lots of other families. Have you ever been there?'

Notes

13

Setting Up a Business in Spain

Bay of Biscay

La Coruna
Lugo
Oviedo
Santander
San Sebastian
FRANCE
Bilbao
Vizcaya
Guipuzcoa
Alava
Vitoria
Pamplona
Navarra
Pontevedra
Leon
Logrono
Orense
Palencia
Burgos
Huesca
Gerona
Zamora
Valladolid
Soria
Saragossa
Lleida
Barcelona
Tarragona
PORTUGAL
Salamanca
Segovia
Avila
Guadalajara
Madrid ✪
Teruel
Castellon
Balearic
Sea
Minorca
Cuenca
Castellon
de la Plana
Palma
Toledo
Caceres
Valencia
Balearic
Islands
Majorca
Ibiza
Badajoz
Ciudad Real
Albacete
Formentera
Alicante
Mediterranean Sea
Cordoba
Murcia
Huelva
Jaen
Sevilla
Gulf of Cadiz
Granada
Almeria
Malaga
Cadiz
Strait of Gibraltar
Ceuta (Spain)

Key statistics

Total surface area:	504,750 square kilometres
Population:	39.3 million
GDP growth:	3.8% (1998)
Per capita GDP:	€12,611 (1998)
Public deficit/GDP ratio:	−1.8% (1998)
Public debt/GDP ratio:	65.6% (1998)
Inflation:	2% (1998)
Unemployment:	18.8% (1998)

Spain's entry into the European Community in 1986 led to significant growth in foreign investment inflow. Throughout the 1980s, the Spanish economy experienced a boom period that brought gains in productivity and innovation.

Spain is one of the European Union's most decentralized nations. It has a federal government and 17 autonomous regional governments, each with its own parliament.

Madrid and Catalonia are generally the primary targets of investment inflows, which grew sharply in Andalucia, Navarre and the Basque region in 1997. Investment in manufacturing (automotive, chemicals and agri-business) accounts for 46 per cent of all inflows, while the financial sector accounts for only 8 per cent of the total.

Foreign investment in Spain is being stimulated by the privatization programme (in telecommunications, energy and transportation), the outlook for sustained economic growth and the country's membership in the European economic and monetary union.

Unemployment, however, remains the highest in the European Union.

The United States is Spain's biggest foreign investor in terms of volume (in excess of €3,048,980,344.75). The principal European investors are the Netherlands, Germany, France, the United Kingdom and Italy.

Recent foreign investment in Spain includes Ford (US), which invested €259,163,329.30 in its plant in Valencia to manufacture the latest version of its Escort model; General Electric (US); Lucent Technologies (US); Continente (Promodes, France), which acquired the Simago supermarket chain for €121,959,213.79; PSA and Renault (France), to produce the Xsara and the new Clio respectively; Pernod Ricard (France), which acquired Larios, the country's top gin distillery for €213,428,624.13; Danone (France), which is building a new plant in Valencia; Deutsche Bank, which injected €60,979,606.89 into its subsidiary; Volkswagen

(Germany), which invested 182,938,820.68 euros to launch the new Polo; and the BYSE Group (Bosch-Siemens, Germany), which invested 91,469,410.34 euros in its Saragossa plant to produce a new washing machine model.

Regulations governing foreign investment

Foreign direct investment is not subject to restriction, provided that relevant information is subsequently furnished for statistical monitoring purposes. Certain business activities, such as those that fall under the realm of national defense, require prior authorization. Investments in areas such as telecommunications, television and radio broadcasting, gambling, and the manufacture of arms and explosives are subject to special regulations.

The following types of investment are subject to disclosure requirements:

— all foreign equity investments in Spanish businesses;
— the establishment of a branch office and amount invested;
— real estate transactions;
— the establishment of, or investment in, a foundation, an inter-company partnership, a partnership or a joint venture if the amount invested exceeds 500,000 pesetas (€3,005,060.52);
— investments in investment trusts and bond subscriptions.

The following types of investment are subject to prior disclosure in addition to that for statistical monitoring purposes:

— investment in tax havens that bring the foreign stake in the Spanish company to more than 50 per cent;
— real estate transactions;
— the establishment of, or equity investment in, a foundation, an inter-company partnership, a partnership or a joint venture.

Principal legal forms

It is possible to conduct business in Spain by establishing a representative office, a branch office or a subsidiary. Subsidiaries must adopt one of the country's existing legal forms.

Corporate law has been reformed twice in recent years, in 1989 (the SA) and in 1995 (the SRL). Prior to the 1989 reform, many businesses opted for the highly flexible SA form. But the SRL form now increasingly used is particularly well suited to the establishment of small and medium-sized undertakings. Today, more than half of all Spanish firms are limited-liability companies.

■ Limited-liability company (SRL – Sociedad de Responsabilidad Limitada)

Requirements of an SRL:

— minimum of two founding shareholders (one if the company is a sole proprietorship);
— minimum share capital of 500,000 pesetas (€3,005.06), fully subscribed and paid in at the time of incorporation;
— relatively strict formalities at the time of incorporation (notarized instrument).

Flexible management:

— at least one director, who may but need not be a shareholder, or a board of directors with at least three members;
— annual general meeting of the shareholders;
— presence of an independent auditor mandatory, except for small firms;
— shareholders' liability is limited to the capital invested;
— for tax and social security purposes, directors who also exercise technical duties within the company are considered employees.

■ Corporation (SA – Sociedad Anonima)

Requirements of an SA:

— minimum of three founding shareholders (one if the company is a sole proprietorship, in two shareholders);
— minimum share capital of 10 million pesetas (60,101.21 euros), fully subscribed and at least 25% paid in at the time of incorporation;
— relatively strict formalities at the time of incorporation (notarized instrument).

Relatively flexible management:

— one or more directors, board of directors if there are more than three directors, with joint authorities, who may be but need not be shareholders;

— annual general meeting of shareholders;
— presence of an independent auditor mandatory, except for small firms;
— shareholders' liability is limited to the capital invested;
— for tax and social security purposes, directors who also exercise technical duties within the company are considered employees.

Note: In Spanish, the term *administrador* is used to designate both directors of SAs and managers of SRLs, while the term *gérante* describes managers working for the company.

Other legal forms

■ General commercial partnership (Sociedad regular colectiva)

Requirements:

— minimum of two partners;
— partners' liability is joint and several and unlimited with respect to third parties;
— incorporating instrument executed in the presence of a notary and registration with the commercial register.

■ Limited partnership (Sociedad comanditaria)

Requirements:

— active partners have unlimited liability;
— limited sleeping partners' liability is limited to the capital invested. They do not play a management role.

Administrative procedures

The following procedures must be followed to establish a business in Spain.

■ Patent search and certification

A patent search on the corporate name must be undertaken with the Central Commercial Register (*Registro Mercantil Central*).

Certification is valid for two months from the filing date, and must be submitted to the notary when the articles of incorporation and bylaws are signed.

Depositing the share capital

The share capital is deposited with a bank or savings and loan association.

Drafting the articles of incorporation and bylaws

They are drawn up by a notary public and must contain the following information: corporate name and legal form, business purpose, registered office, life of the corporation, start-up date, number of founders and their nationality and place of residence, amount of capital, capital contributions, corporate governance (make-up, duties and powers of managing bodies), rules for calling meetings. These instruments are executed by the founders in the presence of a notary.

Registering the company with the Commercial Register

Registration is carried out by the Commercial Register in the region of the company's tax residence, and confers corporate status on the company.

Tax declaration

The business must apply for a tax identification number (*declaracion censal*) from the tax centre with which the company files returns.

Paying the tax on registered capital

The tax on registered capital must be paid within 30 days following the execution of the articles of incorporation and bylaws.

■ Publication

The commercial register handles publication in the *Boletin Oficial del Registro Mercantil*.

Completing these administrative formalities takes from three weeks to a month.

Note: if the company is a sole proprietorship, then certain requirements must be met, otherwise the sole shareholder will be held liable with respect to the third parties.

■ Principal organization/incorporation costs

For an SA with initial capital of 10 million pesetas (€60,101.21), the main incorporation costs are as follows:

— registration with the Registro Mercantil: around 80,000 pesetas (€480.80);
— tax on registered capital of 1%;
— notary fees of approximately 0.2% of capital.

Legal expense fees may be added to these amounts, generally around 200,000 to 350,000 pesetas (€1,202.02 to €2,103.54), depending on the nature and complexity of services rendered and which are negotiated between client and solicitor.

Human resources/labour law

■ Employment contract

Permanent

A written contract signed between the employer and the employee, containing a required minimum of information on job requirements and working conditions.

Fixed-term

May be concluded for a period of six months as provided by law.

■ Length of the working week

Legal maximum of 40 hours.

In certain industry-wide collective bargaining agreements, the working week is set at 37 or 38 hours.

■ Overtime regulations

Eighty hours per annum maximum.

■ Annual vacation period

Thirty calendar days, including Saturdays and Sundays.

■ Paid leave and public holidays

Fourteen days per year. Autonomous communities and municipalities may designate local holidays that replace or add to the list of paid holidays.

■ Wages

A statutory inter-industry minimum wage (SMI) exists.

Annual compensation is paid in 14 monthly instalments, with double pay on the sixth and twelfth months of the year and bonuses (*complementos*) at Christmas and on another date during the year.

■ Social security

The contribution for health and maternity, death and disability, old age, supplemental retirement and family allowance totals 23.8 per cent of gross salary at the employer's charge and 4.7 per cent at the employee's charge. In addition, contributions are paid to cover unemployment, work-related accidents and the employee guarantee fund.

Work-related accidents and the employee guarantee fund are at the employer's charge exclusively.

Supplemental retirement plans are relatively under-developed.

■ Mandatory social security contributions

Overall, social security contributions represent 37.2 per cent of gross salary, of which:

— Employer contribution: 30.8 per cent
— Employee contribution: 6.4 per cent.

■ Employing foreigners

Nationals of the European Union do not need permits to work in Spain, but they must apply for a residence permit that is initially valid for five years. The residence permit may be granted for shorter periods under certain circumstances.

Non-EU nationals must apply for both a work and a residence permit from the Foreign Office of each regional bureau of the Ministry of Labour and Social Security. The single card, issued for a period of six months to five years, is renewable.

Paying taxes

■ Corporate income tax (Impuesto sobre sociedades)

Basic rate: 35 per cent. Reduced rates apply to non-resident companies, which do not have a permanent establishment in Spain, mutual insurance funds, investment companies and co-operatives.

■ Personal taxes (Impuesto sobre la renta de las personas físicas)

There is both a national and a regional income tax. The progressive tax rate starts at 0 per cent, then rises from 18 per cent to 48 per cent (11 brackets).

The autonomous regions may keep a portion of personal income tax revenues to fund their own budgets. If they do not exercise this prerogative, the Spanish government receives the entire amount.

■ Value-added tax (Impuesto sobre el valor anadido)

Depending on the nature of goods and services:

— Reduced rate: 4%, 7%;
— Standard rate: 16%.

■ Economic Activities contribution (Impuesto sobre Actividades Economicas – IAE)

The tax rate varies depending on the type of business, the size of the company and its location.

Businesses that establish operations in the Canary Islands and the Basque region are entitled to investment subsidies, mainly in the form of tax deductions or reduced direct or indirect taxes.

The advantages of establishing an ETVE (holding company)

An ETVE (*Entitad de tenencia de valores extranjeros*) is a regular company whose primary business purpose is to hold equity interests in foreign firms. It may also exercise other activities, particularly finance-related or services rendered on behalf of affiliates.

ETVEs are subject to corporate income tax.

Principal advantage: the holding is exempt from taxes on dividends and capital gains realized on the sale of equity securities.

Prior approval must be obtained from the Spanish tax authorities, and is considered to be granted after three months in the absence of notification.

Primary advantage: dividends and capital gains realized on the sale of equity security investments are tax exempt, provided that certain other conditions are met.

Prior authorization from the Spanish tax authorities is needed, and is considered to have been granted after three months – barring written notification to the contrary.

The holding company may receive dividends paid by its subsidiaries established in EU member countries with no at-source withholding in the originating country and may pay dividends that are not subject to at-source, withholding in Spain to its non-resident shareholders.

Investment incentives

Spain is marked by economic disparities. Certain areas such as the Basque region, Catalonia and Madrid are the powerhouses of the country, while others, which cover three-quarters of Spanish territory, lag far behind in terms of economic development. These under-developed regions receive special assistance.

Foreign firms are entitled to the same treatment as their Spanish counterparts when it comes to competing for grants offered by the European Union, the federal government, the autonomous regions and even municipal governments.

Spain is among the most favoured nations in the European Union when it comes to economic incentives.

The Ministry of Industry and Energy has set up the *Instituto de la Pequena y Mediana Empresa Industrial* (IMPI) to advise and orient small and medium-sized businesses.

■ Industry-specific grants

Regardless of geographic location, special incentives are available to new businesses in various industries. In recent years, grants have favoured shipbuilding, textiles and household appliances. The list of eligible sectors is regularly updated by the government.

Current incentives include interest-rate subsidies, reductions in social charges for jobs created and outright grants. The latter generally cover 20 to 30 per cent of investment costs (which may rise to 50–75 per cent in special cases) in the following sectors:

— agri-food (to improve production and processing infrastructures and stimulate sales);
— energy (to promote energy savings and the use of alternative sources of energy);
— mining (to encourage recycling of mining scraps and improve the safety of facilities);
— research and development.

Applications are reviewed by the Ministry of Industry and Energy.

The Official Credit Institute (ICO) offers low-interest rate loans for investments in various sectors. The ICO offers a special credit line for small and medium-sized businesses (*La Linea PYME del ICO*).

ATYCA (*Apoyo a la Teccnologia la Seguridad y la Calidad Industrial*) offers subsidies of up to 70 per cent for investment in information technology, communications, biotechnology, chemicals, food, pharmaceuticals, environmental protection and industrial development and design.

In addition, the government grants corporate income tax credits to offset investment costs.

■ State hiring and training subsidies

The amount of incentive varies from one year to the next. Usually, the incentives consist of a reduction in social security contribution charges to the employer.

The Spanish government offers a wide array of hiring incentives. These grants are awarded by the National Employment Institute (INEM) and the Labour Department.

The 'local employment initiatives' programme concerns small business start-ups (25 employees maximum) that foster innovation and job creation. Grants of 700,000 pesetas (4,207.08 euros) are offered for each new full-time permanent position that is created. Interest-rate subsidies on loans granted to businesses are also available under this programme.

The programme to stimulate the creation of permanent jobs targets young people under the age of 25, the unemployed over the age of 45 and women in general, especially in sectors where the latter are under-represented. Grants of between 400,000 and 500,000 pesetas (2,404.04 and 3,005.06 euros) are offered for each employment contract signed.

Another programme, aimed at transforming fixed-term employment contracts into permanent jobs, offers employers 550,000 pesetas (3,305.57 euros) for each contract. Internships that turn into full-time permanent jobs also qualify for aid.

Vocational training grants are offered by the Spanish government to offset associated costs. Additional aid is available under the European Social Fund programme.

■ Regional grants

The Spanish government oversees the regional assistance programme, whose main goal is to reduce regional inequalities. The autonomous regional authorities play only an advisory and administrative role with respect to these funds.

■ State aid

Spain is divided into geographic zones:

— economic promotion zones (ZPE) cover Spain's poorest regions (Galicia, Castille-Leon, Castille-la Manche, Asturias, Cantabria, Andalucia, Canary Islands, Murcia, Aragon, Ceuta and Melilla, Extremadura and part of Valencia);
— special zones (ZE) describe regions that have been affected by industrial decline and traditionally under-developed rural areas. They include several provinces in the Aragon region (Huesca, Teruel, Saragossa).

Within these zones, several types and amounts of outright grants are available. In most of Spain, these grants cover 50 per cent of investment outlays, but in some areas they may range from 20 per cent to 60 per cent. The applicant must demonstrate that the investment project is viable and that it will create jobs, in addition to putting up 30 per cent of the total investment outlay.

■ Autonomous regions and municipalities

Potential investors can also play the regions off against one another to obtain the most favourable terms. Local development agencies have been set up in each autonomous region to orient investors.

Certain types of aid, awarded in the form of outright grants, interest rate subsidies, tax breaks (for example in the Basque region and Navarre) and technical support, can be accumulated with state or European subsidies.

This aid is granted and reviewed annually, and selection criteria do not generally vary from one year to the next. Grants promote business start-ups, the modernization of existing facilities and innovation. Applicants must demonstrate that the investment will create jobs. Targeted sectors include agriculture, handicrafts, fishing, business support services, processing, tourism and electronics.

■ European Community grants

For the period 1994–1999, Spain has been granted 26.3 billion euros in structural development aid. In addition, the Cohesion Fund set up by the EU has made 39 billion euros available.

> In Castille-Leon, grants are available for small and medium-sized businesses on the same basis as those offered by the federal government. Grant amounts cover 40 to 50 per cent of investment costs between 20 and 75 million pesetas (from 120,202.42 to 450,759.07 euros). In addition, advances and loans featuring attractive interest rates are available to tide over investors who have qualified for but not yet received grant monies.

Community aid packages include:

— loans granted by the European Investment Bank (EIB) for investment in economically under-developed regions with a view to forming European joint ventures and modernizing or converting existing plants and businesses;
— grants from the European Social Fund (ESF), the European Orientation and Agricultural Guarantee Fund (EAGGF) and the European Regional Development Fund (ERDF) to promote disadvantaged regions such as Galicia, Andalucia and Castille;
— co-financing of half of the costs of research programmes jointly undertaken by companies operating in two different EU member states, provided that one of the two companies is involved in manufacturing.

Interested investors should contact the relevant authorities in the region in which their business is located.

Useful addresses in Spain

Bank of Spain
Alcala 50
28014 Madrid
Tel.: (34 91) 338 50 00

IMPI (Institute of Small and Medium-sized Industrial Businesses)
Instituto de la Pequena y Mediana Empresa Industrial
Paseo de la Castellana, 141
28046 Madrid
Tel.: (34 91) 567 06 45

Official Credit Institute (ICO)
Paseo del Prado
28014 Madrid
Tel.: (34 91) 592 16 00

Spanish Confederation of Small and Medium-sized Businesses
Confederacion Espanola de Pequena y Mediana Empresa
Diego de Leon, 50
28006 Madrid
Tel.: (34 91) 411 61 61

Ministries

Center for the Development of Industrial Technology (CDTI)
Edif Cuzco IV
Paseo de la Castellana, 141
28046 Madrid
Tel.: (34 91) 581 55 84

Ministry of Industry and Energy
Ministerio de Industria y Energia
Paseo de la Castellana, 160
28046 Madrid
Tel.: (34 91) 349 400

Ministry of Labour and Social Security
Ministerio de Trabajo y Seguridad Social
General Labour Office
Calle Agustin de Bethencourt, 4
28027 Madrid
Tel.: (34 91) 535 20 00

Ministry of the Economy
Ministerio de Economia y Hacienda
Direccion General de Politica Comercial e Inversiones Extranjeras
Paseo de la Castellana 162, planta 11
28046 Madrid
Tel.: (34 91) 349 39 83

National Employment Institute (INEM)
Calle Condesa de Venadito, 9
28071 Madrid
Tel.: (34 91) 585 98 88

Secretariat of State for the Economy
Alcala 9, primera planta
28014 Madrid
Tel.: (34 91) 532 04 93

For information on all types of regional aid.

Economy and finance offices for the autonomous regions:

In Andalusia
Consejeria de Economia y
Isla de la Cantiya
Ed Tonetriona
41011 Sevilla
Tel.: (39 954) 46 40 00

In Catalonia
Departemento de Economia y Finanzas
Rambla de Cataluna, 19–21
Barcelona
Tel.: (34 93) 316 20 00

In Madrid
Consejeria de Economia y Hacienda
Plaza de Chamberi, 8
Madrid
Tel.: (34 91) 580 35 00

Gemplus Espana

It takes passion to stay on top.

Xavier Libret, Managing Director of Gemplus Espana

The little plastic rectangle in copper and silicon has managed to insinuate itself into our daily life practically unnoticed. The smart card is everywhere: on charge cards, standard and cell phones, the Internet, pay TV, even on apartment keys. In Belgium, smart cards are already used in health care, while in Portugal they are used to pay for bread and in Korea they get you on the bus. Behind the smart card lurks a Silicon Valley-style success story made in France.

Marc Lassus met Roland Moreno, the inventor of the smart card, at the end of the 1970s. An engineer at Thomson, he developed the concept and founded Gemplus in 1988 with five of his colleagues. The world's leading smart card producer (with market share of 42 per cent), this start-up has multiplied its revenues a hundredfold in 10 years and is forecasting 4 billion francs this year.

To consolidate its leading position, the group went public and is betting on its ability to innovate (it has 350 R&D engineers) and produce (it had produced 1 billion cards in 1998). At the helm of 41 subsidiaries in 27 countries, Gemplus is currently preparing to establish operations in Asia and Eastern Europe. Among its 4,000 employees, some 40 nationalities are represented. This is the archetype of the new generation of French enterprises, which earn the bulk of their revenues abroad. France accounts for only 5 per cent of Gemplus' total sales.

Xavier Libret, an engineer, became acquainted with Gemplus when he responded to an ad in *Le Monde* and was hired by the company in 1990. His background prepared him to some extent for the job with the 'little high-tech outfit'. After finishing his doctorate while working as a researcher for Microcontrole, Xavier took a year off to network in Asia and Latin America. From Tokyo to Rio de Janeiro, he met with company heads to get a better grasp on the business and the life of an expatriate. He began working as a major accounts engineer in Northern Europe, and within two years had garnered an important agreement with Telefonica in Spain. He was then asked to assume the stewardship of the new Gemplus subsidiary based in Madrid, set up to compete for tender offers in Spain and Portugal, as well as to transfer the company's know-how to Latin America. The *societa anonima* has a five-person sales force, three engineers and an administrative support team of two.

'We are very present in the standard telephone and cell phone markets via Telefonica and Airtel. In addition, we are making inroads into the bankcard market with the Spanish Federation of Savings and Loan Associations (the Ceca) and Sistema 4B. The electronic purse is widely used in Portugal and we have been developing the concept to Spain over the last two years. We are also active in the public urban transportation market, where we offer payment cards. With the Internet, e-commerce is our next big challenge. Our financial statements are consolidated by the group, but we have been turning a profit in Spain since we started doing business here.'

For this 36-year-old Frenchman from Toulouse, the secret to business success is 'having the energy, the desire and the taste for doing. It takes passion to stay on top'.

Notes

14

Setting Up a Business in Sweden

RUSSIA

Kiruna

Lulea

Umea

Ornskoldsvik

Ostersund

Harnosand

FINLAND

Gulf of Bothnia

Hudiksvall

NORWAY

Siljan
Falun

Gavle

Aland

Gulf of Finland

Vasteras

Uppsala

Karlstad

Orebro

Stockholm

ESTONIA

Mariestad

Vanern

Nykoping

Vanersborg

Vattern

Linkoping

Skagerrak

Goteborg

Jonkoping

Visby

LATVIA

North Sea

Vaxjo

Kalmar

Kattegat

Halmstad

DENMARK

Karlskrona

Kristianstad

Baltic Sea

LITHUANIA

Malmo

Key statistics

Total surface area:	449,964 square kilometres
Population:	8.8 million
GDP growth:	2.9% (1998)
Per capita GDP:	23,067 euros (1998)
Public deficit/GDP ratio:	2% (1998)
Public debt/GDP ratio:	75.2% (1998)
Inflation:	1.1% (1998)
Unemployment:	8.2% (1997)

Sweden, the largest and most densely populated of the five Nordic nations, is the gateway to the entire Scandinavian region. It serves as a litmus test for investment in the other four nations as well as the growing neighbouring markets of the Baltic countries and the St Petersburg region.

Although it has been a member of the European Union since 1995, Sweden nonetheless opted out of the first batch of euro participants on 1 January 1999. It remains one of Europe's most attractive countries for foreign investors, however. Its infrastructure is modern and efficient, and its R&D expenditures amount to a significant percentage of GDP. The workforce is skilled and an effective programme to deregulate the economy is in place.

Financial services, air and rail transport, telecommunications, electrical power production and pharmaceuticals are among the sectors that have been deregulated to date.

The creation of the Invest in Sweden Agency (ISA) has helped the organization of foreign investments in Sweden.

In the last five years, the number of foreign corporations in Sweden has risen by around 30 per cent, from 2,600 to 3,300 companies. The United States, Norway, the Netherlands and Switzerland lead the list of foreign investors. In 1997, 2,810 businesses were controlled by foreign capital. They employed 239,000 people, 13 per cent of the private sector workforce.

Recent foreign investors include Morton (US), William Resources (Canada), Stagecoach (UK), Scana Industrier (Norway), Notfisk (Norway), and Imatran Voima (Finland).

Regulations governing foreign investment

No preliminary approvals are required to set up or acquire a business in Sweden, although restrictions apply to national defence and other sensitive sectors. For statistical monitoring purposes, those who establish businesses must report their investment to the Central Bank (*Riskbank*) via a retail bank, which must transmit the information within one week.

In some areas, setting up industrial operations requires the prior approval of the National Board for Environmental Protection. Processing may take up to one year for a new investment project and six months for an existing production site.

The Invest in Sweden Agency (ISA) offers a wide range of services and ample information to would-be investors looking for suitable locations, partners or equity investors. The ISA identifies potential investment opportunities in industries where Sweden is well positioned, such as health care, call centres, information technology and systems, telecommunications, digital image processing, the auto industry, wood processing, the environment and the chemicals sector. Subcontracting is widespread, especially in the automotive and health care sectors. Although a cartel of three major food distributors has not made it easy for importers, Swedish consumers are demanding a broader array of imported products to choose from (food and textiles). They also value technological innovations and after-sales service.

Principal legal forms

It is possible to conduct business in Sweden by establishing a representative office, a branch office or a subsidiary. Subsidiaries must adopt one of the country's existing legal forms.

Foreign firms that set up operations in Sweden generally opt for the *Aktiebolag* (AB) form.

■ Limited-liability company (AB – *Aktiebolag*)

Requirements of an AB:

— at least one founder (may be an individual or a corporate entity);
— foreign shareholders may acquire all of the founder's shares, which explains the common practice of buying shell companies to speed up administrative procedures;
— minimum capital of 100,000 SEK (€11,148.89), fully subscribed and paid in (500,000 SEK (€55,744.47) for companies that issue shares or bonds for public subscription);
— administrative formalities are relatively straightforward.

Relatively flexible management:

— a board of directors with at least three members (although a company with capital of less than 1 million SEK can be administered by one or two directors);
— the chairman and at least half of the members of the board must be residents of a European Economic Area member state;
— for companies with a workforce of more than 25, employees appoint two trade union delegates to sit on the board of directors;
— the presence of an outside auditor is mandatory;
— shareholders' liability is limited to the capital invested;
— for tax and social security purposes, the managing director is not considered to be a salaried employee.

Other legal forms

■ General commercial partnership (HB – *Handelsbolag*)

Requirements of an HB:

— minimum of two partners (individual or corporate entity);
— no statutory requirements regarding minimum capital or management (although this information must be specified in the articles of incorporation and bylaws);
— partners' liability is joint and several and unlimited with respect to third parties.

■ Limited partnership (KB – *Kommanditbolag*)

Requirements of a KB:

— one or more partners;
— partners' liability is limited to the capital invested, by agreement with the other partners;
— at least one partner has unlimited liability.

Buying a shell company

It is common practice in Sweden to buy shell companies, usually limited-liability (AB) companies. Interested investors should contact a specialized consulting firm, a law firm or a bank to have the bylaws amended (corporate name, purpose, registered office, etc). The investor can begin doing business immediately, provided that the initial directors (who serve as nominee shareholders) grant a general mandate.

The investor acquires membership rights at their nominal value, and pays consulting and legal fees, which run to around 8,000 SEK (€891.91) for an AB with initial capital of 100,000 SEK (€11,148.89).

Administrative procedures

The following procedures must be followed to establish an AB in Sweden.

■ The corporate name

A patent search should be conducted to verify that the corporate name is not already in use. Contact the Central Patent and Registration Office (PRV – *Patent och Registreringsverket*) based in Sundsvall.

■ Drawing up the articles of incorporation and bylaws

The founding members draw up a notarized instrument (a deed of formation) with the bylaws and articles of incorporation. The memorandum of association contains the draft bylaws, procedures for subscribing to share capital, the nominal value of shares, the date on which shares must be paid in and rules for calling the constitutive meeting.

The articles of association indicate the corporate name, registered office, business purpose (mandatory in Sweden), amount of authorized share capital and the par value of each share, the number of board members and their terms of office, rules for calling the general meeting of the shareholders, the company's fiscal year and the name of the independent auditor. The founders sign the bylaws and articles of incorporation in the presence of a notary.

■ Company registration

An application for registration must be filed with the *Patent och Registreringsverket* within six months after the deed of formation is signed. Capital must be fully paid in and deposited in a special bank account. The company then receives a certificate of registration (*registreringsbevis*).

■ Announcements

The bylaws and articles of incorporation are published in the Official Gazette.

■ Principal organization/incorporation costs

For an AB with initial capital of 100,000 SEK (€11,148.18), registration costs total around 1,200 SEK (€133.79).

Solicitor and consulting fees (minimum 6,000 SEK (€66,893)) may be incurred in addition to the above. The amount depends on the nature and complexity of the services rendered.

Human resources/labour law

■ Employment contract

Permanent

A written contract signed between the employer and the employee, containing a required minimum of information on job requirements and working conditions.

Fixed-term

A contract of a maximum term of six months is allowable under conditions stipulated by law. The contract must be written, failing which it automatically becomes a permanent employment contract.

■ Length of the working week

Although the legal maximum is 40 hours, the actual working week is from 35 to 38 hours under the terms of many collective bargaining agreements.

■ Overtime regulations

Two hundred hours per annum maximum.

Premium of 35 to 70 per cent over the regular hourly wage for overtime, double time for weekend work.

■ Annual vacation period

Twenty-five days per year.

■ Paid leave and public holidays

Ten paid holidays a year.

■ Wages

There is no statutory minimum wage.

Wages are fixed in employment contracts or by collective bargaining agreements for various employment categories and industries.

■ Social security

The Swedish social security system is highly developed. Workers receive benefits covering sickness and maternity, disability, retirement, unemployment and family allowances. Employers may also offer supplemental pension plans.

■ Mandatory social security contributions

Calculated on the basis of both wages and fringe benefits, social security contributions are withheld at source and paid by the employer (the same system applies to personal income tax). They come to about 33 per cent of wage costs. Employers pay an additional 6 per cent to 8 per cent of the basic wage to cover supplemental pension plans.

■ Employing foreigners

Nationals of the European Union and the European Economic Area (except Switzerland) need only a residence permit to work in Sweden. Nationals of other countries must obtain both a work permit and a residence permit from their country's Swedish embassy or consulate office before coming to Sweden. To qualify for these permits, the employer must demonstrate that the foreign applicant possesses skills that are not available in Sweden. The Swedish Immigration and Naturalization Office (AMS) makes the final decision after consulting other government organizations.

The work permit is valid for one year and may be renewed. After one year of residence, foreigners who remain must apply for a long-term residence permit, which is renewable every three years.

Paying taxes

■ Corporate income tax (*Bolagsskatt*)

Corporate tax rate: 28 per cent (whether profits are distributed or not).

■ Personal tax

Income is subject to local taxation, at rates set by municipal governments (between 26.5 and 36 per cent). The average rate is 31 per cent. High-income individuals also pay 25 per cent in state taxes on the portion of their income that exceeds 209,100 SEK. Only 20 per cent of all taxpayers pay the state portion of the income tax.

■ Value-added tax (*Mervärdeskatt*)

Depending on the type of goods and services:

— Zero rate;
— Reduced rates: 6% and 12%;
— Standard rate: 25%.

■ Real estate tax (*Statlig fastighetsskatt*)

Rate: 0.5 per cent of the assessed value of business premises, 1 per cent of the assessed value of industrial property. Deductible from taxable corporate income.

Newly constructed buildings are exempt from real estate tax for the first five years after completion of construction, and pay 50 per cent of the standard rate over the five following years.

Note: There is no business tax.

Investment incentives

Foreign investors are entitled to the same government grants and subsidies as their Swedish counterparts. Grants and loans are available for all business sectors, and tend to support small and medium-sized companies, job creation, training in disadvantaged regions, the research and development of efficient energy systems and exports.

Aid may be accumulated, but the total may not exceed 70 per cent of the total investment cost. Companies that receive these incentive packages may be required to repay them in full or in part if grant eligibility criteria are no longer met, or if they cease to operate. The government does not offer many tax incentives, although social security contributions may be reduced for manufacturing companies that locate in certain areas.

For information on available incentives, investors should contact the National Board for Technical and Industrial Development (Nutek – *Närings-och Teknikutvecklingsverket*). Nutek, established in July 1991, is the result of the merger of the National Industry (SIND – *Statens Industriverk*), Energy (*Statens Energivek*), and Technical Development (STU – *Styrelesen för Teknisk Utveckling*) Boards.

Nutek co-ordinates the regional development offices (*Lansstyrelsen*) located in each of Sweden's 24 counties. The amounts it allocates to the county-based regional development funds depend on the local unemployment rate compared with the number of small businesses as a percentage of the national number. Finally, Nutek also co-ordinates nine regional development and investment companies that acquire equity interests.

■ Regional incentives

Regional grants support the development and competitiveness of existing small and medium-sized businesses (in general, companies with a workforce of less than 200) and business start-ups. Amounts awarded vary with the region in which the company is located. Eleven of Sweden's 24 counties are considered preferential-support areas.

Location grants

In Area 1 (northern and inland Sweden), location grants are available for plant and machinery investment outlays (up to a ceiling of 35 per cent of the total investment outlay). In Area 2 (coastal regions in the north and the western interior), the ceiling is 20 per cent. Temporary pref-erential-support areas have been designated in the north and the south, primarily along the coast, and grant criteria are identical to those offered for Area 2. These grants are taxable.

Since it joined the European Union, Sweden has been eligible for structural fund subsidies. The *Frystad* region (Objective 2) offers small and medium-sized firms investment subsidies of up to 800,000 Skr (€89,191.15).

Development grants are available to offset up to 50 per cent of intangible investment costs, including licences, market research and training. Although the usual ceiling is 500,000 SEK (€55,744.47) per project, exceptions are granted on a case-by-case basis.

Employment subsidies may run as high as 200,000 SEK (€22,297.79) per employee in Area 1, and 120,000 SEK (€13,378.67) in Area 2. Subsidies are also granted to offset the cost of transporting raw materials into and manufactured goods out of remote areas. These subsidies cover between 10 and 50 per cent of these costs, depending on the firm's location and the length of the journey.

Low-interest loans

Enterprise location loans and low interest-rate loans are offered to regional investment development companies that bring private funds into the region.

Reduced social security contributions

Employer social security contributions are reduced by 10 per cent in Area 1 and by five percentage points in Area 2 until 2000. In the north of Sweden, near Kiruna, employer social security contributions have been reduced to zero.

■ General incentives

For small and medium-sized companies

Almi Foretagspartner, which operates under the auspices of the Ministry of Industry and Trade, offers funding for small and medium-sized businesses with capital of 3.5 to 4 million SEK (€390,211.27 to €445,955.73). It also analyses business plans and provides loans with terms of six, nine or 12 years that are interest-free for the first two years.

New companies in any industry can borrow up to 1 million SEK (€111,148.89), provided that the amount does not exceed 30 per cent of its total capital requirements. In this case, company owners must contribute at least 10 per cent of the capital themselves.

Although the minimum loan is 100,000 SEK (€11,148.89), companies headed by women may borrow as little as 25,000 SEK (€2,787.22).

Training grants

The training incentives available to all companies take the form of a wage grant of up to 35 SEK (€3.90) per hour of training, up to a ceiling that varies with the job in question. The Labour Market Board administers all training and recruitment programmes.

Useful addresses in Sweden

Almi Foretagspartner
Dalagatan 100
S-104 35 Stockholm
Tel.: (46 8) 15 14 00

Central Bank
Sveriges Riksbank
Brunkebergs Torg 11
S-103 37 Stockholm
Tel.: (46 8) 787 00 00

Central Patent and Registration Office
Patent och Registreingsverket (PRV)
(company registration)
Storgatan 13
S-851 81 Sundsvall
Tel.: (46 60) 18 40 00

Central Patent and Registration Office
Patent och Registreingsverket (PRV)
(patents, trademarks, designs and models)
Box 5055
S-102 42 Stockholm
Tel.: (46 8) 782 25 00

Export Guarantee Council
Kungsgatan 36
S-103 61 Stockholm
Tel.: (46 8) 701 00 00

Federation of Swedish Industries
Storgatan 19
S-114 85 Stockholm
Tel.: (46 8) 783 80 00

Industrifonden (Industrial Enterprise Development Fund)
Vasagatan 11
S-111 20 Stockholm
Tel.: (46 8) 14 43 45

Invest in Sweden Agency (ISA)
Gustav Adolfs Torg 18
S-103 38 Stockholm
Tel.: (46 8) 676 88 70

Labour Market Office
Sundbybergsvagen 9
S-171 99 Solna
Tel.: (46 8) 730 60 00

Ministry of Finance
Finansdepartementet
Rödbdgatan 6
S-103 33 Stockholm
Tel.: (46 8) 763 10 00

National Board for Environmental Protection
Scheelegatan 24, Box 8163
S-104 20 Stockholm
Tel.: (46 8) 692 21 00

National Board for Technical and Industrial Development
Närings-och Teknikutvecklingsverket (Nutek)
S-117 86 Stockholm
Tel.: (46 8) 681 91 00

National Social Security Office
Socialstyrelsen
Linnégatan 87
S- 106 30 Stockholm
Tel.: (46 8) 783 30 00

National Statistics Institute
Statistika Centralbyràn SCB
Karlavagen 100
S-115 81 Stockholm
Tel.: (46 8) 783 40 00

Stockholm Chamber of Commerce
Stockholms handelskammare
Vaestra Tradgaardsgatan 9, Box 16050
S-103 22 Stockholm
Tel.: (46 8) 613 18 00

Swedish Employers' Federation
Blasieholmsaemnen 4A
S-103 30 Stockholm
Tel.: (46 8) 762 62 90

Swedish Export Council
Exporträdet
Storgatan 19, Box 5513
S-114 85 Stockholm
Tel.: (46 8) 783 85 00

LA CIE (electronique d2)

We wanted to avoid buying a ready-made shelf company to limit the additional expenses. Our investment paid off within two months!

Jean Marchal, Managing Director of LA CIE AB

Philippe Spruch and Pierre Fournier were 26 and 32 years old respectively when they started up electronique d2 in 1989. The Paris-based company specializes in the manufacture of storage peripherals for microcomputers and workstations, a market that is expanding rapidly with the development of multimedia applications. The two entrepreneurs quickly decided to develop their business abroad, and in 1991 they opened their first subsidiary in London. Then came Brussels, Copenhagen, Düsseldorf, Rotterdam, Basle, Madrid and Milan.

In 1995, Electronique d2 took on the North American market via the acquisition of LA CIE, a Portland-based subsidiary of Quantum. The deal came with an exclusive contract with Apple to manufacture and distribute hard drives worldwide under the Apple trademark.

One year later, electronique d2 was trading on the Paris Nouveau Marché.

In April of 1996, the two founders decided to establish operations in Sweden. They felt that Stockholm would provide a better springboard than Copenhagen into Finland and Norway and, in a couple of years, into the Baltic states. Current business conditions are particularly positive for LA CIE. Sweden has as many computers as Spain for a population that is five times smaller.

The job of launching the new company was entrusted to 27-year-old Julien Marchal. He arrived from London, where his first professional experience was as a military-service intern with LA CIE. The Invest in Sweden Agency (ISA) helped him find premises in downtown Stockholm.

'We visited 20 different sites in one day, and our efforts paid off. We found office space for one-third the usual rental price. The ISA also put us in touch with the SE Banken, and we were able to come up with the necessary capital to fund an Aktiebolag without being Swedish residents. We wanted to avoid buying a ready-made shelf company to limit the additional expenses. Our investment had paid off within two months. Gradually, we were able to set up a team, and today there are 12 of us, including four French people who took Swedish lessons and now speak the language.'

The Swedish subsidiary receives products from the parent company, but manages inventories and after-sales service. Delivery is made within a day to IT resellers that sell in turn to public organizations and businesses. Recent clients include Volvo and Saab. The company also offers a maintenance contract and services sites directly.

By June of 1997, revenues for LA CIE totalled 36.1 million SEK, and the company plans to double this figure in its second year of business.

Notes

15

Setting Up a Business in the United Kingdom

Mainland

Kirkwall

Stornoway

Skye

Inverness

Aberdeen

Dundee

Mull

Copar

Atlantic Ocean

Islay

Stirling

Edinburgh

Glasgow

North
Channel

Arran

Dumfries

Newcastle-upon-Tyne

Carlisle

Durham

Middlesborough

Northallerton

ISLE OF MAN

Preston

Kingston upon Hull

Irish Sea

Wakefield

Anglesey

Manchester

Barnsley

Liverpool

Lincoln

Caernarfon

Chester

Derby

Stafford

Nottingham

Shrewsbury

Birmingham

Leicester

Norwich

Llandrindod Wells

Worcester

Warwick

Cambridge

Northampton

Bedford

Ipswich

Carmarthen

Gloucester

Oxford

Hertford

Chelmsford

Swansea

Newport

London

Cardiff

Reading

Kingston

Maidstone

Bristol

Trowbridge

Winchester

Taunton

Lewes

Chichester

Exeter

Dorchester

Newport

Truro

English Channel

North Sea

Skye

Berwick

Key statistics

Total surface area:	242,516 square kilometres
Population:	59 million
GDP growth:	2.3% (1998)
Per capita GDP:	€17,590 (1998)
Public deficit/GDP ratio:	0.6% (1998)
Debt/GDP ratio:	49.4% (1998)
Inflation:	2% (1998)
Unemployment:	6.5% (1998)

Given its strong ties with the United States and Commonwealth nations such as India, Australia and New Zealand, the United Kingdom not only enjoys international economic reach, its own market is very open to foreign investments.

The liberal economic policies pursued for the last 25 years have drawn more than 6,000 European, US and Japanese businesses to the United Kingdom. One-third of Europe's international investment is made there.

Energy is one of the pillars of the economy thanks to major oil fields in the North Sea. The home of activities ranging from healthcare to agri-business, today the UK is at the hub of biotechnology.

The ability of its workforce to innovate and its high levels of productive output make the UK one of the world's top exporters of electronic equipment. More than half of all personal computers sold in Europe are produced in the UK.

Revered institutions like the London Stock Exchange and Lloyd's contribute to making the City of London Europe's biggest financial marketplace, even though the UK is not currently a member of Euroland. The United Kingdom is also traditionally one of the main drivers of mergers and acquisitions.

The United States is the biggest foreign investor, followed by the Netherlands. France is a distant third with 1,800 companies operating on British soil. French companies are very active in the automotive (Peugeot) and automobile parts industries (Michelin), CD ROM publishing, and water (Lyonnaise des eaux) and rail networks (Vivendi) following public-sector privatization. Last year, 483 investment projects made it possible to create or save more than 93, 720 jobs.

Recent investors include Microsoft (US); Seagate Technology (US); Ford (US); Toyota (Japan); Black and Decker (US); Adobe Systems

(US); Fujitsu (Japan); Sodhexo (France), which purchased Gardner Merchant; EDF (France), which acquired London Electricity; and Holzbrink Publishers (Germany), which acquired Macmillan.

Regulations governing foreign investment

Whether it involves a start-up or a take-over, foreign investment is not generally subject to any prior governmental approval mechanism, except in certain key sectors such as national defence, coal mining and railways. The government may seek to block takeovers in other strategically important areas such as telecommunications, radio and television, and banking.

Holdings by the State in recently privatized companies may be in the form of a 'golden share'.

Capital flowing back following the divestment or winding up of a company, or the transfer of earnings abroad, are not subject to any controls.

Foreign firms, like their UK counterparts, must comply with environmental regulations and regulations relating to factory location.

Principal legal forms

It is possible to conduct business in the United Kingdom by establishing a representative office, a branch office or a subsidiary. Subsidiaries must adopt one of the country's existing legal forms.

The vast majority of companies in the United Kingdom are unlisted or private limited companies. PLC (Public limited company) status entitles the company to invite the public to subscribe to shares or bonds.

◼ Private limited company (Ltd)

Requirements of Ltd companies:

— at least one shareholder (it is possible to form a single member private limited company);
— no minimum capital requirement, but in practice two shares for at least £2 (€3);
— no deadline for paying in of capital.

Relatively flexible management:

— at least one director, who may be an individual or a corporate entity, and who may be but need not be a shareholder, or a board of directors;
— a company secretary, who is appointed by the board and may be one of the directors, and whose function is to ensure compliance with administrative formalities (maintenance of records, calling of meetings, etc);
— annual general meeting of shareholders;
— an external auditor to certify the annual accounts;
— shareholders' liability is limited to the capital invested;
— for tax and social security purposes, directors who also exercise a specific management function are considered employees (for example: managing director).

■ Public limited company (PLC)

Requirements of PLC companies:

— at least two shareholders;
— fully subscribed capital of at least £50,000 (€75,154.06), one-quarter of which must be paid up;
— operates like a private limited company but has a board of directors with at least two directors, who may be individuals or corporate entities, and who may be (but need not be) shareholders;
— additional administrative formalities (trading certificate);
— an outside external is required;
— shareholders' liability is limited to the capital invested;
— for tax and social security purposes, directors who also exercise a specific management function are considered employees (for example: managing director).

Other legal forms

■ Partnership

Requirements:

— no corporate personality or status;
— at least two partners and no more than 20 (except for professional practices, such as solicitors);
— partners are liable jointly for all debts and obligations of the firm;
— used for all types of business activities, especially professional practices.

■ Limited partnership

Requirements:

— must be registered;
— limited liability of certain of the partners;
— it is a form rarely used.

■ Unlimited company

Requirements:

— similar to a commercial partnership;
— partners' liability is joint and unlimited.

Administrative procedures

The following procedures must be followed to establish a limited liability company in the United Kingdom.

■ Choosing the corporate name

The registered company name must be filed with the Registrar of Companies after a name and trademark search has been conducted.

■ Drafting the memorandum and articles of association

The memorandum of association indicates the corporate name, registered office, business purpose, amount of authorized share capital and its division, and the limitations on liability. The articles of association set forth the regulations for internal company management and the relations among the shareholders (annual general meeting of shareholders, voting rights, etc).

■ Filing signed memorandum and articles of association and bylaws with the Registrar of Companies

These documents must be filed with the Registrar of Companies together with other specific forms that provide the names and details of the founding board members and the company secretary.

The company comes into existence, ie acquires a corporate personality, when the Registrar delivers the certificate of incorporation.

■ Principal organization/incorporation costs

For a private limited company, incorporation costs come to around £1,200 (€1,803.69) and include:

— filing and registration fees with the Registrar of Companies of around £30 (€75.15);
— miscellaneous expenses (for printing documents, mandatory registrations, seals);
— solicitor fees, which vary depending on the nature and complexity of the services rendered.

■ Processing delays

Incorporation from scratch normally requires a minimum of two weeks. Private limited companies may begin doing business as soon as they obtain the certificate of incorporation from the Registrar of Companies.

Note: Public limited companies may not really begin doing business until they have obtained a trading certificate, which is delivered when the statutory capital requirements have been met.

Acquiring a 'ready-made' company

The potential investor should contact a solicitor, a company registration agent or a chartered accountant. These professionals can recommend an off-the-shelf-company, ie an already formed and registered private limited company that has not done business since it was founded (a 'dormant company').

The administrative procedures required for taking over the company can be effected within 48 hours. The dormant company can be transformed into a bona fide PLC with a certificate attesting that it complies with the statutory capital requirements for public limited companies.

A ready-made company can begin doing business within 24 hours.

The cost of the transaction is at most, £100 to £200 (150.31 to €300.62). Acquiring a ready-made company is the most common way of forming a company in the United Kingdom.

Human resources/labour law

■ Employment contract

Permanent

A written contract signed between the employer and the employee, containing a required minimum of information on job requirements and working conditions.

Fixed-term

There are no restrictions on the number of times this type of contract can be renewed or on its total term.

■ Length of the working week

Legal maximum of 48 hours. Generally, the working week for most categories of workers is between 35 and 45 hours, depending on the terms of applicable collective bargaining agreements.

■ Overtime regulations

These vary with sector and employment category. In general, a 100 per cent premium is paid for overtime hours worked on Sundays and during paid holidays.

■ Annual vacation period

Two to four weeks a year, depending on the terms of the employment contract and length of service.

■ Paid leave and public holidays

Eight days a year.

■ Wages

A statutory minimum wage exists. In addition, wage levels are set either in individual employment contracts or in company-wide agreements. There may also be additional fringe benefits: bonuses, profit sharing, preferential interest-rate loans, supplemental healthcare insurance and retirement or pension schemes, housing, etc.

■ Social security

The Department of Health and Social Security provides coverage for the following: sickness, maternity, disability, death, old age, retirement, and unemployment.

The benefits payout is quite limited, although supplemental benefits and coverage may be granted for industrial injury compensation, welfare and family allowances.

To supplement this coverage, employers often conclude agreements with certain categories of employees providing for supplemental voluntary insurance coverage (pension funds, supplemental health coverage, etc). Today, supplemental insurance is provided for less than 25 per cent of the UK workforce.

■ Mandatory social security contributions

Employer contributions: up to 10.2 per cent of gross salary.

Employee contributions: up to 10 per cent of gross salary, up to a ceiling of £2,500 per year (3,757.70 euros).

■ Employing foreigners

Non-EU nationals must obtain a work permit before entering the United Kingdom to work. Generally, work permits are granted for a period of up to four years.

Paying taxes

■ Corporation tax

— For small companies, a reduced tax rate of 20 per cent on profits that total less than £300,000 (€450,924.39).
— Profits falling between £300,000 and £1.5 million are taxed at a rate of 20 to 30 per cent.

— A tax rate of 30 per cent is levied on profits in excess of £1.5 million (€2,254,621.90).

■ Personal taxes

The marginal rates of personal tax are 10 per cent, 23 per cent and 40 per cent of gross salary (three brackets).

■ Local council tax (Uniform Business Rate)

Calculated on the basis of annual rental value of premises occupied by the business.

■ Withholding income tax at source

Employers withhold personal income taxes at source, calculated on the basis of the wages paid to employees. This is the Pay As You Earn (PAYE) system.

■ Value-added tax (VAT)

— The tax rate on certain consumer goods (staples, books), services (healthcare, training, insurance, public transport) and on exports is zero.
— Reduced rate: 8 per cent on fuel, gas and electricity for residential use.
— Standard rate: 17.5 per cent.

Investment incentives

Aid to industry has declined considerably in the last few years. Northern Ireland continues to offer some of the best financial incentives in Europe. Between April 1996 and March 1997, Northern Ireland attracted foreign investment totalling £500 million (€751,540,659), creating 6,000 jobs.

The European Commission monitors aid for compliance with its guidelines on the proportion of state aid for investment projects that may be offered by member states. Various EU agencies offer grants and subsidized loans, including the European Investment Bank (EIB), the European Coal and Steel Community (ECSC), the Social Fund (ESF) and the European Regional Development Fund (ERDF).

In Great Britain (England, Scotland and Wales), the primary form of aid is capital grants offered by the Regional Selective Assistance (RSA) programme designed to stimulate growth in assisted areas.

The Invest in Britain Bureau (IBB), under the authority of the Department of Trade and Industry, is the best contact for foreign investors in search of information and orientation on who to contact. In its 20 years of existence, the IBB has helped more than 5,000 businesses take root and thrive in Great Britain.

Inward investors with projects outside England can contact regional development agencies such as the Northern Ireland Industrial Development Board (IDB House), Scottish Enterprise or the Welsh Development Agency. Regional and local information offices provide full territorial coverage of the United Kingdom.

■ Enterprise Zones (EZs)

Only seven of the enterprise zones given preferential status by the British government to stimulate industrial and commercial development (the largest being the Isle of Dogs) remain. They include two zones in Scotland (Inverclyde and Lanarkshire), two in north-east England (Sunderland and Tyne Riverside) and three in mining regions (Midlands, Dearn Valley, and Durham).

Businesses based in an enterprise zone are entitled to the following benefits:

— an initial allowance for corporation or income tax purposes of 100% of capital expenditure on the construction, extension or improvement of all industrial and commercial buildings;
— exemption from municipal taxes;
— exemption from training tax;
— speedier processing of planning applications.

The preferential status of enterprise zones lasts for 10 years from its date of designation.

■ Regional and local grants and subsidies

This aid is available for projects in Assisted Areas in the UK, which are divided into two categories:

— Development areas;
— Intermediate areas.

These areas cover Northern Ireland, and parts of England, Scotland and Wales.

Although the differences between the two zones are negligible, grants awarded in development areas tend to be larger than those that go to intermediate areas.

■ Regional Selective Assistance grants (RSA)

This grant programme backs viable development projects that create or save jobs in Assisted Areas. Up to half of the total investment cost may be funded by a grant. To qualify, the company must demonstrate that the project is viable, that it needs the grant to go through, that it will have a positive impact on both the local and national economies and that it will create new jobs or safeguard existing ones.

Once the application is made, the approval process takes from three to six months. The amount of the grant package is negotiated directly between the DTI/Invest in Britain Bureau and the foreign investor, and is limited to half of the total cost of the project.

■ Regional Enterprise Grants (REG)

This grant programme, which has a much lower total budget than the RSA, serves the needs of small firms with fewer than 50 employees that set up operations in depressed areas of Wales, Scotland and certain mining regions.

All kinds of business activities are eligible for financial aid, with the exception of retail trade, banking and insurance. The grant covers up to 15 per cent of the total investment cost, with number of job creations taken into account.

Interested investors should apply to the Department of the Environment.

■ Urban regeneration programmes

Among the principal programmes are Urban Block, City Challenge (under the authority of the Department of the Environment, Transport and the Regions) and English Partnerships.

There are also Urban Development Corporations, which work in conjunction with local authorities to encourage development in certain urban centres. They provide advisory services and financial assistance to firms that are interested in setting up operations in the urban centres in question.

■ Innovation grants

The British government encourages technology transfer from universities and businesses. Under the LINK scheme, the government pays half the eligible costs of pre-competitive research. Since 1994, more than 1,000 projects have been funded under the Realizing our Potential Award programme.

Small Firms Merit Award for Research and Technology (SMART) is an annual competition open to small firms (workforce of less than 50). Winning projects receive subsidies that go as high as £45,000 (€67,638.66), used to finance feasibility studies prior to the implementation of new technologies. The Support of Products under Research (SPUR) programme is similar, although it concerns the development phase for new processes and products.

The government also plays a role in communicating scientific information via Business and Innovation Centres, Innovation Relay Centres and Regional Technology Centres. It also encourages small firms to set up business operations in the UK Science Parks.

As part of the EU's EUREKA programme, British companies in search of industrial partners can receive funding of up to 50 per cent of related costs.

> Note: The LINK scheme should not be confused with Business Links (Scottish Business Shops in Scotland, Business Connect in Wales). Business Links are 'one-stop shops' providing business information and advisory contacts with local partners such as chambers of commerce, local authorities and training outfits. They offer customized assistance to SMEs in the area of sales and marketing, innovation, business start-up, regulations, etc.
>
> The Diagnostic and Consultancy Service will pay up to half the cost of specified forms of advisory services for companies with fewer than 250 employees.

■ Training grants

British companies are under no legal obligation to provide professional training for their workforce. However, the government plays a pivotal role in the training of skilled labourers through the Training and Enterprise Council. Awards and subsidies are available to companies that seek to improve the skills base of their employees.

The National Training Award recognizes achievements in the implementation of training programmes. The Skills for Small Business programme in England and the Small Firms Training Initiative in Wales offer subsidies to cover training costs for businesses that employ fewer than 50 people.

■ Small business support

For small investment projects, Centa offers consulting and limited financial assistance. After having validated the business plan, Centa can also facilitate access to the banks for more sizeable loans.

Loan Guarantee Scheme

The Loan Guarantee Scheme guarantees loans made to small start-up businesses that would not otherwise qualify for traditional bank loans.

Loan amounts fall between £5,000 and £100,000 (€7,515.41 and €150,308.13) over a period of 2 to 10 years. The Treasury guarantees 70 to 85 per cent of the amount borrowed.

Enterprise Investment Scheme (EIS)

A private investor who invests in a new or unlisted company (except in the financial services, real estate and certain other services industries) may deduct 20 per cent of the amount invested from taxable income, up to a ceiling of £150,000 (€225,462.19) per year and per person.

Shares must be held for at least five years to get full relief, failing which, the investor's deduction from taxable income may be disqualified. Normally, EIS investments qualify for relief from capital gains tax if the proceeds are reinvested in a company that qualifies under the EIS (Capital Gains Tax Reinvestment Relief).

Venture Capital Trusts (VCT)

These are investment trusts that are given the same tax treatment as EIS investments. Quoted on the stock exchange, these trusts must be 70 per cent invested in SMEs that qualify for the EIS.

Business Angels

Business Angels, firms or individuals, finance businesses that are too small to attract venture capital or private equity specialists (in general, less than £25,000 pounds (€37,577.03)). A national network, the Local Investment Networking Company (LINC) was established to facilitate contacts between potential investors and investees (SMEs).

Grants for job seekers

Long-term unemployed workers (more than one year of continuous unemployment) and young people under the age of 30 who want to set up a business may qualify for special grants. In addition, specific funding is earmarked for them as part of the Prince's Youth Business Trust and the Prince's Scottish Youth Business Trust.

Prince's Youth Business Trust Grants and Loans

Founded by Prince Charles, the Prince's Youth Business Trust helps disadvantaged young people set up their own business by granting low interest-rate loans or subsidies on a case-by-case basis. The Trust also provides consulting, training and monitoring services.

Useful addresses in the United Kingdom

Business Link
For details of the nearest office, call (44) 121 458 2000.

Centa
4–24 Britannia Street
London WC1 X9JD
Tel.: (44) 171 278 5757

Invest in Britain Bureau
Department of Trade and Industry (DTI)
Kingsgate House
1 Victoria Street
London SW1E 6SW
Tel.: (44) 171 215 25 35

London First Centre
1 Hobhouse Court
Suffolk Street
London SW1Y 4HH
Tel.: (44) 171 925 20 00

National Federation of Enterprises Agencies
A network of 350 agencies offering consulting and training to entrepreneurs.
Tel.: (44) 121 458 2000

Scottish Enterprise
120 Bothwell Street
Glasgow G2 7JP
Tel.: (44) 141 248 27 00

Welsh Development Agency
Principality House
The Friary
Cardiff CF1 4AE
Tel.: (44) 1222 828 860

■ Ministries

Department of Employment
Overseas Labour Section
Caxton House
Tothill Street
Southall
Tel.: (44) 174 259 40 74

Department of Trade and Industry (DTI)
Ashdown House
Victoria Street
London SW1E 6RB
Tel.: (44) 171 215 50 50

■ Other

Companies House
Registrar of Companies
Crown Way
Cardiff CF4 3UZ
Tel.: (44) 1222 38 08 01

Confederation of British Industry (CBI)
Centre Point
103 New Oxford Street
London WCIA IDU
Tel.: (44) 171 379 74 00

Link Secretariat
51 Buckingham Palace Road
London SW1W 9SS
Tel.: (44) 171 215 66 71

Prince's Youth Business Trust
18 Park Square East
London NW1 4LH
Tel.: (44) 171 543 12 34

Bubble Gun Mobile recording studio

> While Great Britain is not Eldorado, if you believe in your project and
> are enthusiastic, you can succeed.
>
> Martine Baratte, Managing Director of Bubble Gun

In June 1997, Martine Baratte founded a mobile recording
studio in London with a French partner. She was driven by the desire to
'work in the music industry'.

Her high school diploma in hand, the young Frenchwoman
from Normandy set off for Manchester, where she worked as an au pair by
day and took correspondence courses in advertising at night. She
returned to Caen to sit for a diploma in sales, then left for London in 1994.
Her dream: to go into business for herself.

'I met a sound engineer who, like me, was working at the
Terminal in Waterloo. We invested together in a mobile recording studio.
Most studios travel in large trucks – we fit everything into a car. This gave
us the advantage of flexibility, and we could go wherever we were needed
very quickly, even outside the country. For the CD, we recorded a variety of
music styles. Dreamtime, a contemporary jazz group, the Westminster
Abbey Choir, Shocktaws in the Vogue studios in Paris, Bobsleigh in
Trégastel, a Viennese group, etc. At the beginning, we worked in partnership while keeping our part-time jobs. This allowed us to test the project
and draw up our business plan.

'A local government agency, the Centa, granted us a £2,000
interest-free loan, and opened the doors to Lloyds. Approval of our project
by this agency was crucial, since we had virtually zero in the way of self-
funding. Lloyds asked us to set up a partnership and granted us a loan of
£9,000, 65 per cent guaranteed by the government. We didn't get a single
outright grant, but an audio equipment studio supported us. Business
Links gave us precious aid in terms of information, advice and follow-up.'

Today, the two partners are paying off their loans and are beginning to make a living from their business. They are thinking of launching a production company by transforming their partnership into a private limited company. Another project in the works is an Internet radio. They have created their own label, Ballyhoo Recording, to commercialize their business in Europe.

'French legislation is overly rigid. I never could have done the same thing there that I have done here,' admits Martine Baratte. 'While Great Britain is not Eldorado, if you believe in your project and are enthusiastic, you can succeed.'

Is the entrepreneurial spirit a stronger force on the UK side of the Channel?

SOS Doctors Ltd

We are overcoming the shortcomings of the English healthcare system. The money taboo doesn't exist here – you can practise medicine and be an entrepreneur.

Alain Batarec, Chairman SOS Doctors

Alain Batarec was a general practitioner in Fleury-Mérogis, then worked at a centre for disabled children in Courcoronnes before joining SOS Médecins in Paris, where he worked for 12 years. In 1994, he decided to found SOS Doctors in London.

■ A healthcare system marked by inequality

'I wanted to export the concept of emergency medicine to England. I did market research on the English healthcare system, which was positive. Today, the English healthcare system is marked by inequality. The National Health Service (NHS) was founded on the principle of free services. The patient doesn't have the right to choose his doctor; the choice is made on the basis of where he lives. It takes a long time to get an appointment and one doesn't spend much time in consultation – sometimes only five minutes – because medical practices are overcrowded. But the patient can't avoid them, since the only way to get to the specialist is through a referral by the generalist.'

'Alongside the public healthcare system,' explains Dr Batarec, 'the private system offers high-quality consultations to those who can pay the price. A visit to a generalist costs between £50 and £80, while a specialist runs from £80 to £120. Less than 25 per cent of the workforce has supplemental healthcare insurance. SOS Doctors, which began as a provider of emergency medical treatment at home, has also become an alternative for many patients, who reject the NHS system but cannot afford private care.

'Based in London, our team of 14 MDs (six different nationalities) all speak several languages – including English of course. Around 30 per cent of our patients are French nationals, and we work with 360 MD correspondents in the main cities in England.

'At the beginning, I partnered with a French MD and an English businessman. We invested £300,000 and then £200,000 more during the development phase. Each of us has a 25 per cent stake in the capital of the Limited company. And we are all on the board. I'm the Chairman. Our General Manager takes care of administrative staff and the switchboard, which has six operators. He also handles communications, while our Managing Director handles management and marketing. Annual revenues total around £500,000 from direct consultations and referrals from the NHS. We will be setting up a unit in Birmingham in the near future, as well as in other cities. The money taboo doesn't exist here. You can practise medicine and be an entrepreneur.'

Notes

Appendices

ICELAND

Norwegian Sea

North Atlantic
Ocean

SWEDEN

FINLAND

Gulf
of
Bothnia

NORWAY

RUSSIA

ESTONIA

Baltic Sea

North Sea

DENMARK

LATVIA

IRELAND

LITHUANIA

NETHERLANDS

BELARUS

UK

POLAND

English Channel

BELGIUM

GERMANY

LUX.

UKRAINE

CZECH

SLOVAKIA

FRANCE

AUSTRIA

HUNGARY

Bay of Biscay

SWITZERLAND

ROMANIA

ITALY

Black Sea

Monaco

SLOVENIA

BOSNIA

CROATIA

SERBIA

CORSICA

Adriatic

BULGARIA

MONTENEGRO

MACEDONIA

PORTUGAL

SPAIN

SARDINIA

GREECE

Aegean

TURKEY

BALEARIC
ISLANDS

Tyrrhenian Sea

ALBANIA

Mediterranean Sea

SICILY

Ionian Sea

Appendix 1 – Tables and charts

The Limited-liability company in the European Union

Country	Name	Minimum number of shareholders	Minimum subscribed capital	Minimum paid-in capital	Independent auditors	Incorporating instrument
Austria	GesmbH	2, unless sole proprietorship	Sch 500,000 (€36,336.42)	50% at the time of incorporation	Mandatory when certain thresholds are surpassed	Notarized
Belgium	SPRL	2, unless sole proprietorship	BFr 750,000 (€18,592.01)	BEF 250,000 at the time of incorporation	Mandatory when certain thresholds are surpassed	Notarized
Denmark	Aps	2, unless sole proprietorship	DKr 125,000 (€16,820.52)	Fully paid in	Mandatory	Notarized or private signature
Finland	OY	1	FM 50,000 (€8,409.37)	50% at the time of incorporation	Mandatory when certain thresholds are surpassed	Notarized or private signature
France	SARL	2, unless sole proprietorship	FFr 50,000 (€7,622.45)	Fully paid in	Mandatory when certain thresholds are surpassed	Notarized or private signature
Germany	GmbH	2, unless sole proprietorship	DM 50,000 (€25,564.59)	50% at the time of incorporation	Mandatory when certain thresholds are surpassed	Notarized

Country	Entity	Members	Minimum capital	Capital payment	Audit	Document form
Greece	EPE	2, unless sole proprietorship	Dr 6 million (€18,461.54)	Fully paid in	Mandatory when certain thresholds are surpassed	Notarized
Ireland	Ltd	2, unless single member limited	No minimum, in practice, one share (€2.54)	Fully paid in	Mandatory	Notarized or private signature
Italy	SRL	2, unless sole proprietorship	L 20 million (€10,329.14)	30% at the time of incorporation	Mandatory when certain thresholds are surpassed	Notarized or private signature
Luxembourg	SARL	2, unless sole proprietorship	LFr 500,000 (€12,394.68)	Fully paid in	Mandatory when certain thresholds are surpassed	Notarized
Netherlands	BV	2, unless sole proprietorship	Fl 40,000 (€18,151.20)	25% at the time of incorporation	Mandatory when certain thresholds are surpassed	Notarized
Portugal	Lda	2, unless sole proprietorship	Es 400,000 (€1,995.19)	50% at the time of incorporation	Mandatory when certain thresholds are surpassed	Notarized
Spain	SRL	2, unless sole proprietorship	Pta 500,000 (€3,005.06)	Fully paid in	Mandatory when certain thresholds are surpassed	Notarized
Sweden	AB	1	SKr 100,000 (€11,148.89)	Fully paid in	Mandatory	Notarized or private signature
United Kingdom	Ltd	2, unless single member Ltd	No minimum, in practice 1 share (€1.5)	Fully paid in	Mandatory	Notarized or private signature

The corporation in the European Union

Country	Name	Minimum number of shareholders	Minimum subscribed capital	Minimum paid-in capital	Independent auditors	Incorporating instrument
Austria	AG	2	Sch 1 million (€72,672.83)	25% at the time of incorporation	Mandatory	Notarized
Belgium	SA	2	BFr 2.5 million (€61,973.38)	25% at the time of incorporation	Mandatory when certain thresholds are surpassed	Notarized
Denmark	AS	1	DKr 500,000 (€67,287.07)	Fully paid in	Mandatory	Notarized or private signature
Finland	OY	1	FM 50,000 (€8,409.37) FM 500,000 if public invited to subscribe (€84,093.96)	50% at the time of incorporation	Mandatory when certain thresholds are surpassed	Notarized or private signature
France	SARL	7	FFr 250,000 (€38,112.25)	50% at the time of incorporation	Mandatory	Notarized or private signature
Germany	AG	1	DM 100,000 (€51,129.19)	50% at the time of incorporation	Mandatory	Notarized

Country						
Greece	AE	2	Dr 20 million (€61,538.46)	Fully paid in	Mandatory	Notarized
Ireland	PLC	7	I£30,000 (€38,092.14)	25% at the time of incorporation	Mandatory	Notarized or private signature
Italy	SpA	1	L 200 million (€103,291.37)	30% at the time of incorporation	Mandatory	Notarized or private signature
Luxembourg	SA	2	LFr 1.25 million (€30,986.69)	25% at the time of incorporation	Mandatory	Notarized
Netherlands	NV	1	Fl 100,000 (€45,378.23)	25% at the time of incorporation	Mandatory	Notarized
Portugal	SA	5	Es 5 million (€24,939.89)	30% at the time of incorporation	Mandatory	Notarized
Spain	SA	1	Pta 10 million (€60,101.21)	25% at the time of incorporation	Mandatory	Notarized
Sweden	AB	1	SKr 100,000 (€11,148.89) SKr 500,000 if public invited to subscribe (€55,744.47)	Fully paid in	Mandatory	Notarized or private signature
United Kingdom	PLC	2	£50,000 (€75,154.05)	Fully paid in	Mandatory	Notarized or private signature

Personal tax rates in the European Union

Country	Tax rate
Austria	10–50% (5 brackets)
Belgium	25–55% (7 brackets)
Denmark	41–58% (3 brackets)
Finland	0% 7–38% (7 brackets)
France	0% 10.5–54% (7 brackets)
Germany	0% 25.9–53% (4 brackets)
Greece	0% 5–45% (6 brackets)
Italy	18.5–45.5% (5 brackets)
Ireland	24 and 46% (2 brackets)
Luxembourg	0% 6–46% (18 brackets)
Netherlands	35.75–60% (4 brackets)
Portugal	15–40% (4 brackets)
Spain	0% 18–48% (11 brackets)
Sweden	31 and 56% (2 brackets)
United Kingdom	10–40% (3 brackets)

Note: These figures do not include solidarity surcharges and other miscellaneous additional taxes levied in certain countries.

May 1999

Corporate income tax rates in the European Union

Country	Tax rate
Austria	34%
Belgium	Standard rate: 39% (40.17%)*. Reduced rate if profits are below BF 13 million. From BFr 0 to 1 million: 28% (28.84%)*. From BFr 1 to 3.6 million: 36% (37.08%)*. From BFr 3.6 to 13 million: 41% (42.23%)*. *A 3% 'crisis tax' (CCC) has been added on to the corporation tax.
Denmark	32%
Finland	28%
France	Basic rate: 33 1/3% + a 'temporary contribution' of 10%, which brings the global tax rate to 36 2/3%. For businesses whose annual revenues exceed FFr 50,000,000, the tax rate is 33 1/3% + 10% + 10%, ie an effective rate of 40%. For SMEs (*PME*): 19% + 10%, ie an effective rate of 20.9% for profits of up to FFr 200,000, provided that such profits are recapitalized.
Germany	30% on distributed earnings (+ solidarity surcharge of 5.5%). 45% on retained earnings (+ solidarity surcharge of 5.5%)
Greece	Standard rate: 35%. Higher rate: 40% for unlisted corporations.
Italy	37% on distributed earnings. 19% on retained earnings. + regional rate of 4.25%.
Ireland	25% on earnings up to I£100,000. 28% on earnings in excess of I£100,000. 10% for manufacturing, information technology and systems, finance and export.
Luxembourg	Up to LFr 400,000: 20%. LFr 400,000 to LFr 600,000: LFr 80,000 + 50% on the portion over LFr 400,000. In excess of LFr 600,000: 30% on total taxable income. A surtax of 4% is levied on income in excess of Lfr 600,000 to finance the employment fund.
Netherlands	35%
Portugal	34%
Spain	Reduced rate for SMEs: 30% up to earnings of PTAS 15 million. Standard rate: 35%.
Sweden	28%
United Kingdom	Standard rate: 30%. Small business rate: 20%.

Note: These figures are provided for information only and may vary on the basis of location. Investors are advised to inquire into local regulations.

May 1999

VAT rates in the European Union

Country	Reduced rate	Standard rate
Austria	10%	20%
Belgium	1%, 6%, 12%	21%
Denmark		25%
Finland	12%–17%	22%
France	2.1%, 5.5%	20.6%
Germany	7%	16%
Greece	4%, 8%	18%
Italy	4%, 10%	20%
Ireland	4%, 12.5%	21%
Luxembourg	3%, 6%, 12%	15%
Netherlands	6%	17.5%
Portugal	5%, 12%	17%
Spain	4%, 7%	16%
Sweden	6%, 12%	25%
United Kingdom	8%	17.5%

Zero rates in Austria, Belgium, Denmark, Finland, Ireland, Portugal, Sweden and the United Kingdom.

The applicable VAT rate is that of the country to which the goods or services are being delivered. This transitory system is expected to be phased out when rate disparities are reduced between member countries, to be replaced with a system whereby the applicable rate is that of the country from which the goods or services are exported.

May 1999

Conversion rates/euro and Euro Area currencies

1 euro =

> 6.55957 French francs
>
> 40.3399 Belgian francs
>
> 1.95583 German marks
>
> 166.386 Spanish pesetas
>
> 0.787564 Irish pounds
>
> 1936.27 Italian lire
>
> 40.3399 Luxembourg francs
>
> 2.20371 Dutch guilders
>
> 13.7603 Austrian schillings
>
> 200.482 Portuguese escudos
>
> 5.94573 Finnish markka

These are irrevocable rates (regulation 2866/98 of the 31 December 1998 Board meeting).

After a three-year transition period (1999–2001), euro coins and bank notes will become legal tender as of 1 January 2002.

Since 1 January 1999 all bank money (cheques, remote interbank payments, transfers of funds, payment and credit card transactions, direct debits, telepayments) can be issued in euros.

Conversion rates/euro and non-euro area currencies

1 euro =

> 0.6653 British pounds
>
> 7.4314 Danish kroner
>
> 8.9695 Swedish kronor
>
> 325 Greek drachmas
>
> 1.0928 US dollars

April 1999

Table comparing the status of holding companies in Belgium, Luxembourg and the Netherlands

	Belgium	Luxembourg Holding 29	Luxembourg SOPARFI	Netherlands
Business activities	No restrictions	Investment firm	No restrictions	No restrictions
Ruling	No	No	No	Yes
Registration fees	0.5% of capital	1% of capital	1% of capital	1% of capital
Thresholds	5% of the subsidiary's capital or going price of at least LUF 50 million	None	10% of the subsidiary's capital or going price of at least Lfr 50 million	5% of the subsidiary's capital
Required holding period for tax exemption of dividends	1 year	None	1-year holding commitment	1 year
Double-tax treaties	Yes	No	Yes	Yes
Exemption of dividends paid to the holding company	95% of all dividends are non-taxable	100%	100%	100%
Exemption from capital gains tax on the sale of holding equity interests	Yes	Yes	Yes, provided that 25% of the capital is held or going price of at least Lfr 250 million	Yes
Taxation of the subsidiary comparable to local taxes	Comparable to Belgian taxes	Not applicable	Comparable to Luxembourg taxes	Comparable to Dutch taxes

May 1999

Appendix 2 – Experts' names and addresses

With special thanks to the solicitors and experts consulted in the 15 European Union member states.

■ AUSTRIA

Béatrix Hebenstreit
Poste d'Expansion Economique
Reisnerstrasse 50
A-1030 Vienna
Tel.: (43 1) 712 63 57

■ BELGIUM

Nauta Benoît Feron
Nauta Dutilh
Chaussée de la Hulpe, 177/6
1170 Brussels
Tel.: (32 2) 673 00 07

■ DENMARK

Frantz Dahl
Geelskovparken 52, St
Postbox 6
DK-2830 Virum
Tel.: (45) 45 83 09 04

■ FINLAND

Laura Susi-Gamba
Wäntsilä Power Finance Oy
John Stenbergin Sata 2
PO Box 196
Fin 00531 Helskinki
Tel.: (358 9) 709 5660

■ FRANCE

Maître Patrick Bignon
Archibald Andersen
41, rue Ybry
92576 Neuilly sur Seine
Tel.: (33 0)1 55 61 10 10

Maître Anne Garola-Giuglaris
12, rue de la Paix
75002 Paris
Tel: (33 0) 1 42 61 57 71

■ GERMANY

H Werner Lignitz
Brandenburgische Strasse 38
10707 Berlin
Tel.: (49) 30 892 70 70

■ GREECE

Constantinos Karagounis
Karagounis et Partners
Valaoritou 18
10671 Athens
Tel.: (30 1) 36 26 821

■ IRELAND

Gerald Fitzgerald
30 Upper Pembroke Street
Dublin 2
Tel.: (353) 1 82 90 00 00

■ ITALY

Pierre Destefanis
Mazars et Guerard
Via Morigi, 5
20123 Milan
Tel.: (39 2) 80 68 511

■ LUXEMBOURG

Eric Breuillé
Credit Lyonnais Luxembourg
26 A, boulevard Royal
B.P 32 L-2094 Luxembourg
Tel.: (352) 47 68 31 321

■ NETHERLANDS

Maître Guy-Martial Weijer
Nauta Dutilh
Weena 750
Pastbus 110
3000 BC Rotterdam
Tel.: (31) 10 224 00 00

■ PORTUGAL

Antonio Vilar
rua Centa, 118–20
4050–190 Panto
Tel.: (351) 2339 47 10

■ SPAIN

Rafael Alonso
Nauta Dutilh
Plaza Marquès de Salamanca 3 y 4
28006 Madrid
Tel.: (34 1) 435 97 64

■ SWEDEN

Johanna Chaouat
Zanders Eurolawyers
Grev Turegaran 14, III
Box 5288
S-102 46 Stockholm
Tel.: (46) 8 463 99 40

■ UNITED KINGDOM

Carla Putok
MBP Law Limited
25 Burton Street
W1X 7DB London
Tel.: (44) 171 495 38 65
Tel.: (Paris) 01 47 27 65 06

Sarah Jones
Clifford Chance
200 Aldersgate Street
EC1 A4JJ London
Tel.: (44) 171 600 1000

Regus Business Centres

Introduction

Regus is Europe's largest operator of fully serviced business centres with a global network of more than 200 centres in 40 countries, each offering immediately available, fully equipped and furnished offices on short flexible terms: by the day, week or month.

Regus offers a low risk, cost effective and instant means of achieving a national and international presence. Clients range from multinationals accessing new markets or utilizing business centres to reduce property overheads, to start ups requiring comprehensive facilities and flexibility. By removing the complexities involved in managing office facilities, Regus allows companies to focus on their core business – hiring a Regus office is as simple as renting a car or hotel room.

Facilities

All centres include fully furnished reception areas, meeting rooms complete with audio-visual equipment and videoconferencing facilities, and fully equipped kitchens. State of the art technology allows for instant Local and Wide Area Network (LAN/WAN) access. All offices are fitted with high quality furniture and workstations, exceeding EC Health and Safety requirements ensuring an ergonomic and healthy working environment.

Staffing

Experienced support staff are on hand to manage enquiries and appointments, and to organize travel arrangements. In addition, they can provide additional business services such as desk top publishing, presentations and translations. Most Regus centres employ a number of multilingual staff. The provision of fully trained secretarial staff at each centre will often save clients the added cost of hiring their own support staff.

Products and Services

Regus offers the following services throughout its business centres:

Regus Offices

Regus Offices provides instantly available, fully furnished offices on a short term, flexible basis. Clients can walk in and start work, without long-term commitment, start up costs or fixed ongoing overheads. Regus Offices are ideal for those clients who are conducting projects and need to expand quickly in a specific location or require overspill space temporarily.

Regus Link

Regus Link is essentially a telephone-based service, where clients are given a personalized telephone answering service which passes messages and calls directly through to the recipient's home, office or voice mail address. From only £150 per month, clients can benefit from a prestigious mailing address, fax service and the use of Regus offices and boardrooms when necessary. This service is aimed at those clients who need a presence in a prestigious location, without any of the costs associated with having an office there.

Regus Meeting Rooms

Bookable by the hour, meeting, conference and training rooms are available in every centre worldwide. Able to accommodate from 2 to 20 people (and up to 100 at selected locations), rooms are equipped with a range of options including: flipcharts, overhead projectors, slide projectors, LCD projectors, TV and video, videoconferencing, and catering packages.

Regus Videoconferencing

Regus is the largest provider of public access videoconferencing facilities in Europe and has the ability to network with thousands of videoconferencing studios globally.

Regus Touchdown

Regus Touchdown offers clients a private office for a day or half a day, where and when the client needs it. Situated in most of the Regus centres around the world, Touchdown provides a fully operational office environment and support staff for clients wishing to conduct their business over the course of several hours. Touchdown is operated on a membership basis

Regus Netspace

Netspace is 'your own business centre on your own terms', billing clients on a revolutionary price-per-head basis. Netspace is geared towards companies which need a minimum of 50 workstations and want serviced business accommodation for one year or more.

The Regus Worldwide Network of Business Centres

Argentina
Buenos Aires

Austria
Vienna x 3

Belgium
Antwerp x2
Brussels x5

Brazil
Rio de Janeiro
Sao Paulo x 2

Chile
Santiago

China
Beijing x 2
Hong Kong
Shanghai

Czech Republic
Prague x 3

Denmark
Copenhagen x 3

Egypt
Cairo

Finland
Espoo
Helsinki

France
Bordeaux
Lyon
Nice
Paris x 9
Strasbourg
Toulouse

Germany
Berlin x 6
Bremen
Cologne x 2
Dortmund
Dresden
Dusseldorf x 3

Eschborn
Essen
Frankfurt x 5
Hamburg x 3
Hanover
Mainz
Mannheim
Munich x 4
Nuremberg
Stuttgart x 2

Greece
Athens

Hungary
Budapest x 2

Ireland
Dublin

Israel
Tel Aviv

Italy
Milan x 4
Rome

Japan
Tokyo x 2

Latvia
Riga

Luxembourg
Luxembourg

Malaysia
Kuala Lumpur

Mexico
Mexico x 2

Morroco
Casablanca

Norway
Oslo x2

Philippines
Manila

Poland
Warsaw x 3

Portugal
Lisbon x2

Republic of Panama
Panama City

Romania
Bucharest

Russian Federation
Moscow
St. Petersburg

Singapore
Singapore

Slovakia
Bratislava

South Africa
Cape Town x 2
Durban
Johannesburg x 2

Ukraine
Kiev

Spain
Barcelona x 2
Madrid x 3

Sweden
Gothenburg
Malmo
Stockholm x 3
Uppsala

Switzerland
Geneva x 2
Zurich x 2

Tanzania
Dar Es Salaam

Thailand
Bangkok

The Netherlands
Amersfoort
Amsterdam x 5
Arnhem
Eindhoven
Hilversum
Hoofddorp
Maastricht
Rotterdam x 2
The Hague
Utrecht x 2

Turkey
Istanbul

U.A.E.
Dubai

UK
Basingstoke
Birmingham x 3
Brentford
Bristol x 3
Cambridge
Cardiff x 2
Chertsey
Crawley

Croydon
Dartford
Doxford
Edinburgh
Fleet
Frimley
Gatwick
Glasgow
Harrow
Heathrow
Leatherhead
Leeds x 3
London x 17
Luton
Maidenhead
Manchester x 4
Milton Keynes
Norwich
Oxford
Potters Bar
Reading x 3
Sheffield
Slough x 2
Southampton
St. Albans
Staines

Stockley Park
Swindon
Uxbridge

USA
Atlanta x 2
Boston
Chicago x 2
Denver
Glendale
Irvine
Los Angeles
Miami
Minneapolis
New York
Northern Virginia
Phoenix
Redwood Shores
Reston
San Francisco
San Jose
Washington

Vietnam
Hanoi
Ho Chi Minh City

For more information:

International Freephone: 00 800 5222 5333
Or International Direct Dial   +44 (0)1784 898 444
Email: contact@regus.com   www.regus.com

Index